GOING WILD IN THE KITCHEN

GOING WILD

in the

KITCHEN

by
GERTRUDE PARKE

Illustrated by the author

DAVID McKAY COMPANY, INC.
NEW YORK

GOING WILD IN THE KITCHEN

COPYRIGHT © 1965 BY GERTRUDE PARKE

LIBRARY OF CONGRESS CATALOG CARD NUMBER: 65-21596
MANUFACTURED IN THE UNITED STATES OF AMERICA

Contents

CHAPTER 1

Going Wild--

Although American food is never really bad, neither does it often reach the heights of *haute cuisine*. All too often it is simply inoffensive and mediocre. I recently heard one friend, who travels this country regularly on business (and goes frequently to Europe for pleasure—and good dining), say that you can move across the United States constantly and while no meal will prove fatal, neither will it remain in your memory.

I believe that the convenience foods, all too alluring and available on our grocery shelves, have tended to spoil the cuisine in many an American home. Not that I am completely against them. Heaven forbid! They have saved my life on too many occasions. But too many of us rely on them so completely that we fall into deplorable culinary ruts and fail to use our imaginations to create the delicious, different meals that we can, if we only turn to what our native land so readily produces.

Many of us are much closer to the source of excellent American foods than we realize. Let me explain. Our home is on the shore of Lake Erie. Behind us are stretches of woodland, and beyond those are open fields. In my family, we are ardent fishermen, hunters, and gatherers of the wild bounty in fruits and vegetables, which Nature has provided with such prodigal generosity in this country. In my dooryard garden, I have planted a variety of herbs—just a step from garden to kitchen.

Now you have the setting out of which this book grew.

1

Are you near a lake—not necessarily one of the Great Lakes? Do you spend at least part of the year close to a stream, where you can catch trout in the spring and go ice-fishing in midwinter? Is there woodland within your reach, and are there fields, no longer used for pasture, where wild strawberries ripen in June? Are you, perhaps, blessed with friends who go forth with rod and gun, and return to lay a gift of fish or game on your doorstep?

If you are lucky enough to live in a house, even in the suburbs, surely you have a spot somewhere outdoors where you can grow a portion of what you put into the supper pot. And those with scarcely more than a few inches of ground to call their own can perhaps resort to a patch of herbs to add inspiration and country-fresh flavor to many meals.

If vacation time is your only chance to experience the deep satisfaction of fishing or hunting for provender, or gathering food from your surroundings, take advantage of it. Make part of your holiday memories the meals that you and your family search for and create together.

Fifty-two-weeks-a-year city dwellers don't have to despair any more about the chance to enjoy many kinds of native bounty. Even supermarkets today carry a wide variety of fish, game, and native produce, and you find bird and game farms across the country increasingly advertising what they will ship to your door.

For all of you, with this wealth of wild, fresh foods available, it is posssible that you are neglecting opportunities to serve dishes that will surprise and delight your family and friends. Why not go wild in your own kitchen? Try it, it's fun.

Although the heart of this book is concerned with fish—and the pleasures of catching them—and game and birds of all kinds, every important meal starts with appetizers or soup. Moreover, if you are a hunter or fisherman, you often have bits and pieces of bounty remaining that you'd like to use, but that aren't sufficient for a main dish. Into the soup pot they can go, or they can provide the makings of appetizers that are fresh and different. Follow me, and see.

APPETIZERS

Chestnuts and Bacon

Makes 12 snacks

12 chestnuts   12 strips bacon, 2″ x 1″

1. Remove the shells and skins of the chestnuts, using one of the methods on page 152.

2. Cover with boiling water and simmer until tender. Drain.

3. Cut the bacon into strips and fasten around the chestnuts with toothpicks.

4. Put under the broiler until the bacon is crisp.

Marinated Fiddleheads

Serves 10 to 12

These make an unusual hors d'oeuvre.

2 quarts fiddleheads, washed thoroughly
3 cups water
Juice of 1 lemon
5 tablespoons wine vinegar
½ cup salad oil

1 teaspoon salt
1 stalk fennel, chopped
2 stalks celery, chopped
5 coriander seeds
A few peppercorns

1. In a saucepan, combine the water, lemon juice, vinegar, oil, salt, fennel, celery, coriander seeds, and peppercorns, and bring to a boil.

2. Add the fiddleheads. Simmer for 20 minutes, or until ferns are tender.

3. Drain, cool, and place in refrigerator until ready to be served.

Leeks as Hors D'Oeuvres

Using the white part of the leeks only, simmer in salted water until tender. Cool, then marinate overnight in French dressing. Serve with cocktails.

Pickled Mushrooms

Serves 6 to 12 for cocktails

Serve as hors d'oeuvres, or in salad.

1 pound small mushrooms
1 teaspoon salt
Freshly ground black pepper
6 whole cloves

1 teaspoon each, chopped
  tarragon leaves, parsley
  and oregano
1 clove garlic, crushed
1 cup white wine vinegar

1. In a saucepan, combine the salt, pepper, cloves, tarragon, parsley, oregano, garlic, and wine vinegar. Simmer for 5 minutes. Strain.
2. Add the mushrooms and simmer 10 minutes longer.
3. Pour into small hot, sterilized jars and seal.

Cream Tart with Leeks

Serves 6 for lunch or makes 18 cocktail snacks.

This is similar to the traditional Quiche Lorraine, but contains no cheese. Serve it for lunch or at the cocktail hour. If the latter, bake in a rectangular tin and cut into bite-sized squares.

Pastry for a one-crust pie
  (see page 214)
2 cups leeks, white parts only,
  sliced
3 tablespoons butter

4 strips bacon
2 cups cream
4 eggs, lightly beaten
½ teaspoon salt
A little freshly grated nutmeg

1. Line pie tin with pastry. Bake in 450° oven for 5 minutes.
2. Cook the bacon until crisp and lay aside on paper towels to drain.
3. Melt the butter, add leeks, and simmer gently until soft but not brown.
4. Add eggs, cream, salt, nutmeg, and finally the leeks, and mix.

5. Arrange the bacon on the pastry. Pour the mixture over it.

6. Bake at 450° for 15 minutes. Reduce temperature to 350° and bake another 10 minutes. Test as for custard, by putting a knife blade in the edge. If blade comes out clean, the quiche is done. The center may still be a little runny, but as it actually cooks a little after it comes out of the oven, it will set. Serve warm.

Raw Mushrooms

Raw mushrooms are a most delicious dish. If you can find those called *Caprinus Macaceous* growing around a maple stump, gather every one of the fragile little treasures, and you are in for a treat. They have a flavor that is like nothing else. Perhaps the nearest descriptive word for them is "nutty." Certainly they taste not at all like the usual mushroom.

For a dressing mix a little olive oil and vinegar, add a dash of salt and pepper, and dip the mushrooms in this, eating the caps and discarding the stems.

Eat freshly picked mushrooms immediately as they do not keep well.

Stuffed Mushroom Caps

Makes 12 to 16 snacks

12-16 small field mushrooms
2 strips bacon
2 tablespoons minced onion

1 tablespoon chopped chives
1 tablespoon chopped parsley
2 teaspoons sherry

1. Pick only the smallest mushrooms so that when each cap is filled, it is bite-size.

2. Wash the mushrooms. Remove and chop the stems. Invert the caps to dry while preparing the filling.

3. Cut bacon into small pieces and sauté in a skillet. Remove it, cook onion in the fat for a few minutes, then add the mushroom stems.

4. Remove from fire, add the herbs, and moisten mixture with sherry.

5. Place the caps, gill side up, in a shallow buttered baking dish, spoon the filling into the caps, and crumble the bacon on top.

6. Bake in a 350° oven for 20 minutes. Serve hot.

Smoked Pheasant Pâté

Serves 4 for cocktails

You see this in small cans at high prices in a fancy grocery store. Why not make your own?

Actually, any game bird will do—partridge, woodcock, or whatever is on hand. I make only a small quantity at a time and store it in a small jar in the freezer.

1 pheasant liver, cooked
½ cup cooked pheasant
1 slice bacon
2 shallots, sliced fine

Hickory-smoked salt
Freshly ground black pepper
Brandy
Melba toast rounds

1. If pheasant or other game bird liver is not available, use chicken or even calves' liver. Grind together with pheasant meat, using the finest blade on your grinder.

2. Try out the bacon, discard, and use the fat to cook the shallots, being careful not to brown.

3. Add this to the pheasant mixture, season with pepper and salt, mix again and add as much brandy as necessary for the proper consistency. I usually use my electric mixer or give the paté a second or two in the blender to insure smoothness.

4. Chill. Serve on Melba toast rounds at cocktail time.

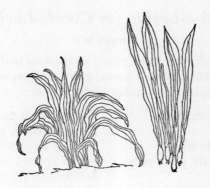

SOUPS
Chestnut Soup

Serves 4 to 6

There are three ways of preparing chestnuts. Look on page 152 and take your pick.

1 pound prepared chestnuts
Bouquet garni of:
    2 celery stalks, leaves and
      all
2 sprigs of parsley
2 or 3 sprigs thyme

Salt and freshly ground pepper
2 cups chicken broth
½ cup cream
3 tablespoons sherry
Whipped cream

1. Tie the herbs together for easy removal later.
2. In a soup kettle combine the chestnuts, herbs, and seasonings, and cover with boiling water. Simmer until chestnuts are very soft.
3. Remove the bouquet garni and either sieve the soup or run through a blender.
4. Add the chicken broth and cream, and bring to a boil.
5. Add the sherry and serve at once, topped with salted whipped cream.

Cock-a-Leekie (or Cockie-Leekie)

Serves 6 to 8

This delicious Scotch soup, made of chicken and leeks, is practically a meal in itself. With a tossed salad and toasted rolls, it could well serve as a lunch or Sunday night supper.

1 small stewing chicken
Butter
6 cups chicken broth
6 to 8 leeks, white parts only, sliced

A few sprigs parsley, chopped
1 sprig thyme, chopped
1 small bay leaf
1 cup cooked rice
Salt and freshly ground pepper

1. Cut up the chicken and brown well in butter. Add the broth and simmer, skimming as necessary, until tender.
2. Strain the soup and return to saucepan. Cut all the chicken meat off the bones and add to the soup together with the leeks, parsley, thyme, and bay leaf.
3. Simmer for 1 hour, then add the rice and salt and pepper to taste. Remove bay leaf and serve.

Jellied Mulberry Soup

Serves 4

1 quart ripe mulberries, washed and drained
¼ cup sugar
1 quart elderflower wine
3 whole cloves

A dash of salt
A few mint leaves
2 tablespoons unflavored gelatin
4 tablespoons cold water

1. In a saucepan, combine the mulberries and sugar, and mash lightly. Add the wine, cloves, salt and mint leaves. Simmer until berries are soft. Strain the liquid.
2. Moisten the gelatin with the cold water, pour the hot liquid over it, and stir to dissolve thoroughly. Pour mixture into flat pan and let stand in refrigerator to set.
3. Cut the jelly into cubes and serve in bouillon cups with sprigs of mint on top.

Mushroom Bisque

Serves 6

3 tablespoons butter
1½ cups mushrooms, coarsely chopped
3 tablespoons flour
½ teaspoon dry mustard

2 cans chicken broth
¼ cup sherry
¼ cup heavy cream
Whipped cream for topping
Paprika

1. In a saucepan melt the butter, add the mushrooms and simmer for a few minutes.
2. Add the flour and dry mustard. Stir, gradually add the chicken broth, and cook until thick and hot.
3. Add the sherry and heavy cream.
4. Bring to the boiling point, and serve topped with whipped cream sprinkled with paprika. If you prefer a smooth soup, run it through your blender.

Fish Bisque

Serves 4

This, again, is a mouth-watering dish to be made from almost any kind of fish, or from several kinds. We have used bass or walleye, with perhaps a rock bass or a blue pike thrown in.

Fish to serve 4 when filleted
4 cups fish stock
Sprig of thyme
3 tablespoons butter
1 tablespoon flour

1 cup heavy cream
Parsley or chervil, minced
Salt and fresh ground pepper
Crumbled crackers

1. Fillet the fish. Make fish stock, using heads, tails, bones. Follow recipe for fish stock, page 27.
2. Strain the stock, add the fillets, and simmer until they flake. Remove fish and chop very fine, or put through blender with some of the stock.
3. Melt the butter, stir in the flour and cook until smooth. Add the stock, bring to a boil, then add the fish, cream, parsley or chervil, and salt and pepper to taste.
4. Heat thoroughly, pour over crackers into a hot tureen and serve.

Nettle Soup

Serves 4

2 cups nettle leaves
2 tablespoons butter
1 teaspoon minced onion

4 cups chicken broth
Salt
Lemon or sour cream, salted

1. To pick the nettles, use a pair of gloves and a pair of shears. Pick enough so that you will have 2 cups of the tender top leaves, firmly packed.
2. Pour boiling water over nettles to remove the "sting." Drain and chop.
3. Melt the butter in a saucepan and sauté the onion for a minute or two, being careful not to brown.
4. Add the broth and the nettles, and salt to taste. (I like to run the soup through the blender for a second or two.) Simmer for a few minutes.
5. Serve topped with either a lemon slice or a spoonful of salted sour cream per portion.

Bouillabaise

Serves 6

A delicious way to use up odds and ends of fish. In fact, a variety improves the flavor. We use bass, rock bass, carp, and pike, and sometimes add fresh crab meat or shrimp.

1½ pounds fish
½ cup olive oil
6 onions, sliced paper thin
1 small clove garlic
1 bay leaf
Few sprigs thyme
3 or 4 cloves
4 crushed peppercorns

2 cups dry white wine
2 cups water
1½ teaspoons salt
1 tablespoon lemon juice
Grated rind of ½ a lemon
3 tablespoons chopped parsley
French bread, sliced
    and toasted

1. In a kettle, combine olive oil, onions, garlic, bay leaf, thyme, cloves, and peppercorns. Simmer for 5 to 10 minutes, add the wine and water, and cook for another 10 minutes. Strain, return to kettle,

and put in the fish, adding enough water to cover. Add the salt, lemon juice, lemon rind, and parsley. Simmer for about 30 minutes, or until the fish flakes. If soup becomes too thick, add more water.

2. Pour bouillabaise over toasted French bread slices and serve at once.

Leek and Sorrel Soup

Serves 4

6 wild leeks, white part only
2 tablespoons butter
1 can chicken broth

3 potatoes, sliced paper thin
A handful sorrel leaves
½ cup heavy cream

1. Wash, peel and slice the leeks.
2. In a saucepan melt the butter and cook the leeks for a few minutes.
3. Add the chicken broth, and simmer while peeling and slicing the potatoes. Add to the soup.
4. Add the sorrel leaves and continue to cook over a low flame for half an hour, or until leeks and potatoes are tender.
5. Purée the soup in a blender or put through sieve to insure smoothness.
6. Add the cream. Reheat and serve.

Sorrel Soup

Serves 4

Sorrel is the plant with clover-like leaves also known as sour grass. It grows wild everywhere and is easily come by.

½ cup sorrel leaves, firmly
    packed
4 cups rich chicken broth

2 egg yolks, well beaten
2 tablespoons sherry

1. Heat the chicken broth, add the sorrel, and simmer for 5 minutes.
2. Slowly pour the soup over the beaten egg yolks, whipping briskly to prevent curdling.
3. Return to saucepan and heat but do not boil.
4. Add the sherry and serve.

French Leek Soup
Serves 4

4 slices French bread
Sweet butter
1 cup leeks, white part only
3 tablespoons sweet butter

5 cups boiling water
Salt and freshly ground pepper
Grated Parmesan cheese

1. Toast the bread in a slow oven. Butter and keep hot.

2. Sauté the leeks in melted butter until transparent and golden in color, add the water, and simmer for 20 minutes. Put soup through sieve or purée in blender. Season to taste. Reheat.

3. Place a slice of toast in bottom of each soup bowl. Ladle the soup over it. Pass the grated cheese.

Fish Chowder #1
Serves 8

Here is a chowder that lends itself to almost any combination of fish. I have made it with bass, perch, pike—and in an emergency have stretched it with salmon from a can.

The advantage of this kind of dish is that occasionally, when you come home with an odd assortment of fish and there is not enough of any one kind to serve as a main course, you can make this chowder, which I assure you is most tasty; and if there is a surfeit of it, you can freeze it and delight your family with it in winter, when the summer's fishing is nothing but a memory.

3 pounds fish, scaled and
    cleaned
4 good-sized potatoes, sliced
4 tablespoons butter
3 onions, sliced paper-thin
1 small clove garlic

1 sprig thyme
Water
Dry white wine
Salt and freshly ground pepper
Toast slices
Garlic butter

1. Melt the butter and cook the onions until soft. In a saucepan, combine the potatoes, onions, garlic, thyme, and fish. Cover with half water and half wine, and simmer until the fish and potatoes are soft. Add salt and pepper to taste. Remove the garlic.

2. While the chowder is cooking, heat a tureen, spread the toast with garlic butter, and place in the bottom. Pour chowder over the toast and serve at once.

Fish Chowder #2

Serves 4 to 6

Here is another chowder to be made of an assortment of fish.

2 pounds fish, scaled and
cleaned
2 cups each, dry white wine
and water, or
4 cups water
1 bay leaf
2 onions, sliced thin
2 carrots, sliced

1 clove garlic, crushed
A sprig or two parsley
1 sprig of thyme
2 whole cloves
Salt and freshly ground pepper
Buttered toast
Butter

1. In a saucepan, combine the wine and water, add the bay leaf, onions, carrots, garlic, parsley, thyme, and cloves. Season with salt and pepper to taste. Simmer for 15 to 20 minutes.

2. In the meantime, arrange the fish in a buttered flame-proof casserole, and when the bouillon is done, strain it over the fish. Cover and simmer gently for 30 minutes, or until the fish flakes.

3. Pour the chowder into a hot tureen, over toast. Dot the top generously with butter, and serve.

Spring Fish Soup

Serves 6 to 8

This is a good lunch or supper dish and, like bouillabaisse, may be made of a variety of fish.

3 or 4 pounds fish for fillets
6 cups fish stock
Several sprigs thyme
1 bay leaf
5 or 6 scallions, finely cut

½ cup diced celery
3 or 4 carrots, julienne
1 cup new peas
1 teaspoon salt
Freshly ground pepper

Make fish stock, of the bones, heads and tails. See recipe, page 27. Strain the liquid into a soup kettle, add bay leaf, scallions, celery, carrots, peas, and salt, and pepper. Simmer for about 20 minutes. Then add the fillets and simmer for 10 to 15 minutes more, or until the fish flakes. Serve in warmed soup plates.

Fish Soup

Serves 6

They tell me this is a common dish in Scandinavian countries, where it is made of codfish, but since pike and bass is what we have here, we make it of either one, and enjoy it immensely. It is a delicious hot-weather dish, and can serve as a simple lunch, served with a salad and toasted cheese sandwiches.

Pike or bass fillets, about 3
   pounds, sliced
2 onions, sliced
1 clove garlic, chopped
Water
½ teaspoon salt

1 teaspoon each, finely chopped
   chervil and thyme
A few chives, cut fine
Chopped parsley
2 cups sour cream

1. In a kettle, combine the onions, garlic, and fish, barely cover with water, add salt, and simmer until fish is tender and flakes easily. Place in a serving dish and chill.

2. Combine chervil, thyme, chives, parsley, and sour cream, check the seasoning, spoon mixture over the fish, and serve.

Vichyssoise

Serves 4

This is delicious made from wild leeks and served cold. I find six leeks enough, as they are strong even though small.

6 leeks, the white parts only,
   sliced
½ an onion, sliced
2 tablespoons butter
2½ potatoes, diced

2 cups chicken broth
1 cup milk
¾ cup heavy cream
Minced chervil

1. Combine the leeks and onion and cook lightly in butter. Add the potatoes and the chicken broth.

2. Simmer until vegetables are tender, then sieve or run through blender.

3. Add milk and cream.

4. Serve hot or cold, sprinkled with the minced chervil.

Cream of Nettle Soup

Serves 6

1 pound nettle leaves	Salt and freshly ground pepper
4 cups chicken stock	1 cup half-and-half cream

1. Using method described on Page 10, pick a pound of tender nettle tops.

2. Pour boiling water over them and let drain. Bring the chicken stock to a boil and simmer nettles in it for 5 minutes. Run through blender.

3. Add the half-and-half cream, check the seasoning, reheat and serve.

Cold Strawberry Soup

Serves 6

A delicious way to start a meal on a hot summer day.

1 quart wild strawberries	1 tablespoon cornstarch
4 cups water	2 tablespoons cold water
4 tablespoons sugar (approx.)	Thick sour cream

1. Simmer the berries in the water for 20 minutes. Add sugar, adjusting the amount to the sweetness of the berries. Mix the cornstarch and cold water, stir into the hot soup, and simmer for another 10 minutes. Let cool.

2. Serve ice cold, topped with a spoonful of sour cream per serving.

Turkey Soup

Serves 6 to 8

Turkey bones and scraps	Few sprigs parsley
Water	4 or 5 peppercorns
Celery leaves	1 teaspoon salt
1 onion, quartered	½ cup raw rice
2 carrots, cut up	1 cup cream
1 bay leaf	½ pint oysters

1. In a kettle, combine the turkey bones and scraps with enough water to cover, add the celery leaves, onion, carrots, bay leaf, pars-

Continued on page 16

ley, peppercorns, and salt. Simmer gently for an hour, or until the meat falls away from the bones.

2. Strain the turkey broth, return to kettle and cook the rice in it until tender. Add the cream, bring to a simmer again, then add the oysters. Cook only until oysters begin to curl. Pour the soup into a hot tureen for serving.

Pheasant Soup

Serves 4

Pheasant bones, skin, and leftover meat	Celery leaves
A few sprigs parsley	Salt
A few sprigs thyme	2 or 3 peppercorns, crushed
1 bay leaf	Water, or
1 onion	Half water and half chicken stock,
2 carrots	to cover
1 or 2 cloves	¼ cup sherry

1. In a kettle, combine the pheasant bits with the parsley, thyme, bay leaf, onion, carrots, cloves, celery leaves, salt, and peppercorns. Barely cover with water, or half water and half chicken broth, and simmer for 2 hours.

2. Strain the broth, add the sherry, heat, and serve with cheese Melba toast.

Game Bird Soup with Rabbit

About 1½ quarts

This is a time-honored recipe and its ingredients may be adjusted to whatever game you have available.

1 small rabbit	1 bay leaf
2 pheasants or grouse, exclusive of breasts	3 whole cloves
	A dash of mace
3 slices salt pork	Salt and freshly ground pepper
2 quarts water	1 cup dry white wine
3 celery stalks	¼ cup raw rice
4 or 5 sprigs parsley	2 carrots, julienne
3 or 4 stalks lemon verbena	½ cup fresh or frozen peas

1. Cut up the rabbit and the birds. Wash, dry, and set aside.
2. Cube the salt pork and try it out in the soup kettle. Add the meat and brown it well.
3. Pour in the water, add the herbs, seasonings, and wine, bring to a boil, and simmer for 3 hours, skimming when necessary.
4. Strain the soup through cheesecloth and return to kettle.
5. Again bring to a boil, then add the rice. When rice is about half-done, add the vegetables and continue cooking until they are tender.
6. Adjust the seasoning, add bits of the meat, and serve.

Rabbit Soup

Serves 4 to 6

Leftover rabbit, can be made into this delicious hearty soup:

Leftover rabbit meat and bones	1 bay leaf
Soup bone	4 cans chicken broth
¼ lb. salt pork	1 cup dry white wine
3 carrots, cut into pieces	1 cup diced potatoes
1 onion, quartered	½ cup finely diced celery
1 clove garlic	½ cup sliced carrots
Few sprigs each of parsley and thyme	Salt and freshly ground pepper

1. Remove all meat from the bones and set it aside. In a kettle, combine the bones, a good-sized soup bone, and the salt pork. Add the carrots, onion, garlic, parsley, thyme, and bay leaf. Cover with water, then simmer until almost dry.
2. Add the chicken broth and white wine. Simmer for 20 minutes more.
3. Strain the broth and adjust the seasoning. Add the potatoes and continue to simmer until potatoes are almost tender. Add the celery and carrots and cook for 20 minutes longer. Then put in the rabbit meat.
4. Heat thoroughly and pour into a hot tureen.

Wild Duck Soup

Serves 4

During the hunting season, when wild duck is so abundant, the breasts alone are used for a main dish and the leftovers, in the form of bones, skin, and scraps, can be made into a delicious soup.

Duck bones, scraps, skin from 2 ducks
1 large onion, quartered
2 or 3 carrots, cut up
Sprig of thyme
1 stalk celery and leaves
Salt and freshly ground pepper
Wild rice, if available
Sprig or two of parsley

1. In a soup kettle combine the duck scraps and bones with the onion, carrots, thyme, celery, and parsley. Cover with cold water and slowly bring to a boil. Simmer for about 2 hours.

2. Strain the soup. Add leftover bits of meat, season to taste.

3. Add any wild rice left over from previous duck dinner.

4. Heat and pour into a hot tureen.

Game Bird Soup

Serves 6 to 8

2 birds—pheasant, grouse, or partridge—except for the breasts
2 quarts water
1 cup dry white wine
Few sprigs each of parsley and thyme
A bunch of sorrel
Salt and freshly ground pepper
½ cup fresh tomato purée
¼ cup raw rice
2 tablespoons flour
2 tablespoons sherry

1. After the breasts have been removed to be used for another dish, cut up the birds and place in a soup kettle with the water and wine. Add the herbs, season with salt and pepper, and simmer for 2 hours, skimming as needed.

2. Strain the soup through cheesecloth and return to kettle.

3. Add the tomato purée and rice, and simmer until the rice is done.

4. Blend the flour with a little water and add to the soup. Bring to a boil, add sherry, and serve.

CHAPTER 2

Fish

To all of us who live close to Nature, the coming of spring means many things: the swelling of buds on the trees, the delicate, woodsy fragrance rising from the earth after a spring rain, and those impossibly hopeful last-minute additions to the order from the seed catalog.

To those of us who live on Lake Erie, spring—or more specifically April—is marked in a most exciting way by the arrival of *Osmerus mordax,* the American smelt.

Some two dozen species of this tasty little fish, native to Lake Ontario, have now been introduced into other Great Lakes as well as some inland lakes. An old "smelter" will tell you that there is no way of knowing when the smelt will appear, for they run for no rhyme or reason and stop as suddenly as they start. It is a mysterious something in the air, a feeling in the bones, that tells one that tonight is a good night?

We may have had an early dinner and are enjoying our coffee in front of the fire, when we hear the tinkle of a bell outside: Hank and Betty have come for us with their smelt-mobile, and we know that the smelt are running.

Let us describe this ingenious device, the smelt-mobile, of which a small sketch appears, at this chapter's head. Essentially an orange crate, mounted on wheels with broad rims which will not sink into the sand, it has a tongue with a crosspiece forming a handle by which it may be pulled from position to position on the beach. This tongue is topped with a board which serves as a counter on which we clean the fish, which then go immediately into the frying pan.

19

Incidentally, I am not of the school that believes, with the late Robert Tristram Coffin, in flipping the fish straight from the water into the frying pan. Neither do I go along with the woman who, in a cookbook written years ago, stated that the smelt should remain whole, "the insides being pulled out through the gills." She must have had more nimble fingers than I.

Our camp is divided in two on this subject: those who believe that the smelt must be scaled within an inch of its life, with casual disregard of other areas, and those to whom scaling is a waste of time better spent in catching, and therefore eating more smelt. But we all feel that the cavity should receive careful attention. And there is no disagreement about the fact that fresh-caught smelt, hurried from the lake to the frying pan, is food fit for the gods.

Inside the smelt-mobile there are sharp knives for scaling and cleaning, a bag of seasoned flour, fat for frying, an iron skillet, and a turner for flipping the crisp, delectable morsels over to brown on the other side. There are paper plates to hold the sizzling fish until they can be bitten into. There is a towel on which the fastidious may wipe their fingers. And in the corner is a bottle from which everyone swigs with relish. Beer is traditional at a fish fry, so that is provided too.

By the time we join our friends on the beach, they will already have started a fire which will serve two purposes—to cook the fish and to warm the fingers of the fishermen. We keep it going with driftwood, which gives those who are not "sweeping" something to do.

In some places where the smelt go up streams or canals to spawn, dip nets are used; but here, along the lake shore, a seine is the thing. Ours is thirteen feet long, the netting sufficiently fine to prevent the small fish from slipping through but strong enough to handle a good haul. The netting is fastened at the ends to upright poles which are manipulated by the fishermen who sweep it slowly towards the shore, keeping the lower edge close to the bottom as they move.

Two people man the seine, maneuvering it for a wide sweep. They stand hip-high in the water and slowly bring it to shore with, they hope, a catch. There may be a mere handful of smelts, there may be none, or it may be one of those unforgettable occasions when the beach is covered with hundreds of glittering, curling fish.

As some of us are sweeping, others are replenishing the fire or cleaning the catch. One person cooks—someone who is expert at the nearly impossible task of regulating a beach fire so that the fish are golden and crisp and delectably tender.

We eat in between chores as the spirit moves and as our appetites dictate.

As the moon rises, we stand around the fire, and the breeze from the lake grows chilly. We have eaten our fill, all available pails are filled, and suddenly the run is over. The fire is put out, the gear packed, and we return home to deal with the catch.

Smelts Cooked on a Beach Fire

Serves any number of fishermen and passers-by

Smelts—as many as can be
   caught and cleaned during
   a given period

Seasoned flour
Vegetable shortening
Butter

1. After the fire has been well established, push the burning embers to one side at the edge, so that a flat bed of coals is made on which to cook.
2. Shake the fish, which have been cleaned and ready, in a bag of seasoned flour.
3. Melt vegetable shortening in a skillet placed over the coals, adding a little butter. (Butter burns too easily to be used alone, but we add it for flavor.) When the fat is hot, lay the fish in it side by side until the pan is full. (Oven mitts are recommended as protection for this job.)
4. As the smelts cook, shake the skillet gently back and forth so they do not burn; when crispy and brown on one side, turn and brown on the other side. Cook 4 or 5 minutes on each side, depending on the fire and the size of the fish.
5. Serve immediately. To be eaten with the fingers, accompanied by whatever liquid refreshment you prefer.

To Freeze Smelts

Method #1

Clean the fish as for cooking, wrap in meal-sized packages, and freeze at once. If the catch is a good one, by the time the last of the fish has been taken care of and the kitchen straightened, the sun may be up. In this case, try:

Method #2

Wash the fish well, place them whole in ice cube trays, cover with water, and freeze. The frozen blocks may then be wrapped, and stored in the freezer, to be thawed as needed. When the smelts are thawed, cleaned, and cooked, they will taste as fresh as if they had just been caught.

Method #3

This is the easiest way of all, and the results are almost as good as #2. Wash the smelts and pack in freezer bags—enough in each bag for one meal. Freeze, and thaw as needed.

French Fried Smelts

Serves 4

| 20 smelts | Lemon wedges, or |
| Seasoned flour | Tartar Sauce |

1. Clean and dry the smelts and shake them in flour.
2. Fry in deep fat at 365° for 4 minutes.
3. Serve at once with lemon wedges or Tartar Sauce (see page 161).

Pan Fried Smelts

Serves 4

One method is to sprinkle the smelts with buttermilk half an hour before cooking. This supposedly adds to their crispness. Another method is to let them stand on a wire rack for half an hour after they have been floured, to give them a crisper crust.

16 to 20 smelts   Butter
Seasoned flour   Lemon wedges

1. Clean and dry the smelts. Shake them in a bag of seasoned flour.
2. In a skillet, melt the butter and brown the fish on both sides over a fairly hot flame. This will take only a few minutes.
3. Serve the smelts immediately, while crisp and hot with lemon wedges—although there are those who claim that even lemon distracts from their perfect flavor.

Shirred Smelts

Serves 4

Use individual ramekins for this; allow 4 or 5 fish per person.

16 to 20 smelts   Salt
4 teaspoons white wine   Mornay Sauce
Lemon juice

1. Butter the ramekins, arrange the fish in each separately, then add the wine, a dash of salt, and a few drops of lemon juice.
2. Bake in a 350° oven for about 15 minutes. If the smelts are large, twenty minutes may be required.
3. In the meantime, make a Mornay Sauce (see page 155), spread over the fish, and place the ramekins under the broiler to brown. Serve piping hot.

Smelts Au Gratin

Serves 4

16 to 20 smelts
2 tablespoons butter
4 mushrooms, sliced
2 tablespoons bread crumbs

2 teaspoons chopped parsley
2 or 3 tablespoons dry white
   wine
Salt and freshly ground pepper

1. In a skillet, melt the butter, add the mushrooms, cover and simmer over a low fire until mushrooms are tender. Add bread crumbs and parsley to make a sauce. Check the seasoning.

2. Butter a baking dish. Arrange the smelts in this and pour the wine over them. Spread the sauce on top.

3. Bake in a 350° oven for 20 minutes, or until the smelts are cooked through and brown.

Baked Stuffed Smelts

This is a rich dish—a dozen fish should serve 3 or 4. Leave the heads and tails on, for a more attractive appearance.

12 smelts
1 pound fresh crab meat
Salt

2 tablespoons fresh lemon juice
Lemon wedges

1. Mix the crab meat with lemon juice and salt to taste. Salt the cavities of the fish and stuff with the crab meat. Sew up the cavities, and arrange the smelts in a buttered baking dish.

2. Bake in a 400° oven for 20 minutes. Serve with lemon wedges.

Smelts Brochette

16 snacks. Serve as appetizers.

4 smelts
4 slices bacon

Salt and fresh ground pepper

1. Cut cleaned smelts into ½ inch pieces. Cut bacon into pieces of like size. Arrange them on skewers, alternating the fish and the bacon. Season to taste.

2. Bake in a 450° oven until bacon is crisp and the fish brown.

3. Replace the skewers with toothpicks, spearing just enough on each for a mouthful. Serve piping hot.

Baked Smelts

Serves 4

16 to 20 smelts   ¼ cup bread crumbs
2 tablespoons butter   Salt and freshly ground pepper
Shallots, chopped fine

1. Clean and dry smelts and arrange in a shallow baking dish.
2. In a saucepan, melt the butter and cook the shallots briefly.
Add bread crumbs, salt, a dash of pepper, and sprinkle mixture over
the fish.
3. Bake in a 350° oven until smelts are brown. This will take 15
to 20 minutes, depending on the size of the fish. Serve with Butter
Sauce (see page 144) or Tartar Sauce (see page 161).

Bass

Everyone in my family looks forward to the time when the bass
season opens in our area. We have smallmouth bass here, which,
as every fisherman knows, provide great sport. This fish, the *Nicrop-
terus dolomein,* is a member of the sunfish family, and runs to
about five pounds at the most.

We find them lurking in the cool depths along the edge of a
reef, or hiding deep in holes farther out in the lake. True fishermen
seem to know by instinct where these holes are, so that when these
experts are out on the lake, we try to note their position and, by
lining up landmarks, try to pick the same spots. Of course one has
to consider the question of bait and the time of day, as well as the
temperament of the bass. No one has a satisfactory explanation of
why they stop hitting at a certain moment. Perhaps it is the un-
certainty that makes it all so fascinating.

There are different opinions as to the best method of catching
the smallmouth. Some cast, using a dry fly, others prefer a spinning
rod. We like to drift, using diamond-back soft-shelled crabs as bait.
In any case, the hook must be set firmly or you can kiss your bass
goodbye.

Perhaps the very best time to fish for smallmouth bass is at dawn, when the water is cold and rough. The fish will hit your hook like a bolt of lightning, and then the fun begins. The sight of a bass leaping out of the water to try to shake the hook out of his mouth is a thrill of excitement for the fisherman.

Those who prefer a more peaceful form of bass fishing can go out near the shore in the early summer, just as the sun is setting, and cast for the fish which come in at that time to feed. But we like the early morning fishing best.

When the alarm goes off at dawn, at first we are tempted to turn it off and say, "It's not going to be good fishing today; it's too hot (or cold);" or "it's too foggy (or bright). Let's go tomorrow." But having conquered this cowardly temptation, we struggle into our clothes, dressing in several layers which we can remove one by one as the air on the lake turns from icy cold to uncomfortably hot, as it can do in a few hours. We gulp hot coffee, pouring more into a thermos for a late breakfast in the boat, snatch a packet of sandwiches from the refrigerator, collect our fishing gear, and we are off, feeling very superior to the slug-a-beds we have left at home happily dreaming under their warm blankets.

The delicious morning air rushes by us, fresh and moist, and as we head for our fishing spot we breathe deeply, pulling that intoxicating freshness into our lungs, deciding that we wouldn't have missed this for anything, fish or no. As we turn off the motor and settle down, the shore is lost in the morning mist and we have the lake to ourselves, except for a lone fisherman who eyes us speculatively from a distance, wondering if our spot might prove to be better than his.

As we drift, we feel that we have been transported to a different planet and have left the cares of the world behind us. We think of nothing at all except possibly what we are going to do with the fish we are going to catch.

When fishing for bass, there are two important things we never fail to do: put the fish in a net over the side of the boat to keep them fresh, and skin and clean them immediately on getting them home.

Directions for skinning fish are on page 298-299.

Here is a basic recipe that you may want to use for the dishes below requiring fish stock. For a richer stock, use the recipe for FISH FUMET on page 151. Court Bouillon, on page 59, is used to poach a fish, and some of the liquid may be used in making the fish sauce.

Fish Stock

2 pounds of raw fish, bones,
    heads, skin, and scraps
5 or 6 peppercorns
1 teaspoon of salt
1 or 2 sprigs of parsley
1 or 2 sprigs of thyme

1 onion (optional)
Water to cover
1 cup of dry white wine
    (optional) to replace
1 cup of water

1. Put the fish in a kettle with the other ingredients. Cover with water or water and wine.
2. Simmer for 45 minutes, strain.

Baked Bass

Serves 4 to 8

If you have a fairly large bass, try baking it, using this French recipe.

1 large bass, skinned and clean
1 clove garlic, cut
Salt and freshly ground pepper
Tomatoes, ripe but not soft,
    sliced

2 tablespoons chopped parsley
½ cup bread crumbs
¼ cup melted butter

1. Rub the fish inside and out with garlic and season with salt and pepper.
2. Place the bass in a buttered baking dish, and cover with tomato slices. Combine the parsley, bread crumbs, and butter, and spread over the tomatoes.
3. Bake in a 350° oven for 30 minutes. Serve with wine sauce (see page 161).

Bass with Almond Sauce

Serves 2 to 4

1 bass   Parsley butter
Salt and freshly ground pepper   Almond Sauce

1. Fillet the bass and season with salt and pepper. Place in a buttered oven dish and spread them with parsley butter (see page 144).

2. Bake the bass in a 375° oven for 20 to 25 minutes.

3. Remove the fish to a hot serving dish. Serve with Almond Sauce (see page 144).

Bass Stuffed with Kasha

Serves 6 to 8

Kasha, or buckwheat groats, is a grain cereal well worth trying if you have not already done so. The groats can be bought in many grocery and food specialty shops, especially those carrying kosher foods, and are usually sold in three sizes, fine, medium or whole. We like the small size, but that is a matter of preference. Serve kasha as a delicious substitute for rice—it is a happy accompaniment for any food.

1 4-pound bass, cleaned, cavity   2 hard-cooked eggs, chopped
   salted   Few sprigs parsley, chopped
2 tablespoons butter   2 thin slices salt pork
1 onion, minced   ½ cup water
2 cups cooked kasha (see recipe   1 cup sour cream
   page 29)

1. Melt the butter and cook onion until transparent but not brown. Add the kasha, chopped eggs, and parsley. Mix thoroughly and stuff the bass.

2. Arrange stuffed fish in a buttered baking dish, top with salt pork, and add small amount of water.

3. Bake in a 350° oven for 30 minutes, basting occasionally. Pour sour cream around the fish and bake for 10 minutes more.

4. Arrange fish on hot serving platter and pour the sauce around it.

Basic Kasha Recipe

1 cup buckwheat groats   4 tablespoons butter
1 egg, lightly beaten   2 cups chicken or beef broth
1 teaspoon salt   Sweet butter

1. Coat groats with the egg and add salt.
2. In a skillet, melt butter and add the groats-and-egg mixture. Stir and cook gently until groats are golden and quite dry. (This extra toasting adds greatly to their flavor.)
3. Pour boiling broth over groats, cover tightly, reduce flame, and simmer gently for 15 to 20 minutes, or until all liquid has been absorbed. The groats should be tender but not mushy.
4. Add a generous amount of sweet butter and serve as an accompaniment to meat or fish. Kasha can also be eaten as a cereal with cream; added to soup; topped with gravy; or any way that appeals to your fancy. Kasha as a fish stuffing is unusual, but once you have tried it, you will use it often.

Bass Fillets Provençal

Serves 4

4 bass fillets   4 ripe tomatoes, cut up
2 tablespoons butter   2 tablespoons chopped chives
6 mushrooms, sliced   2 tablespoons basil
1 onion, sliced   1 small clove garlic
1 carrot, chopped   Salt and freshly ground pepper

1. In a skillet, melt the butter and sauté the mushrooms, for a few minutes. Add the onion, carrot, tomatoes, herbs, garlic, and salt and pepper. Simmer for 10 minutes. Remove garlic.
2. Place the fillets in a buttered baking dish. Pour sauce over them.
3. Bake in 350° oven for 20 to 30 minutes, or until the fish flakes.

Bass with Herbs

Serves 4

1 bass, cleaned
4 tablespoons butter
1 small clove garlic, crushed
1 or 2 onion slices, minced
2 or 3 sprigs parsley, chopped

1 teaspoon tarragon leaves,
   chopped
Salt and freshly ground pepper
2 tablespoons lemon juice

Prepare the bass for pan-frying (see page 297-298).

1. In a skillet, melt the butter and add the garlic, onion, parsley, and tarragon. Simmer for a minute or two.

2. Season fish with salt and pepper and cook gently in the herb-butter mixture until tender.

3. Place the bass on a hot serving dish. Add lemon juice to the sauce in the skillet, re-heat, and pour over the fish.

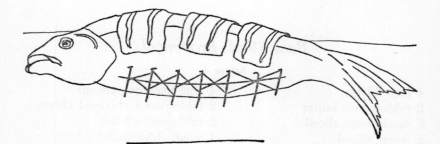

STUFFED FISH

READY FOR THE OVEN

Bass Fillets Italienne

Serves 6

6 bass fillets
Salt and freshly ground pepper
½ cup dry white wine
3 tablespoons olive oil
2 small onions, sliced thin
12 stuffed olives, sliced
1 tablespoon capers

1 tablespoon pimento, chopped
2 ripe tomatoes, cut up
1 tablespoon vinegar
1 teaspoon salt
Water
Parsley

1. Arrange fillets in a buttered baking dish, season with salt and pepper, and pour wine around it.
2. Make the following sauce:
Heat the oil in a skillet, add the onions, and simmer until transparent but not brown. Add the olives, capers, pimento, tomatoes, vinegar and salt. Simmer for 20 minutes, add a little water if sauce becomes too thick.
3. Spread the sauce over the fillets, and bake in 350° oven for 30 minutes. When ready to serve, sprinkle with minced parsley.

Bass Stuffed with Forcemeat

Serves 4 to 6

1 large bass
1 cup ground raw fish
½ cup medium thick cream
    sauce

2 tablespoons soft butter
1 egg, lightly beaten
Salt and freshly ground pepper
½ cup dry white wine

1. To make the forcemeat, combine ground fish with the cream sauce, butter, and egg. Beat until very smooth, preferably in electric blender.
2. Stuff the bass, arrange in a buttered baking dish, season with salt and pepper, and add the wine.
3. Bake in 350° oven for 35 minutes. Serve with Piquante Sauce (see page 160).

Bass with Tarragon

Serves 4

4 bass fillets
1 onion, chopped
Few sprigs each of parsley, dill,
   and tarragon

Salt and freshly ground pepper
½ cup fish fumet (see page 151)
¼ cup dry white wine
Butter

1. Arrange the fillets in a heat-proof serving dish and season with salt and pepper. Combine onion, parsley, tarragon, and a bit of dill. Sprinkle over bass.

2. Pour the fish fumet and wine around the fillets, dot with butter and bake in 350° oven for 30 minutes.

Bullheads and Catfish

I class these together since they belong to the same family. When they are small, no one, not even an expert, can tell the difference; but when they are grown, it is a different story.

The catfish grows to tremendous size, 97 pounds being the record here. The European catfish, called the sheat fish, has been known to go as high as 400 pounds. Other catfish of interest are the tiny South American species which lives as a parasite in the gills of other fish; and the African catfish, or thunderfish, which goes back to early Egypt. This one delivers a severe electric shock if molested.

The bullhead, which we fish for here, weighs only one to two pounds at best, but makes delicious eating. In fact, it is considered the best of all pan fish. Most fish markets carry them already skinned and cleaned, ready for the skillet.

Here we find them in muddy, reedy streams back from the lake shore. The best fishing for them is in late spring and early summer, and again in early fall. Since this fish is a bottom feeder and is most active at night, that is the time to go out. As they say in the South, "Mosquitoes and bullheads go together like love and marriage."

BULLHEADS

The bullhead will take almost any bait. It is essential, however, that the bait be on the bottom of the stream, not in the mud or so high up that the fish will ignore it. When your bullhead is hooked, hold it behind the head with your left hand and wear a glove on the right one to remove the hook. Otherwise you are almost sure to receive a painful sting from the barbels.

To prepare for cooking, clean and skin the bullhead; split it unless it is very small.

Bullheads Sauté

Serves 4

4 small bullheads, cleaned and   Butter
    split   1 teaspoon salad oil
Seasoned flour

1. Shake bullheads in bag of seasoned flour.
2. Melt butter in a skillet and add the oil. When hot, put in the fish and cook them until they are crisp and brown. Serve with Sauce Meunière (see page 155).

French Fried Bullheads

Serves 4

2 to 4 bullheads, depending on   Milk and
    size, cleaned   fine bread crumbs, seasoned
Milk and breading mixture, or   to taste with
1 egg   salt and freshly ground pepper

1. Split the bullheads lengthwise; if large, split the halves. Season with salt and pepper.
2. Dip fish in milk, then in breading mixture, or:
2. Beat the egg with a little milk, dip fish in this, then in seasoned bread crumbs.
3. Fry bullheads in preheated deep fat at 370° for about 6 minutes, or until crisp and brown. Serve with lemon wedges or Hot Tartar Sauce (see page 161).

Bullheads Au Gratin

Serves 4

2 or 4 bullheads, depending on
size, cleaned and split
2 cups fine bread crumbs
1 cup grated cheddar cheese
2 tablespoons melted butter

2 tablespoons sherry
¼ onion, chopped fine
Salt and freshly ground pepper
Milk

1. Arrange bullheads in a buttered baking dish.
2. Combine bread crumbs, cheese, butter, sherry, onion, and salt and pepper to taste. Moisten with enough milk to hold the mixture together, and spread over fish.
3. Bake in a 350° oven for 30 minutes, or until the fish flakes.

Bullheads in White Wine

Serves 4

2 pounds bullheads
2 cups white wine
2 cups water
2 scallions, cut fine, including
green ends
1 sprig thyme, chopped
1 small bay leaf

1 teaspoon salt
3 tablespoons butter
3 tablespoons flour
2 cups stock
2 egg yolks
½ cup cream

1. In a kettle combine the wine, water, scallions, bay leaf, and salt. Simmer for 20 minutes. Cut bullheads into serving pieces and add to broth. Poach until the fish flakes, about 10 minutes. Remove fish to hot serving dish. Keep hot. Strain the stock.
2. Melt the butter, stir in flour and cook for a minute or two. Slowly stir in 2 cups of the stock in which the fish cooked.
3. Combine egg yolks with cream and heat lightly. Beat in a little of the hot sauce, then pour mixture back into saucepan. Bring to a boil but do not cook.
4. Pour some of the sauce over bullheads. Sprinkle with thyme. Serve the rest of the sauce in a sauce boat.

Bullheads in Fennel Sauce

Serves 6 to 8

4 pounds bullheads
1 onion, quartered
1 bay leaf
2 carrots, sliced

Few sprigs each, parsley and
    thyme
Water
Salt and freshly ground pepper

1. In a kettle combine the bullheads, onion, bay leaf, carrots, parsley and thyme. Cover with water, season with salt and pepper to taste, and simmer gently for 15 minutes, or until the fish flakes. Transfer to a hot platter. Garnish with fennel branches, and serve with Fennel Sauce (see page 150) made with the stock.

Carp

In the late spring the carp come into shallow water to spawn. Great numbers of these huge fish can then be seen leaping into the air quite near the shore.

On the reef at one end of our bay, where the carp are found splashing about in quite helpless fashion, boys of all sizes gather, armed with sticks or spears. The fish they catch are either discarded, taken home to be eaten, or used to fertilize a rose bush, depending on the inclination, or possibly the nationality, of the fisherman.

There is a distinct prejudice against carp in the minds of a great many people, something which I believe has to do with its unattractive appearance. I have known people to shudder at the thought of touching one. However, if you can overcome this repugnance, you will find that carp has many culinary possibilities.

There are two things to remember in preparing carp for the table. First, it must be absolutely fresh. The Japanese appreciate this; every household of any size has a fish pool in the garden out of which a carp may be pulled at dinner time. Secondly, the fish must be skinned. Otherwise the skin of carp, as of bass, will give a strong "fishy" flavor to the flesh.

Having done this, fillet the fish and proceed with the recipes following.

Carp in Beer

Serves 8

This is possibly the most traditional way of cooking carp. Use about 4 pounds of fish. As carp is generally very large, this may be less than a whole fish.

4 pounds carp fillets, cut in serving pieces
Salt
3 cups beer
2 onions, thinly sliced
1 bay leaf

6 peppercorns
1 lemon, sliced
1 tablespoon flour
1 tablespoon butter
1 tablespoon sugar

1. Sprinkle the fish with salt and let stand for half an hour.
2. Place the fish in a saucepan, pour in the beer and add onions, bay leaf, peppercorns, and lemon. Simmer until fish is tender, from 30 to 45 minutes. Remove to a hot platter.
3. Make a roux of flour and butter and stir into the broth. Add sugar. Simmer until hot.
4. Pour sauce over the fish and serve.

Carp Roe

Allow about 3 or 4 ounces per person

This is the most delicious part of the carp.

Roe
Water
Vinegar
Salt
Batter

Nutmeg
Grated lemon peel
Chopped parsley
Lemon wedges

1. Simmer roe for 15 minutes in equal parts of slightly salted water and vinegar and then drain them.
2. Dip the roe in batter seasoned with a dash of nutmeg and lemon peel. Fry in deep fat preheated to 375° for 3 minutes.
3. Sprinkle with parsley and serve with lemon wedges.

Kedgeree of Carp

Serves 6

Good for using leftover carp.

2 cups cooked carp, flaked   ¼ cup cream
2 cups cooked rice   Salt
4 hard-cooked eggs, chopped   Paprika
4 tablespoons butter, melted

Combine carp, rice, eggs, butter, and cream. Add salt and paprika to taste, mix well, and heat in a double boiler.

Carp with Vegetables

Serves 4

4 pieces carp fillet   Salt
¼ cup celery, diced   Seasoned flour
1 carrot, sliced paper thin   Paprika
1 onion, sliced paper thin   Chervil, chopped fine
2 ripe tomatoes, chopped

1. Arrange diced celery, carrots, and onion in bottom of buttered baking dish, add the tomatoes, and sprinkle with salt.
2. Dip carp fillets in seasoned flour and arrange on top of vegetables in the baking dish. Sprinkle with paprika and more salt.
3. Bake uncovered in a 375° oven for 40 minutes, basting with pan juices as it cooks, allowing the top to brown.
4. Transfer to a hot serving dish and sprinkle with chervil.

Carp in Red Wine

Serves 6

About 3 pounds carp, filleted   A few green onion tops, cut fine
2 tablespoons butter   1 cup dry red wine
1 onion, thinly sliced   1 cup water or fish stock
½ cup mushrooms, sliced   Chopped parsley
1 clove garlic, crushed

1. Cut the carp fillets into serving portions and arrange in a shallow buttered baking dish.

2. In a saucepan, melt the butter, add the onion and cook for a minute or two. Add mushrooms, garlic, and onion tops and simmer for a few minutes more. Add wine and the water or stock, stir until heated through, and pour the sauce over carp.

3. Bake in a 350° oven for 30 minutes or until the carp flakes.

4. Sprinkle with parsley and serve.

Frogs' Legs

Back in our fields runs a shallow, muddy stream, making its sluggish way to the lake. Here we look for soft-shelled crabs for bait once the bass season opens; here too are to be found occasional catfish to grace our table.

In the spring, when the bullfrog sings his love song on soft hazy nights, our thoughts turn to FROGS' LEGS SAUTÉ. Accordingly, we set out after dark, armed with our "frogging" gear, and head for the swamp or the stream nearby, either of which may be a likely spot for a good catch. The frogs we have here are smaller than those which are raised commercially, but their flavor is infinitely superior, since those served even in fine restaurants have generally been frozen.

The game laws differ in different sections of the country and each amateur "frogger" has his own method of catching his prey. I suggest that, unless the game warden is one of your party—or perhaps particularly if he is—you make sure you abide by the rules. In some places a bright beam of light is used to blind the frog so that he is easily captured. In others this is against the law. In some places the frogs are speared, or picked up by means of a long pole with a clip on the end. I have also seen them simply caught by hand.

Frogs' Legs Salad

1. Boil frogs' legs in half milk and half water until tender. Remove all meat from bones, dice and chill.

2. Combine meat with any good mayonnaise, sprinkle with a few drops of lemon juice, and serve over slices of tomato aspic. Garnish with water cress.

Frogs' Legs Poulette

Serves 4

20 frogs' legs
1 cup salt water and
1 cup milk, combined
3 tablespoons butter
3 shallots, chopped fine
1 carrot, chopped fine
4 mushrooms, sliced
1 tablespoon flour

½ cup fish stock (or chicken
    broth)
¼ cup white wine
Salt and freshly ground pepper
Parsley, minced
Lemon juice
3 egg yolks, lightly beaten
3 tablespoons cream
1 tablespoon sweet butter

1. Soak frogs' legs in salt-water-and-milk mixture for one hour. Drain and pat dry.

2. Melt butter in a saucepan, add shallots, carrot, and mushrooms, and cook a few minutes. Add frogs' legs and cook until tender. Remove from pan and keep hot.

3. Stir flour into the saucepan in which frogs' legs have cooked, then slowly add fish stock or chicken broth. Add the wine, the salt and pepper, stir until thick and hot, then add lemon juice to taste and the minced parsley. Combine egg yolks and cream, then slowly add the hot sauce, stirring as you pour. Add the sweet butter, return to saucepan, reheat, and pour sauce over frogs' legs. If you prefer, the meat may be removed from the bones and added to the sauce, to be served on toast or in patty shells.

Frogs' Legs in Tomato Sauce

Serves 4

16 to 20 frogs' legs
Olive oil
Cream
Seasoned flour
1 onion, sliced very thin

1 ripe tomato
1 clove garlic, whole
Lemon juice
Salt and freshly ground pepper

1. Heat olive oil in a skillet. Dip frogs' legs in cream, then in flour. Brown in the oil. Continue to cook gently until tender. Remove to a serving dish and keep hot.

2. Add the onion, tomato, and garlic clove to the oil in the skillet and simmer until sauce is well cooked. Remove garlic, add a dash of lemon juice, adjust the seasoning, and pour sauce over the frogs' legs.

Frogs' Legs Fricassee

Serves 4

Adjust the number of frogs' legs according to their size.

20 frogs' legs	2 egg yolks
3 tablespoons butter	2 tablespoons cream
¾ cup chicken stock	Hot buttered toast, cut in
¼ cup dry white wine	triangles

1. In a skillet, melt the butter and brown the frogs' legs lightly. Add chicken stock and wine and simmer for 20 minutes, or until tender. Arrange on a serving dish over toast. Keep hot.

2. Beat the egg yolks and cream together, then slowly add the hot liquid from skillet, beating constantly so as not to curdle. Return to stove. When thick and hot, pour sauce over the frogs' legs.

French Fried Frogs' Legs

Serves 4

16 to 20 frogs' legs	1 egg, lightly beaten, and
Salt and freshly ground pepper	2 tablespoons milk
Fine bread crumbs	

1. Season the frogs' legs with salt and pepper, and roll in bread crumbs. Then dip in the egg-and-milk mixture, and roll again in the crumbs.

2. Fry in deep fat at 375°, allowing about 3 minutes to brown nicely. Serve with Maitre-d'hôtel Sauce (see page 155).

Frogs' Legs Sauté

The simplest way to prepare frogs' legs is to sauté them. Shake them in a bag of seasoned flour and cook in butter until tender and brown. Serve with lemon wedges or Tartar Sauce (see page 161).

Frog Legs' Provençal

Serves 4

This is a traditional recipe which may be found in one version or another in any cookbook.

16 to 20 frogs' legs   1 clove garlic, crushed
5 tablespoons butter   Lemon juice to taste
Salt and freshly ground pepper   Minced parsley

1. Season frogs' legs with salt and pepper and sauté in melted butter in a skillet until tender and brown. Arrange on a hot platter. Keep hot.
2. Add garlic to the butter in the pan, brown butter lightly, then add lemon juice and minced parsley. Pour over the frogs' legs.

Frogs' Legs with Seafood

Frogs' legs combine well with crabmeat or scallops to make casseroles. A good sauce, a little wine, some herbs, and you have a delicious dish.

Perch

After the smelt fishing is over there comes a brief lull, then we find that the *Perca flavescena,* or yellow perch, are biting.

In New England, one finds a white perch (*Morone americana,* if you are interested) which is more of a game fish than the yellow perch. Both these fish are increasing to the point of being regarded as Public Enemy No. I by conservationists, who beg the fishermen to keep all they catch, down to the tiniest babies, so as to give other fish a chance.

Yellow perch travel in schools and like to hug the bottom of shallow, reedy waters. We find a likely patch of reeds and stay there, sitting quietly in our boat, our hooks, baited with minnows, near the bottom. A nibble shows the fish is interested. But we wait. A premature move may scare him away. Once there is a harder nibble, give a gentle jerk to set the hook, and pull him in. To keep him fresh, place him in a net hanging over the side of the boat, re-bait the hook and wait again. If the perch are hitting, it won't be a long wait. You will have enough for supper and some to give your neighbor.

Perch with Wine Sauce

Serves 4

4 large perch, cleaned
2 tablespoons butter
Seasoned flour
3 tablespoons dry white wine

3 tablespoons butter
2 tablespoons flour
1 cup milk
Few sprigs dill

1. Dust perch with seasoned flour. In a skillet, melt the butter, add perch, and brown very lightly on both sides. Add the wine and cook slowly for about 10 minutes. Transfer to a serving platter and keep hot.

2. To make sauce, melt additional butter, stir in flour, add the milk, wine, and butter left in the pan after cooking perch. Stir until smooth, thick and hot. Adjust seasoning.

3. Pour sauce over the fish. Garnish with fresh dill.

Pan Fried Perch

Serves 4

4 perch—more if small
Seasoned flour

Butter and vegetable shortening
(in equal amounts)

1. Shake fish in a bag of seasoned flour, coating them thoroughly.

2. Melt butter and shortening in a skillet. Cook fish over rather brisk fire, watching carefully that they do not burn. Brown, then turn and brown the other side. Allow about ten minutes in all, unless they are large ones.

3. Serve while crisp and hot with Black Butter with tarragon vinegar (see page 145) or with Tartar Sauce (see page 161).

Perch with Sauce Meunière

Fry as for PAN FRIED PERCH (see above), and serve with Sauce Meunière (see page 155).

Perch Amandine

Serves 4

4 large perch, cleaned
2 tablespoons vegetable
  shortening
2 tablespoons butter

¼ cup almonds, blanched and
  slivered
1 tablespoon lemon juice

1. In the butter and shortening, pan fry the perch (as on page 43), arrange on a serving platter, and keep hot.
2. Add the almonds to the fat in which the perch was cooked, stir, and continue cooking until golden brown. Add lemon juice and pour sauce over the fish.

Marinated Perch

Serves 4

4 large perch, cleaned

White wine marinade (see
  page 212)

1. Arrange perch in a flat flame-proof dish and cover with marinade. Allow to stand 2 or 3 hours.
2. Place over a low flame, bring to a boil and simmer for 15 minutes. Drain. Keep fish hot.
3. Serve with hot Tartar Sauce (see page 161), or Hollandaise (see page 149).

Pike

There is a great local confusion about the name of a fish we catch here in Lake Erie, since "pike" and "pickerel" are used interchangeably.

Actually, we have the pickerel (*Esox niger*) and the grass pickerel or grass snake (*Esox vermiculatus*), both of which are scorned by local fishermen but which are considered good eating elsewhere provided they are filleted.

What we fish for is *Stizostendion vitreum,* or the walleye, and we refer to them as "pike" or "yellows." This fish is actually a member of the perch family and is both exciting to catch and delicious to eat.

We go out on the lake about a mile and a half and troll for them in the early evening. We use a heavy sinker to go deep down, and have found a Yellow Sally baited with a night crawler the most successful thing to use. If we feel a nibble, we give the pike plenty of time to swallow the bait before we set the hook.

Pike may leap in the air like a bass, or it may sulk on the bottom and then decide to run. You never know. One thing you can be sure of is that he will give you a tussle.

Sometimes pike may be found near the shore at dusk on summer evenings, or in the early morning. They travel in schools so that one strike will usually be followed by others. All in all, this is a very satisfactory fish from the viewpoint of the fisherman as well as the cook.

Pike Aux Fines Herbes
Serves 4

1 pike, cleaned and scaled
Marinade, 1 part vinegar to 5
   parts water
Salt

1 onion, sliced very thin
Few sprigs parsley
¼ cup vinegar
1 bay leaf

1. Cut pike into ¾-inch slices. Cover with marinade and let stand for one hour.
2. Arrange slices in a skillet, add salt, onion, parsley, vinegar, and bay leaf, and simmer gently until the fish flakes.
3. Transfer to serving dish. Serve with Sauce aux Fines Herbes (see page 148) or Caper Sauce.

Pike in Sour Cream—I
Serves 4

1 pike, scaled and cleaned
Seasoned flour
Butter

1 cup sour cream
Buttered bread crumbs

1. Remove the head if you wish, and roll fish in seasoned flour. Brown in a skillet in hot butter, then transfer to a buttered casserole.
2. Spread with sour cream, cover over with bread crumbs, and bake in a 400° oven for another 20 minutes, testing for doneness with a fork. When the fish flakes, it is ready.

Pike in Sour Cream—II

Serves 4

1 pike, cut in slices ¾-inch thick	Butter
	Buttered bread crumbs
Salt and freshly ground pepper	Grated cheese
1 onion, sliced very thin	1 tablespoon lemon juice
1 cup sour cream	

1. Season fish with salt and pepper, arrange in buttered baking dish and cover with raw onion slices. Pour sour cream over fish, dot with butter, and bake in a 350° oven, basting with the cream until done or about 20 to 25 minutes.

2. Combine bread crumbs with grated cheese to taste and sprinkle over the fish. Slide dish under the broiler to brown. Transfer slices to a hot platter.

3. Add lemon juice to liquid in the pan, adjust seasoning, bring to a boil, and pour sauce over the fish.

Baked Pike with Forcemeat

Serves 4

This is a recipe from an old cookbook.

1 whole pike, cleaned for cooking	Salt and freshly ground pepper
	1 egg, beaten
1 cup raw boned pike meat	Bread crumbs
½ cup medium Cream Sauce	Few sprigs parsley, minced
1 egg, lightly beaten	Melted butter
2 tablespoons soft butter	

1. To make forcemeat, grind the raw boned pike and combine with cream sauce, egg, and soft butter. Beat until very smooth or run through a blender. Season with salt and pepper to taste.

2. Rinse the whole pike, dry well, stuff with the forcemeat and skewer it with its tail in its mouth. Brush with egg and spread with bread crumbs seasoned with salt and pepper and mixed with minced parsley. Pour melted butter over the fish.

3. Bake in a 350° oven for about 30 minutes. Serve with any good fish sauce.

Pike in Aspic

Serves 4

This is an excellent dish to serve as an extra at a buffet supper; or it can be one of the many dishes at a Smorgasbord.

2 pounds pike fillets
2 peppercorns
1 teaspoon salt
Few sprigs parsley
1 bay leaf

Dill weed to taste
Water to cover
Unflavored gelatin
Fish stock
Mayonnaise

1. In a saucepan, combine the pike, peppercorns, salt, parsley, bay leaf, and dill. (We like enough dill for its flavor to predominate, but that is a matter of taste.) Add cold water to cover, and simmer until fish is tender.

2. Remove fish to serving dish. Strain the stock.

3. Dissolve the gelatin, using 1 tablespoon for each cup of hot stock, pour over fish and let it set. Serve cold with a good mayonnaise. If you wish, the fish may be cut into pieces, arranged in a fancy mold with pimento, sliced ripe olives, truffles, etc., added for decoration, and unmolded when the aspic has set. Serve with Cucumber Sauce (see page 147).

Pike with Oyster Forcemeat

Serves 6

1 whole pike, cleaned for
    cooking
½ pint oysters, chopped
3 tablespoons melted butter
½ teaspoon salt

¾ cup fine bread crumbs
½ cup milk
Pinch of mace
3 cups court bouillon (see page
    59)

1. Wash the pike, dry inside and salt the cavity.

2. Combine the oysters, bread crumbs, milk, butter, salt, and mace. Stir over a low flame until mixture is very smooth. Run through blender if you have one.

3. Stuff pike with this forcemeat, skewer or sew the opening together, and put fish in a baking dish. Add court bouillon.

4. Cover and bake in a 350° oven for 30 minutes, or until the fish flakes. Serve with Oyster Sauce (see page 156).

Baked Yellow Pike
Serves 4

1 yellow pike, cleaned, scaled, Salt and freshly ground pepper
 head removed ½ cup white wine
1 onion, sliced thin ½ cup water or fish stock
4 carrots, sliced thin 4 bacon or salt pork slices

1. Arrange fish on a buttered baking dish and place onion and carrots in the cavity and around the edges. Season with salt and pepper, add wine and the water or fish stock, and cover with bacon or salt pork slices.

2. Bake in a 350° oven for 45 minutes. Serve with Dill or Egg Sauce (see pages 150 and 148).

Baked Pike in Red Wine
Serves 4

For this we usually fillet the fish.

2 large or 4 small fillets 3 tablespoons butter
Salt and freshly ground pepper Few sprigs parsley, minced
6 shallots, chopped fine 2 tablespoons dry red wine
3 or 4 mushrooms, chopped fine

1. Arrange the fillets in a buttered baking dish. Season with salt and pepper.

2. In a skillet, melt the butter and cook shallots and mushrooms for a minute or two. Add the parsley and wine.

3. Pour sauce over the fish and bake in a 350° oven for 30 minutes.

Fried Pike
Serves 4

1 pike, prepared for cooking 1 egg, lightly beaten, and
Batter, or bread crumbs
Flour Onion butter
 Lemon slices

1. Slice pike into ¾-inch-thick pieces and dip in batter; or dredge with flour, dip in beaten egg, and roll in fine bread crumbs.

2. Fry in deep fat at 370° for 5 to 8 minutes, or until golden brown. Drain.

3. Arrange on serving platter, spread with onion butter (see page 144), and garnish with lemon slices.

Pike with Oyster Sauce

Serves 4 to 6

Here, again, is an old recipe. It may seem too simple to be good, but the oyster sauce makes it something special.

1 pike, prepared for cooking, head and tail left on
Soft butter
Salt and freshly ground pepper
Flour
Melted butter and water, combined

1. Spread fish with butter, season with salt and pepper and dredge with flour. Arrange in buttered baking dish.

2. Place in a hot (450°) oven. When flour begins to brown, baste with butter and water. Bake 40 minutes in all. Serve with Oyster Sauce (see page 156).

Fillet of Pike in Egg Sauce

Serves 4

4 pike fillets, plus heads and bones
1 slice lemon
1 bay leaf
1 small onion, sliced
1 sprig parsley
1 sprig chervil
½ cup dry white wine
Fish broth
1 tablespoon cornstarch
2 hard-cooked eggs, sliced

1. Place fillets, plus fish heads and bones, in a saucepan with enough water to cover them. Simmer for 15 minutes.

2. Strain the broth, add lemon, bay leaf, onion, parsley, chervil, and wine, and simmer for another 5 minutes. Add pike fillets and simmer until tender—10 to 15 minutes, depending on thickness of the fillets. Remove fish from broth and keep hot.

3. Again strain the broth and simmer until reduced to about half. Thicken with the cornstarch mixed with a little cold water. Stir sauce until thick and hot.

4. Add egg slices and pour over the fish. Serve at once.

Baked Sheepshead

I remember well when I lugged a large sheepshead triumphantly into the boat. It was the largest fish I had ever caught and I expected to be complimented on my lucky catch.

But my arrival at the dock was met with uproarious laughter and I was advised to plant my prize under a shrub for fertilizer, or better still, drop it back into the lake. I did that.

However, it turned out to be one of those "they laughed when I sat down at the piano" deals, because here is a recipe for baked sheepshead at which no one will laugh.

1 sheepshead	1 mild onion, sliced paper thin
3 tablespoons butter	Salt pork slices
Salt and freshly ground pepper	

1. Prepare the fish for cooking immediately upon bringing it home. The head may be removed or not, as you prefer.

2. Place a flame-proof baking dish directly over a low fire. Brown the butter in it, remove from stove, and lay the fish in the butter. Season with salt and pepper inside and out, and arrange onion slices both inside the cavity and on the outside. Place salt pork slices over the onion.

3. Bake in a 375° oven for 30 minutes, basting occasionally with the fat in the pan.

Trout

This tantalizing game fish of the salmon family provides the most exciting fishing and delicious eating. Its unpredictability exasperates the fisherman and at the same time fascinates him.

The particular trout you will fish for depends on your geographic whereabouts. In the western part of the continent you may fish for the *Cutthroat Trout*, which is known by at least seventy other names and is a small trout living in coastal waters and inland lakes and streams, in the Rocky Mountain area and along the Pacific coast from California to southern Alaska. This fish is very amiable and will take any kind of bait—a fly, a worm, or a spinner. In the West, you will also find the beautiful *Golden Trout* which lives in lakes at high altitude and is fished for in the summer after the snow has receded. The *Dolly Varden* is a larger trout, 10 pounds not being unusual, and is easy to catch by either casting or trolling.

Perhaps the best known trout in the United States and Canada is the *Rainbow Trout,* originally found only on the Pacific coast but now widely distributed. It is found in secluded mountain lakes where it is caught with a bait-casting rod, and in swift-running streams where fly or spinning rods are used.

The *Brown Trout,* introduced here from Europe, is found in the lakes, streams, rivers and ponds of the northern United States and southern Canada. For this, use dry or wet flies, spinning lures, or natural bait.

The *Brook* or *Speckled Trout* is found from Labrador down to the Great Lakes region, and also in smaller quantities all over the United States except in the South. It occasionally inhabits some cold lakes but is usually found in streams. It will take a dry or wet fly and is a good fighter.

When dry-fly fishing, select the fly nearest to whatever insect the trout feeds on at the time. The trout lies with its head upstream, so the fly should be cast above the fish, gently, so as not to alarm it. Let it float down on the current in a natural manner; if there is no strike, carefully lift the fly, dry it if necessary (there is a silicone spray on the market for this purpose), and cast again.

The *Lake Trout* or *Salmon Trout,* is widely distributed in large, cold, very deep lakes in Canada and the Great Lakes region, and is found in a few western lakes as well. The best fishing for "lakers" is in the spring when the ice is out of the water and a few warm days have made the trout active. In July and August the fisherman is plagued with black flies, and therefore those months had best be avoided. Cold weather in the fall brings good fishing again. This fish can run from 20 to 50 pounds though the average is much smaller. The method of fishing depends on the temperature and depth of the water. This trout cruises in water from 40° to 50°. In the spring and fall the fish comes to the surface, and a fly or bait-casting rod can be used. When the weather grows warm the fish retreats to colder depths, which in the case of a very cold, deep lake might be only twelve or fourteen feet down but otherwise might be the bottom. Troll slowly under these conditions, using artificial lures, worms, or minnows, and getting the hook just above the floor of the lake.

Whatever kind of trout you are after, you will find it thrilling sport and very satisfactory from the culinary standpoint, too.

Pan Fried Trout
Serves 6

6 rainbow trout, cleaned, heads and tails on
1 egg, well beaten
Fine bread crumbs

Salt and freshly ground pepper
4 tablespoons butter
1 teaspoon salad oil

1. Dip trout in egg and roll in bread crumbs. Season with salt and pepper.

2. Fry in combined butter and oil until the fish flakes and is brown. Serve with Tartar Sauce (see page 161), or Sauce Aux Fines Herbes (see page 148).

Lake Trout in Wine
Serves 4

4 fillets of lake trout
Seasoned flour
4 tablespoons butter
1 teaspoon salad oil

1 onion, sliced paper thin
1 cup dry white wine
1 egg yolk, beaten

1. Roll the fillets in flour and brown in the butter and oil. Arrange in a baking dish.

2. Cook the onion in the butter and oil until transparent but not brown. Arrange the onion slices over trout and pour the wine around it.

3. Cover and bake in a 350° oven for 35 to 45 minutes. Remove fish to a serving platter and keep hot. Strain the sauce.

4. Slowly stir the sauce into the egg yolk, return to saucepan, and cook over a slow fire until thick and hot. Check the seasoning and pour the sauce over the trout.

Whole Baked Trout

Serves 6

1 3-pound lake trout, cleaned   Salt and freshly ground pepper
   head and tail left on   Few sprigs thyme
1 lemon, sliced   Salt pork, sliced thin, to cover

1. Place a sheet of tin foil on a cookie sheet, oil the foil, and place the trout, its cavity seasoned with salt and pepper, on it. Fill the cavity with lemon slices and thyme. Cover fish with salt pork slices.

2. Bake at 400° for 25 minutes, or until the fish flakes. Serve with Egg Sauce (see page 148).

Baked Trout with Oyster Stuffing

Serves 4

4 brown trout, cleaned, heads   Melted butter
   and tails on   Salt and freshly ground pepper
Oyster stuffing (see page 68)

1. Make oyster stuffing using half the recipe given. Fill the cavities and sew them up. Brush the fish with melted butter and sprinkle with salt and pepper.

2. Bake at 350° for 30 minutes. Garnish with water cress and lemon slices.

Trout Meunière

Serves 4

4 brook trout, prepared for   ½ cup butter
   cooking   3 tablespoons lemon juice
Seasoned flour   4 tablespoons parsley, minced
4 tablespoons vegetable oil

1. Roll trout in seasoned flour and brown in the oil in the skillet. Cook until the fish flakes, remove to a serving platter, and keep hot.

2. Brown the butter, add the lemon juice and parsley. Pour it hot over the trout. Garnish with lemon slices.

Baked Brook Trout

Serves 4

4 trout, prepared for cooking
2 tablespoons vegetable
   shortening
2 slices bacon

2 tablespoons lemon juice
2 tablespoons butter, melted
Minced parsley
Freshly grated nutmeg

1. Season cavities with salt and pepper. Brown the fish quickly in hot shortening. Arrange in baking dish, cover with bacon slices, and sprinkle with lemon juice and melted butter.
2. Bake at 350° for 30 minutes, or until the fish flakes. Serve on a hot platter. Sprinkle minced parsley over fish and grate a little nutmeg on top.

Poached Trout

Serves 6

6 rainbow trout, prepared for
   cooking
Court bouillon (see page 59)
2 tablespoons butter

2 tablespoons flour
1 egg yolk, beaten with
1 tablespoon heavy cream
Salt and freshly ground pepper

1. Simmer trout in court bouillon for 10 minutes. Remove to a serving dish and keep hot.
2. Melt butter, stir in flour, and cook for a minute or two. Add two cups of the court bouillon in which the trout cooked. When thick and hot, pour it slowly into the egg yolk and cream mixture. Return to saucepan and reheat. Add salt and pepper to taste and pour sauce over the trout.

Cold Poached Trout

Poach trout as directed above, but allow to cool in the court bouillon. Serve with mayonnaise to which capers have been added, or with any cold fish sauce.

Pan Fried Trout with Mushrooms
Serves 4

4 brown trout, cleaned, heads
   and tails on
Seasoned flour
4 tablespoons butter

1 teaspoon salad oil
6 mushrooms, sliced
2 tablespoons lemon juice

1. Roll trout in seasoned flour; fry in butter and oil until the fish flake and are brown. Remove to a serving platter; keep hot.

2. Sauté mushrooms in the fat until tender. Add the lemon juice and pour mixture over the trout.

FISH IN GENERAL

These recipes may be used for whatever fish you have on hand.

Baked Fish
Serves 4 to 6

1 3-pound fish, cleaned
Salt and freshly ground pepper
1 cup fish stock
1 cup dry white wine
1 sprig, each, parsley and
   thyme

1 bay leaf
1 small onion, sliced thin
1 egg yolk, beaten with
¼ cup cream
Buttered bread crumbs

1. This is a good size for baking. Remove head and tail to make fish stock. Fillet the fish if you wish, in which case add the bones to the stock pot.

2. Butter a flame-proof oven dish, arrange the fish in it, add salt and pepper to taste, and cover with the fish stock and wine. Add parsley, thyme, and bay leaf, place a few onion slices on top, and simmer gently, covered, for about 12 minutes. Fish should be tender but should not fall apart.

3. Pour off the liquid and reduce it to one-half the quantity. Add the egg yolk and cream mixture. Correct the seasoning. Heat the sauce and pour over the fish.

4. Sprinkle bread crumbs over the top and bake in a 450° oven for 15 minutes.

Fish Cakes

Serves 4

For this, I use any leftover cooked fish and follow the general methods for codfish cakes.

2 cups flaked fish
2 cups mashed potatoes
Salt and freshly ground pepper
2 tablespoons chopped parsley

2 teaspoons chopped thyme
1 egg, well beaten
Butter

1. Use instant mashed potatoes, following directions on the box, or left over mashed potatoes. Combine the potatoes, fish, salt, and pepper to taste, parsley, thyme, and egg. Mix well.

2. Form into cakes and sauté in butter until hot and brown. Serve with Tomato Sauce (see page 160) or Piquante Fish Sauce (see page 160).

Fish Cutlets

Serves 4

2 cups cooked, flaked fish
3 tablespoons butter
2 tablespoons chopped onion
3 tablespoons flour
1 cup light cream

Salt and freshly ground pepper
3 egg yolks, lightly beaten
Prepared breading mixture
Deep fat

1. Melt the butter and cook onion for a minute or two.

2. Add flour and cream, season with salt and pepper, and stir the sauce over a low fire until smooth, thick and hot.

3. Stir a little of the hot sauce into the egg yolks, then slowly add to the rest of the sauce. Mix well and return to the fire for a minute or two. Add the flaked fish.

4. Pour the mixture into a shallow pan and place in refrigerator until cold and firm.

5. Shape into cutlets, roll in a breading mixture, and fry in deep fat at 390° for 3 or 4 minutes.

6. Drain on a paper towel and serve piping hot with a Tomato Sauce (see page 160) or Anchovy Sauce (see page 145).

Devilled Fish in Shells

Serves 4

This is an excellent basic recipe, and may be used with lobster meat, salmon, or shrimp.

2 cups cooked fish, flaked
4 tablespoons butter
1 tablespoon chopped onion
3 tablespoons flour
1 cup rich milk, or half and half
Salt and freshly ground pepper
½ teaspoon dry mustard

1 sprig thyme, chopped
1 tablespoon lemon juice
1 teaspoon Worcestershire
    Sauce
1 sprig parsley, chopped
1 egg, beaten
3 tablespoons sherry

Use any type of fish—bass, carp, or whatever you have.

1. Melt the butter, cook the onion until transparent, and stir in flour and milk. (I like to use half milk and half cream, but this is not necessary.) Season with salt, pepper, dry mustard, thyme, lemon juice, Worcestershire Sauce, and parsley. Continue cooking until thick.

2. Stir a little of the hot sauce into beaten egg, then beat egg mixture into the sauce. Add the sherry, then the fish, and mix well. Fill the shells or individual ramekins.

3. Bake in a 300° oven for 15 or 20 minutes.

Creamed Fish on Toast

Serves 4

Any fish—about 2 pounds
3 tablespoons butter
3 tablespoons flour
1½ cups fish stock

½ cup cream
2 tablespoons sherry
Toast triangles
Anchovy butter

1. Poach the fish. Reserve the liquid in which it cooked. Remove all fish from the bones.

2. In a skillet, melt the butter and stir in the flour, add the fish stock, cream and sherry, and stir the sauce until smooth, thick and hot. Put in the flaked fish and heat thoroughly. Serve on toast triangles, spread with anchovy butter.

Fish Curry

In India, where curries originated, curried fish, chicken, and meat are flavored with individual spices, and the chutney served with these dishes is made fresh for each meal.

In this country, we use ready-made curry powders and buy chutney in jars. With the making of a good curry so simplified for us, we should use this way of adding delicious variety to our menus more often.

While discussing curries, let me urge you to buy imported curry powder. It is not too expensive and adds an indefinable something to the dish that domestic curry powders lack.

If you wish, you can make a curry the day before and store it in the refrigerator. Such a period of waiting blends the flavors and, I believe, improves the dish.

I like to cook the rice for my curries Indian style. However, plain boiled rice is quite satisfactory. If you are in a hurry you can also use instant rice.

Serves 4

Fish for 4 people   1 cup raw rice
Curry Sauce (see page 146)   1 jar chutney

1. I start by cooking the fish. If it is already cooked, just cube it. Then I make a Curry Sauce, add the fish and keep this hot in the top of a double boiler while cooking the rice.
2. Serve the curry and rice in separate dishes; or put the curry in the center of a large platter and surround with the rice. Chutney is a "must" with curry; also serve as many of these as you care to: shredded cocoanut, chopped toasted almonds, salted peanuts, baked bananas, crisp crumbled bacon, chopped sweet pickles, chopped hard-boiled eggs.

Court Bouillon for Fish

There are different recipes for court bouillon. This is the one I use for fish, shell fish, and sweetbreads. Any court bouillon which is left over can be frozen and used again.

6 cups water	1 bay leaf
2 cups dry white wine	A few celery leaves
2 tablespoons salt	2 or 3 sprigs parsley
6 peppercorns, crushed	3 cloves
1 onion, thinly sliced	2 or 3 slices lemon

1. Use either all water or water and dry white wine. I like to use them in the proportions given above. Add salt to taste, peppercorns, onion, bay leaf, celery leaves, parsley, cloves, and lemon. Simmer for 30 minutes.

2. Strain the bouillon and poach fish in it. Remember fish should never boil. When planning to serve fish cold, allow to cool in the bouillon: it will have a delightful flavor and be pleasantly moist.

3. For serving fish hot, use the bouillon in making the sauce.

Fish Fillet Sauté

Serves 4

Use any fillets. Pike, bass or perch are good.

Butter	Salt and freshly ground pepper
4 fish fillets	Parsley
Mayonnaise	Lemon

1. Melt the butter in a skillet or flame-proof casserole with a detachable handle.

2. Spread the fillets with any good mayonnaise, preferably one you have made yourself. Season to taste with a little salt and pepper and sauté fish for about 15 minutes, depending on its thickness. (The mayonnaise insures a deliciously moist fish, and adds to the flavor as well.) Serve piping hot, garnished with chopped parsley and lemon wedges.

Fish Fillets in White Wine—I

This is a simple, delicious way of dealing with any fish you may have on hand.

4 fish fillets, plus heads, tails, bones
Water to cover
Few sprigs each, thyme and parsley
Chives to taste
2 tablespoons butter

2 or 3 scallion tops, finely chopped
2 or 3 mushrooms, sliced
Salt and freshly ground pepper
White wine
Fish stock

1. Fillet your fish, and make a fish stock by simmering the heads, bones, and fish scraps, in water, with thyme, parsley and chives added.

2. In a skillet melt the butter and arrange the fillets in it. Add the scallion tops and mushrooms, season with salt and pepper, and cover with ½ white wine and ½ fish stock.

3. At this point I diverge from the usual method, which is to cut out a circle of paper to fit the pan, cut a small hole in the center, butter the paper, and fit this closely over the fish. I ignore this probably important but tedious step, and merely cover the pan with a tight-fitting lid.

4. Simmer the fish for 10 to 12 minutes.

5. Remove to a serving dish and keep hot while making any of the following sauces:

Sauce A

2 tablespoons butter
1 tablespoon flour

Liquid from poached fish

Cream butter and flour and add to the liquid in the pan. Stir until smooth and hot and pour sauce over the fish.

Sauce B

2 tablespoons butter
1 tablespoon flour
Liquid from poached fish
2 egg yolks, lightly beaten

1/3 cup cream
Toasted almonds or
Pickled nasturtium seeds

Cream butter and flour, add to liquid in the pan and stir until thick and smooth. Combine eggs yolks and cream and slowly pour in the hot liquid, stirring as you pour. Return sauce to the fire and heat through, but do not allow it to boil. Pour over the fish, sprinkle with toasted almonds or nasturtium seeds and serve.

Sauce C

This is a more elaborate finish, but one you might like to try. I assure you that it is very good.

1 recipe for Sauce B, plus   3 tablespoons whipped cream
1 can small seedless white grapes,
    drained

To recipe B, add the grapes, fold in the cream, and pour some over the fish. Place under the broiler and brown lightly. Serve immediately.

Fish Fillets in White Wine—II

Serves 4

4 fish fillets   Chives to taste, chopped fine
4 potatoes, parboiled, sliced   Salt and freshly ground pepper
Few sprigs each of chervil and   1 cup dry white wine
    tarragon, chopped fine   Buttered bread crumbs

1. Cover bottom of a buttered baking dish with a layer of potato slices.
2. Combine chervil, tarragon, and chives, and sprinkle over the potatoes. Season with salt and pepper. Arrange a layer of fish on top of herbs and season again.
3. Pour wine over the fish, cover with bread crumbs, and bake in a 400° oven for 30 minutes.

Fish Casserole

Serves 4

We use any cooked fish for this: pike, perch or bass.

2 cups flaked cooked fish
2 tablespoons butter
Few thin onion slices
2 tablespoons flour
2 cups milk or
1½ cups milk and

½ cup cream
Few sprigs parsley, chopped
2 green onion tops, cut fine
1 tablespoon sherry
Buttered bread crumbs

1. Place the fish in a buttered casserole.
2. In a skillet, melt the butter, add onion, and cook until transparent but not brown. Stir in the flour, add the milk and simmer until sauce thickens. Add parsley, onion tops and sherry and pour sauce over the fish. Cover with bread crumbs.
3. Bake in a 350° oven for 20 minutes, or until bread crumbs are brown and the fish bubbly.

Cold Fish Loaf

Serves 6

This is a delicious luncheon or supper dish made of cooked fish of any kind. Use home-made mayonnaise.

3 cups cold cooked fish
1 cup mayonnaise
1 tablespoon each, tarragon,
    parsley, and chives,
    chopped

8 ripe or green olives,
    chopped, or
4 hard-boiled eggs, chopped
1 teaspoon capers
Sliced tomatoes
A few sprigs chervil

1. To the mayonnaise add tarragon, parsley and chives.
2. In the dish in which you intend to serve it, place a layer of fish and cover with a layer of mayonnaise. Repeat, ending with a layer of mayonnaise. This may be varied by the addition of ripe or green olives, hard-cooked eggs, capers, and so on.
3. Serve cold, surrounded by tomato slices.

Fish Omelet

Serves 4

1 cup cooked fish, flaked
2 tablespoons each butter and flour

1 cup rich milk or light cream
5 eggs for omelet

1. Combine the butter, flour, and milk or light cream to make a cream sauce. Add the fish, beat and keep hot.
2. Make an omelet, and when this is done use half the fish for filling, folding the omelet over. Turn out on a hot serving dish and pour remaining fish mixture around it.

Pickled Fish

Serves 4

Serve as a refreshing hot weather dish, or make a smaller amount to serve as an appetizer.

2 pounds fish, in thick slices
1 cup olive oil
½ cup vinegar
6 crushed peppercorns
¼ teaspoon salt
1 bay leaf

4 onions, sliced thin
Lime juice
Salt
4 tablespoons olive oil
1 garlic clove

1. Make a sauce as follows: Combine olive oil, vinegar, peppercorns, salt, bay leaf, and onions, and simmer for 30 minutes. Cool.
2. Sprinkle lime juice over fish slices and season with salt.
3. Heat olive oil in a skillet and sauté garlic clove in it for a few minutes. Remove garlic and brown the fish slices in the oil. Cook for about 10 minutes or until the fish flakes.
4. Pour a little of the cool sauce into a deep glass dish. Cover this with fish slices, pour in more sauce, and add more fish. Repeat until all the fish is used, ending with sauce.
5. Let stand overnight in the refrigerator. Serve cold.

Fish Flakes in Shells

Serves 6

3 cups cooked, flaked fish
¾ cup home-made mayonnaise
  (see page 180)
½ teaspoon salt
1 teaspoon Worcestershire
  Sauce

½ teaspoon dry mustard
2 teaspoons capers
Sprig of parsley and a few
  tarragon leaves, chopped
Buttered shells
Whipped cream

1. Combine mayonnaise, salt, Worcestershire Sauce, dry mustard, capers, parsley, and tarragon.
2. Combine mayonnaise and flaked fish and fill the shells. Top with more mayonnaise, to which has been added an equal amount of whipped cream.
3. Bake in 350° oven for 20 minutes.

Kedergee

Serves 4

2 cups cooked fish (any kind)
2 cups hot cooked rice
2 hard boiled eggs, chopped

3 tablespoons chopped parsley
Salt and freshly ground pepper
½ cup cream

1. Combine fish and rice. Add the eggs and parsley, season with salt and pepper to taste and moisten with cream.
2. Place mixture in a buttered casserole and bake in a 325° oven for 20 minutes.

Hot Fish Loaf

Serves 6

2 cups cooked fish, flaked
2 tablespoons butter
2 tablespoons flour
1 cup top milk or
½ cup cream and
½ cup milk

Salt and freshly ground pepper
1 cup soft bread crumbs
2 tablespoons each chopped
  parsley and chives
1 egg, beaten
Fish sauce, according to
  preference

1. Combine the butter, flour, milk, salt, and pepper to make a white sauce. Add the fish, bread crumbs, parsley, and chives; add beaten egg last. Pour mixture into a buttered loaf pan, which in turn is placed in a pan of hot water, to be put into the oven.
2. Bake at 350° for about 50 minutes.
3. Serve with any fish sauce. We like Dill Sauce (see page 150).

Puerto Rican Fish

Serves 4

2 pounds fish, cut into thick slices	1 8-oz. can tomato sauce
½ cup olive oil	1 tablespoon vinegar
6 onions, sliced paper thin	1 bay leaf
¾ cup water	1 teaspoon salt
12 sliced stuffed olives	3 or 4 tablespoons olive oil
1 tablespoon capers	1 clove garlic
2 tablespoons sliced pimentoes	Salt

1. Make a sauce as follows: Heat oil in a skillet and add the onions, water, olives, capers, pimentoes, tomato sauce, vinegar, bay leaf, and salt. Simmer for one hour. Meanwhile, prepare fish.
2. Slightly season fish slices with salt. Heat more oil in a skillet and cook garlic in it for a few minutes. Remove the garlic, add the fish slices, and sauté for 10 minutes, or until the fish flakes.
3. Remove to a hot platter and pour the hot sauce over it.

Seafood Casserole

Serves 6

This may be made from any fish you have caught. If the catch is small, supplement by opening a can of crab meat, shrimp, or lobster. Leftover fish may also be used.

4 cups fish	Buttered bread crumbs
2 cups Béchamel Sauce (see pages 141-142)	Grated cheese

1. Arrange the fish in layers in a buttered casserole with the Béchamel Sauce. Top with bread crumbs and cheese.
2. Bake in a 350° oven until brown and bubbly, 30 to 40 minutes.

Stuffed Baked Fish

Serves 6 to 8

As a rule we use yellow pike for this delectable dish. However, any kind of fillets can be substituted for the whole fish, provided there are two fairly large pieces of the same size to hold the stuffing.

To go to the other extreme, we were once given a very large salmon trout fresh out of a northern lake. We stuffed and baked it, and it was a sensational *pièce de résistance* for dinner. Baked whole, surrounded by tiny baked tomatoes and garnished with fennel and water cress, it was a beautiful still life.

But as to the method:

Herb Stuffing for Baked Fish

Serves 6 to 8

1 whole fish, cleaned
½ cup butter
1 shallot, chopped
1 teaspoon chopped onion
1 cup soft bread crumbs,
    soaked in milk and
    squeezed dry

2 or 3 mushrooms, chopped
1 tablespoon each, thyme,
    fennel, chives, chopped
Salt and freshly ground pepper

1. Melt the butter, add the shallot and onion, and cook for a minute or two. Add the bread crumbs, mushrooms, and herbs, season with salt and pepper to taste, and mix thoroughly.

2. Place stuffing in the cavity of the fish, or between two fillets, and bake according to directions on page 67.

Stuffing #1

Serves 6 to 8

1 whole fairly large fish
2 cups soft bread crumbs
½ cup melted butter
2 tablespoons chopped parsley

2 teaspoons each chopped
   sweet pickle and capers
Salt and freshly ground pepper
Salt pork strips
Fish sauce

1. Make a stuffing of the bread crumbs, butter, parsley, pickle, and capers. Season with salt and pepper.
2. Wash and dry the fish. Salt the cavity and pack the stuffing in lightly. Sew the fish up, or skewer opening together.
3. Place the salt pork strips over the fish, and bake in shallow buttered dish in a very hot (550°) oven for 15 minutes, or until brown. Turn oven down to 425° for about 45 minutes more. My method for baking a large fish is to use a cookie sheet, cover this with foil, and arrange the fish on it katty-corner. When done, it is easy to transfer to a platter. If you first butter the foil it will not stick. Any good fish sauce may be served with this, such as Almond Sauce, Egg Sauce, or Dill Sauce (see pages 144, 148, 150).

Stuffing #2

Serves 6 to 8

1 whole fish
1 can cooked wild rice
1 can cleaned shrimp, minced
1 teaspoon capers, chopped

2 tablespoons parsley, chopped
2 tablespoons melted butter
Salt and freshly ground pepper

1. Combine rice and shrimp, add capers, parsley, butter, and salt and pepper to taste.
2. Stuff the fish and bake according to directions given above.

Baked Fish with Oyster Dressing

Serves 6 to 8

This "receipt" is from an old cookbook and is easy and delicious.

1 fish, whole, cleaned
Salt and freshly ground pepper
1 pint oysters
½ cup rolled crackers
½ cup milk

¼ teaspoon freshly ground
   pepper
¼ teaspoon celery salt
Tiny pieces of butter

1. "Take a fine fish and soak it in salt water for ten minutes. Season it slightly with salt and pepper, and fill it with as much of the following dressing as possible. Tie with a string, and roast, basting often."

2. Dressing: Mix the oysters, crackers, milk, pepper, celery salt and butter. Mix very carefully, fill the cavity, and spread the dressing on top of the fish also.

3. For a 3- to 5-pound fish, I would suggest a 350° oven for about 30 minutes.

Oyster Stuffing for Baked Fish

Serves 6 to 8

This will stuff a large fish. If fish is small, cut the recipe in half. The stuffing may also be placed between two fillets which are then skewered together for baking.

1 fish
8 small oysters, chopped
¼ cup bread crumbs
1 anchovy, chopped fine
1 teaspoon chopped parsley
½ teaspoon chopped tarragon

3 tablespoons cream
1 tablespoon sherry
2 egg yolks, lightly beaten
4 tablespoons soft butter
Salt and freshly ground pepper

1. Combine the oysters, bread crumbs, anchovy, parsley, tarragon, cream, sherry, egg yolks, and butter. Add salt and pepper to taste. Mix thoroughly and stuff the fish to be baked.

Mushroom Stuffing for Baked Fish

Serves 6 to 8

1 whole fish, cleaned, or two
   fillets
½ onion, chopped
5 or 6 mushrooms, chopped
3 tablespoons butter

2 tablespoons chives, cut fine
1 cup soft bread crumbs
¼ cup Rhine wine
Salt and freshly ground pepper

1. Melt butter in a saucepan and simmer the onion and mushrooms for a few minutes. Add the chives, bread crumbs, wine, and salt and pepper. Mix well.

2. Season fish cavity with salt, and spread with stuffing, or place stuffing between two fillets. Skewer together, place the fish on a baking sheet covered with foil, and bake in a 350° oven for 30 minutes.

ICE FISHING

Ice fishing is becoming increasingly popular. In some places along the lake you see the strange sight of cars parked far out on the ice; tents and other shelters erected; fishermen walking about or pulling sleds on which their gear is piled. Occasionally a snow toboggan equipped with a motorcycle engine is seen where the ice is not safe for heavier vehicles.

It requires a long steady freeze to build up a safe ice layer. The New York State Conservation Department advises fishermen to observe the following rules for safety: don't go out unless the ice is at least four or five inches thick; keep automobiles off of the ice; do not venture out on thin ice, or fish by yourself; be careful of old or cracked ice; if the ice starts breaking, lie flat on your stomach and push yourself carefully to safer ice; look out for thinly-iced holes that other fishermen have cut and stay away from inlet and outlet areas and channels where currents keep the ice in a dangerous condition.

Ice fishermen who go some distance to fish, and therefore plan to spend the day at it, may possess small shacks on runners. These may be equipped with stoves, benches—which may be long enough for sleeping if the hardy fisherman spends the night—covers for the ice holes so that they do not freeze overnight and therefore require re-cutting, and any additional comforts the individual may deem desirable. A power saw for cutting the holes saves time and energy.

It is necessary, of course, to dress warmly, and if possible in layers, so that one's clothing can be adjusted as the weather changes as it is sure to do. The feet get cold first, and a good pair of insulated rubber pacs that lace, under which two pairs of wool socks can be worn, is ideal. A parka hood, warmly lined, plus a scarf, will keep the cold winds from the neck and ears. Warmly lined gloves are, of course, a must.

You will need a windbreak of some kind. We use an old duck blind, and we have a small gasoline stove. We select our spot and cut the hole in the ice. During a cold winter the ice can be as much as thirty inches thick. We pull our gear out on a sled, adjust our windbreak, and start fishing.

If the day is bright, you will need sunglasses. You may also get a sunburn. Sometimes, if the day is cloudy, the fishing is especially good, as the light through the hole in the ice brings the fish up to the surface.

To cover the subject briefly, we use either a tip-up or just a hand line. The advantage of the tip-up is that one fisherman can take care of several hooks, since a flag pops up when a fish has taken the bait. Minnows or cut up worms are good bait and can be purchased near at hand.

We find perch, smelt, and walleye here; occasionally a bass. In some places in Ontario—Lake Simco, for example—white-fish, lake trout, and herrings are caught.

Whatever your luck brings you, fresh-caught fish in the middle of winter is indeed a treat.

CHAPTER 3

Game Birds

Many game birds are ruined when left to the mercies of an inexperienced cook. It is vital to treat them with respect for their individual flavors, textures, and tenderness (or lack of it!), when you handle them in the kitchen.

If you buy your birds from a game farm, you can assume that they will be in good shape for cooking and not need special tenderizing treatment. When you get them on the wing, however, that's another matter. Who knows what their texture will be and how long they have been on this earth? If you, your husband, or friends, have enjoyed the sport of bagging the game, with the attendant mystery as to the bird's past history, follow the simple rules given below.

In the matter of hanging: This is best done in a refrigerator, where the temperature is controlled and will be between 38 and 42 degrees. Of course, a butcher's walk-in is ideal, but not always available. Birds should be aged from 3 to 6 days to develop the best flavor and texture.

The age of the bird is an important consideration in selecting the recipe to be used. A young pheasant has a pliable spur. The breastbone of a young partridge will break easily, and the leg will be plump near the foot. The claws of a young bird are sharp; those of an old one are blunted.

71

The young bird may be roasted or broiled; the old should be braised or stewed. A meat tenderizer helps in the case of the latter. Puncture the inside of the cavity deeply and thoroughly with a fork. Rub the tenderizer well into the holes and let the bird stand for one hour before cooking. You may even do this the day before cooking, but in that case put the bird back in the refrigerator until it is needed. You will find that a tough old customer is tremendously improved by tenderizing. If you are treating a turkey or goose, allow it to stand in the refrigerator for 12 to 24 hours.

All game birds are lean, it is advisable to cover the breast with slices of salt pork or two thicknesses of cheesecloth dipped in oil. Basting with butter, butter and water, or chicken stock will keep your bird deliciously moist.

Generally speaking:

1 pheasant	will serve	3 or 4
1 guinea hen	will serve	2 to 4
1 partridge	will serve	1
(if very large)	will serve	2
1 quail	will serve	1
1 woodcock	will serve	1
(two to a person is better)		
1 grouse	will serve	1

Powdered ginger rubbed on the inside of the cavity improves the flavor.

Stuff the bird with cool stuffing just before cooking. Otherwise bacteria will start working and render your bird unpalatable, if not unsafe to eat.

Serve small game birds on fried bread or toast spread with lemon butter to absorb the delicious juices.

Baste with wine and use the pan drippings for the sauce.

Grain cereals seem to go especially well with game birds: rice, wild or brown; buckwheat groats; barley or hominy; or spoon bread made with stone-ground cornmeal.

Pass wild jellies or preserves.

Garnish the platter with herbs from your herb garden—lemon verbena, chervil, salad burnet, or wild grape leaves. In fact, any interesting leaves from the woods makes an attractive garnish— avoiding poison ivy, I should hope!

Bread Sauce (see page 143) is traditional with game birds. Champagne or Burgundy should accompany them.

Wild Duck

Duck hunting has always been so popular that at one time it threatened to exterminate the birds. However, the regulations now set up to protect them, if observed conscientiously by each hunter, will preserve our water birds so that this sport can continue to be enjoyed.

As far back as Ancient Egypt, ducks and geese were hunted for sport, and as a means of livelihood as well. Wild geese, pintail ducks, and widgeon existed in countless numbers, and were baited in especially chosen pools.

At a later time, hunters merely hid in the bullrushes and stunned the birds with a club or a form of boomerang.

Here on Lake Erie, long before there is a hint of fall in the air, the hunters are busy erecting blinds on either point of the bay on which we live. They are made of any concealing material, dried rushes and evergreen boughs being favorites. When the duck season opens, we hear the sound of shots in the early dawn and we snuggle down in our warm beds, knowing that we have friends who consider it a pleasure to sit for hours in a cramped position in a cold wet blind, and will subsequently leave an offering of ducks on our doorstep. Our share in this is to issue an invitation to a duck dinner. We get mostly mallards, black ducks, pintails, and teals here.

To dress a wild duck, see page 309-310.

Duck cooking is a most controversial subject; there are those who claim that a duck should be merely carried through a warm room. Others believe the birds should be soaked in soda and water overnight, before being roasted for 2 or 3 hours.

We believe in neither extreme. Having tried all ways and taken all sorts of advice, we have concluded that about 45 minutes in a 350° oven is right for us.

Braised Wild Duck

Serves 4

See the end of this chapter, pages 105, 108, for stuffings.

2 wild ducks
Stuffing
1 cup chicken broth

1 cup dry white wine
1 onion, sliced thin
A sprig thyme

1. Stuff the ducks and place them in a roasting pan. Add the chicken broth, wine, onion, and thyme.

2. Bake, covered, in a 350° oven for 45 minutes, basting occasionally. Remove cover and bake for another 20 minutes or so, renewing the pan liquid if it cooks away.

3. Transfer to a hot platter and serve with wild rice, accompanied by a tossed salad. Pass spiced plums.

Wild Duck with Orange Sauce

Serves 4

Since domestic Duck a l'Orange is a favorite of ours, I was led to experiment with wild duck, as follows.

Breasts of 4 ducks
½ cup olive oil
¼ cup dry white wine
2 onions, sliced thin

A few sprigs parsley
Salt and freshly ground pepper
Butter

1. Combine the oil, wine, onions, parsley, and salt and pepper, and marinate the duck breasts in the mixture.

2. Drain, wipe the pieces dry with a paper towel, and sauté gently in butter until tender, or 20 to 30 minutes.

3. Arrange ducks on a hot platter and pour Hot Orange Sauce (see page 157) over it. Garnish with orange slices and sprigs of lemon verbena.

Breast of Wild Duck

Serves 4

If you have an abundance of ducks, serve just the breasts and use the rest for Duck Soup or Salmis.

4 duck breasts	1 cup chicken stock
Butter	1 teaspoon cornstarch
Salt Pork, sliced	1 tablespoon sherry

1. In a skillet melt the butter and brown the duck breasts. Remove to a baking dish and set the skillet aside to use again. Lay a slice of salt pork on each duck breast. Pour the stock around the duck.

2. Bake in a 425° oven for 15 minutes. Arrange on a serving dish and keep hot.

3. To the butter in the skillet, add the juices from the oven dish in which the duck was baked. Stir in cornstarch mixed with a little water. Bring to a boil, add the sherry, and pour sauce over the duck. Risotto is good with this, plus a tossed salad.

Roast Wild Duck

Serves 4

2 ducks	Salt and freshly ground pepper
2 carrots, chopped fine	2 onions
2 stalks celery, chopped fine	½ cup chicken stock
1 small can chopped ripe olives	½ cup Madeira wine
¼ cup olive oil	1 tablespoon cornstarch

1. Combine the carrots, celery, and olives, and sauté the mixture in olive oil for a few minutes. Spread it in a roasting pan. Sprinkle lightly with salt and pepper.

2. Arrange the ducks on top, place an onion in each cavity, brush the tops with olive oil, and season with salt and pepper. Pour the chicken stock and wine around the ducks.

3. Roast in a 350° oven for 35 to 45 minutes. Arrange ducks on a serving platter and keep hot.

4. Strain the pan juices and thicken with the cornstarch mixed with a little water. Pass in a sauce boat. Serve with wild rice.

Wild Duck Casserole

Serves 4

Should you, by any chance, have any wild duck left over, which is unlikely, here is a happy way to deal with it.

2 cups duck meat, cut in slices
2 tablespoons butter
2 shallots, finely chopped
1 cup duck gravy
1 small can chopped ripe
   olives

½ cup sherry
1 tablespoon lemon juice
A little thyme
Less rosemary
Salt and freshly ground pepper
Buttered toast points

1. Melt butter in a saucepan, add shallots, and cook until transparent but not brown. Stir in the gravy, add the olives, sherry, lemon juice, herbs, and seasoning. Cook until blended.

2. Arrange duck slices on the bottom of a buttered casserole. If you are short, the amount can be stretched by adding sautéed mushrooms or green peas, provided you don't overdo the stretching. Pour the gravy over the duck.

3. Bake in a 350° oven for 25 minutes, or until heated through. Serve on buttered toast points. Pass spiced crab apple jelly.

Roast Wild Duck with New Peas

Serves 4

2 ducks
Powdered ginger
Celery stuffing (see page 107)
Few sprigs each parsley and
   thyme

2 shallots, cut up
Soft butter
3 cups new peas, frozen
Salt and freshly ground pepper

1. Rub the inside of the duck cavities with powdered ginger. Stuff with celery stuffing, omitting the garlic. Truss birds and put in roasting pan with a few sprigs of parsley and thyme. Add the shallots. Spread the breasts with soft butter, and season with salt and pepper.

2. Roast for 30 minutes in a 350° oven.

3. Surround the ducks with frozen green peas lightly seasoned with salt and pepper. Cover the pan and continue cooking for another 15 or 20 minutes, or until peas are done.

4. Remove ducks to a hot platter, surround them with the peas, and pour the hot pan juices over them.

Wild Duck Stew

Serves 4

2 ducks, cut into serving pieces	1 onion, sliced
1 cup red wine	Flour
2 peppercorns, crushed	Salt and freshly ground pepper
2 teaspoons salt	Olive oil or butter
Few sprigs each, thyme,	Water to cover
parsley and chervil	Mushrooms
1 bay leaf	Rice

1. Place ducks in a bowl and cover with marinade consisting of the wine, peppercorns, salt, a sprig or two of parsley, thyme, and chervil, bay leaf, and onion. Allow to stand in the refrigerator overnight.

2. Drain and dry the meat. Dust the pieces with flour, season with salt and pepper, and brown in olive oil or butter. Add the strained marinade and water and simmer, covered, until the meat is tender, or about an hour. Serve with rice and mushrooms.

Rice Ring with Wild Duck

Serves 4

I keep referring to "left-over" wild duck, which may seem unlikely; but we have found that leftovers do occur more often than you would think. As I have mentioned elsewhere, if ducks are plentiful, only the breasts are served; or if you have an odd number of ducks, such as three for four people, the extra one is cooked along with the others and is therefore classified as "leftover." It can be used in several delightful ways, including this one.

This recipe may be used for any game bird, although I would not use the olives except for wild duck.

Leftover duck meat, bones, scraps
1 onion, sliced
2 carrots, sliced
1 bay leaf
Few sprigs each, parsley and thyme
3 cloves
½ clove garlic

3 cups chicken broth
1½ cups raw rice
4 tablespoons butter
1 onion, minced
2 cups tomato purée
1½ cup duck stock
Béchamel Sauce
1 can chopped ripe olives

1. Remove all meat from the bones, cube, and set aside. Put the bones, onion, carrots, bay leaf, parsley, thyme, cloves, garlic, and the chicken broth in a soup kettle. Simmer for two hours, adding water if the liquid gets too low.

2. Cook the rice, using the method for Risotto: In a heavy skillet, melt the butter and gently cook the minced onion until transparent but not brown. Add raw rice and stir over a low fire for a few minutes. Add the tomato purée, cover tightly, and simmer until rice is done. It will be dry and fluffy, having absorbed the liquid.

3. Moisten rice with duck stock, mix well, and pack firmly in a buttered ring mold. Keep hot.

4. Make a Béchamel Sauce (see page 141-142), using the duck stock as the liquid called for, and add the ripe olives. Put in the duck meat, and heat thoroughly.

5. Turn out the rice ring onto a serving platter and fill center with the duck. Garnish with herbs from your herb garden.

Wild Duck in Wine

Serves 2

2 wild ducks, breasts only   ½ cup brandy
Seasoned flour   1 small can chopped ripe olives
Olive oil   2 tablespoons chopped parsley
1 onion, chopped fine   1 tablespoon chopped chervil
1 cup dry red wine   Salt and freshly ground pepper

1. Dust duck meat with seasoned flour and brown in a skillet in olive oil. Remove to a baking dish.

2. Simmer onion in the oil until transparent but not brown. Add the wine, brandy, olives, parsley, chervil, and salt and pepper. Cook for one minute, adjust the seasoning, and pour over the duck meat.

3. Bake, uncovered, in a 350° oven for about ½ an hour, basting occasionally with the sauce.

4. Transfer to a hot platter, garnish with garden cress, and pass the sauce in a sauce boat. Serve with fried hominy.

Wild Goose

In late October, we hear the *honk-honk* of the wild goose as the V-shaped formations head south. So far no one has laid a goose on our doorstep, but it could happen any day. I can think of nothing more delectable to grace our Thanksgiving table than one of these majestic birds, complete with a black walnut or a sage and onion stuffing, and accompanied by wild plum jelly.

Jellied Goose

Follow the recipe for Jellied Grouse (see page 83-84), using 2 cups of diced cooked wild goose.

Roast Wild Goose—I

Serves 6 to 8

Wild goose is not as fat as the domestic variety, so it is desirable to place slices of salt pork on the breast of the bird before putting it in the oven.

1 wild goose, plucked and cleaned	1 carrot, sliced
Salt pork slices	1 stalk celery, including leaves
1 or 2 onions, sliced	Few sprigs parsley
	Cornstarch or flour

1. Stuff the goose, using black walnut or sage-and-onion stuffing (see pages 107 and 109).

2. Spread the bird with salt pork slices and roast in a hot (400°) oven until browned. Then add the onion, carrot, celery and parsley, cover, and continue roasting until goose is tender, or about 25 minutes per pound.

3. Strain the pan juices and, if you wish, thicken with cornstarch or flour. Serve with sweet potatoes and grape jelly.

Roast Wild Goose—II

Serves 6 to 8

This recipe was given to me by a friend who claims this is the only satisfactory way to deal with a large goose, which to her way of thinking is bound to be tough. I don't agree (see Roast Wild Goose—III) but here is her method for any goose of good size.

1 goose, plucked and cleaned	Salt
Boiling water	1 or 2 onions

1. Put the goose in a large kettle, cover with water, add salt and onion, and simmer for about 2 hours.

2. Drain and cool enough so that you can handle it. Stuff the bird with sage-and-onion stuffing (see page 109) and roast in a 350° oven for 3 hours.

3. Remove to a hot platter while you make pan juice gravy. Serve with mulberry jelly on the side.

Roast Wild Goose—III

Serves 6 to 8

This recipe gives you potato stuffing, which is especially good with goose.

1 goose, plucked and cleaned
Tenderizer
2 cups mashed potatoes, instant or homemade
1 cup soft bread crumbs
1 teaspoon salt

1 cup chopped onion
3 tablespoons butter
2 tablespoons chopped fresh sage
2 eggs, lightly beaten
¼ cup ground salt pork
Freshly ground pepper

1. Prepare goose by applying tenderizer and letting it stand overnight.

2. Combine mashed potatoes with bread crumbs, salt, onion cooked slightly in butter, sage, eggs, and salt pork. Grind in a little pepper. Stuff the goose loosely and truss.

3. Roast in a 375° oven for 20 to 25 minutes per pound. Pass ginger-apple relish.

Fricassee of Goose

Serves 4

This is a delicious dish made of leftover goose and the parts discarded in roasting.

2 cups leftover goose
Neck, wings, feet, gizzard and heart
1 onion
Few sprigs each, parsley and thyme
3 cloves

1 bay leaf
3 peppercorns
1 teaspoon salt
4 tablespoons goose fat
4 tablespoons flour
Goose gravy

1. Put the goose neck, wings, etc., in a kettle with water to cover. Add the onion, herbs, spices, and salt. Simmer gently for 2 hours to extract all the flavor. Strain the stock. Pick off any scraps of meat left on bones.

Continued on next page

2. In a saucepan, melt the goose fat, stir in the flour, and cook for a minute or two. Slowly stir in the goose stock and cook until smooth, thick, and hot. Add the goose gravy and pieces and leftover goose. Bring to a boil.

3. Serve on a deep platter surrounded by buttered noodles. Pass rose geranium jelly (see page 273).

Grouse—Partridge—Quail

I have grouped these birds together, partly because the recipes that follow are interchangeable and partly because what is called grouse in one part of the country may be called partridge or quail in another.

For example, in the southeastern states, the grouse is referred to as mountain pheasant. The prairie chicken and the heath hen of the West, now, alas, practically extinct, are really grouse. In the Northeast, the ruffed grouse is called partridge. In the West, the terms mountain quail and mountain partridge are interchangeable. In the spruce forests of Canada and the northern United States, the grouse is called spruce hen, partridge, or spruce grouse.

Whatever bird you have in your locality and whatever you call it, you are assured of good hunting and an epicurean feast.

Ruffed Grouse

The ruffed grouse (*Bonasa umbellus*) is found all over the United States except in the Deep South. The bird's presence can be detected by its drumming mating call which is not made by similar birds. Ruffed grouse are found in the deepest forest and the most impenetrable thickets. A tangle of elderberries and wild grapes near a stream will attract these birds. They feed at dawn on wild fruit, and emerge again to feed late in the afternoon, going to roost at dusk.

A dog is essential to flush the grouse out of his thick cover, and the hunter must be ready to shoot at the flash of a wing. Because of the bird's massive wing muscles, he needs no "warming up" period but takes off at full speed, giving the hunter no time to aim.

Grouse with Grapes

Serves 4

2 grouse, plucked and cleaned	1 teaspoon cornstarch
Salt and freshly ground pepper	¼ cup port wine
4 slices salt pork	½ teaspoon grated orange rind
1 cup chicken stock	1 cup seedless white grapes

1. Arrange the grouse in a roasting pan, season with salt and pepper, and lay the strips of salt pork over the breast. Pour the stock around them.

2. Roast at 350° for 30 minutes or until tender. Transfer to a serving platter and keep hot.

3. Mix the cornstarch with a little water, stir into the pan juices to thicken the gravy, add the port, orange rind, and grapes, and heat through. Correct the seasoning. Pass gravy in a sauce boat.

Jellied Grouse

Serves 4 to 6

2 grouse, plucked and cleaned	2 cups stock
1 onion	1 tablespoon plain gelatin
Rosemary, a few leaves	Truffles, sliced
3 peppercorns	Stuffed olives, sliced
2 cloves	2 eggs, hard-cooked, sliced
Salt and freshly ground pepper	

1. Remove the breasts from the grouse. Put them, as well as the rest of the birds in a kettle with the onion, rosemary, peppercorns, cloves, salt, and pepper. Cover with water and simmer until grouse breasts are tender. Remove them and cube. Continue to simmer the rest for 2 hours in all. Strain.

Continued on next page

2. Make an aspic of the stock and the gelatin, and spoon a little into the bottom of a mold that has been rinsed with cold water. Place in refrigerator to thicken. Then arrange the truffle, olive, and egg slices on the aspic, pressing them down slightly. Cover with another layer of aspic and put back in refrigerator to set. Then place a layer of grouse meat on the aspic. Cover with more aspic and again allow to set. Continue until all the grouse and aspic are used up, ending with the aspic. Replace in refrigerator until firmly set.

3. Unmold on a platter and surround with garden cress. Pass mayonnaise.

Grouse in Wine

Serves 4

Partridge, plover, grouse, praire chickens (which, as a matter of fact, are practically extinct), snipe, and ptarmigan, can all be prepared in the same ways. Simply adjust your recipes to the kind of birds you have at hand.

2 grouse, plucked and cleaned	½ cup chicken broth
Salt and freshly ground pepper	2 tablespoons butter
Pecan stuffing (see page 108)	2 tablespoons flour
Salt pork strips	2 tablespoons currant jelly
½ cup sherry	

1. Season the grouse lightly and fill cavities with pecan stuffing. Lay a slice of salt pork on the breast of each bird, and place them in a buttered baking dish. Pour the sherry and broth around the birds.

2. Cover and roast in a 350° oven for about 40 minutes, basting occasionally. Transfer to a hot platter.

3. Thicken the pan juices with a roux of butter and flour, add the jelly, and stir until jelly is melted and the sauce is thick and hot. Pass the gravy in a sauce boat. Serve wild rice.

Partridge

The true partridge belongs to the Old World, having been brought to this country from the Himalaya Mountains. It is the Hungarian partridge, referred to by hunters as "the Hun" and by scientists by the entrancing name *Perdix perdix perdix*. It is smaller than a grouse but larger than a bobwhite.

This bird is not too plentiful, but can be found in the Great Lakes region and across the plains, where it lives in the stubble fields and grassy plains of the open spaces. It takes a good dog to find the birds and the hunter will need a long-range shot.

Partridge Cutlets

Serves 4

You may also make these of pheasant or any other game bird. Cutlets are a good way to use up leftovers, or to make a little game go a long way.

2 cups cooked partridge meat
3 tablespoons butter
2 shallots, finely chopped
3 tablespoons flour
1 cup chicken stock
Salt and freshly ground pepper

3 egg yolks, lightly beaten
Prepared breading mixture, or
1 egg beaten with a little milk, and
Dry bread crumbs

1. Grind the meat.
2. Melt the butter and cook the shallots in it for a few minutes, add the flour, stir, and slowly pour in the stock. Continue stirring until smooth, thick and hot. Salt and pepper to taste.
3. Stir the hot sauce slowly into the egg yolks, return to the fire for a minute or two, and add the partridge meat. Pour mixture into a pan and allow to cool in the refrigerator.
4. When quite firm, shape into cutlets, and roll them in a breading mixture, or dip in egg beaten with a little milk, then in bread crumbs.
5. Fry cutlets in a deep fat at 390° for 4 minutes. Sauté in butter if you prefer. Serve immediately with Port Wine Sauce (see page 157).

Broiled Partridge

Follow the recipe for Broiled Quail on page 88.

Partridge Breasts in Wine

Serves 4

2 or 3 large partridges, plucked
  and cleaned
Butter
2 onions, sliced
1 bay leaf

Few sprigs each, parsley and
  thyme
3 peppercorns
3 cups chicken consommé
Freshly ground pepper
2 tablespoons sherry

1. Remove the breasts from the partridge and sauté in butter until brown. Keep hot.

2. Put the rest of the birds in a kettle with the onions, parsley, thyme, bay leaf and peppercorns. Pour in the consommé and simmer for 2 hours to extract all the flavor from the meat and bones. Strain stock. Add freshly ground pepper to taste.

3. Reduce stock to 1 cup, add the sherry, and return the partridge breasts to the sauce to heat. Transfer to a hot platter. Serve with wild rice and mushrooms.

Cold Partridge Pie

Serves 2 to 4

2 partridges, plucked and
  cleaned
Salt pork, about 1 slice per
  breast
1 onion

Salt and freshly ground pepper
Bacon slices
Water cress
Sliced tomatoes

1. Remove the breasts from the partridges. Place the rest of the birds in a kettle, cover with water, and simmer for an hour or two to make a rich stock. Strain.

2. Grind the salt pork, and the onion, mix well, and season with salt and pepper. Spread mixture over the patridge breasts.

3. Line a casserole with bacon slices, place partridge breasts over them, cover with another layer of bacon slices, and fill the dish to the top with stock.

4. Bake in a 275° oven for 3 hours, renewing the stock if necessary.

5. Allow the pie to cool, place a weight on top to pack it down firmly, and place in refrigerator until you are ready to serve it.

6. Slice the pie, arrange on a platter, and garnish with water cress and sliced tomatoes.

Braised Partridge

1 partridge per serving,   Salt pork slices
   unless large   Salt and freshly ground pepper
                       Buttered toast squares

1. Pluck, clean and truss the birds for cooking. Cover the breasts with salt pork, and roast in a 400° oven for 30 minutes.

2. Serve on toast squares, with a gravy made of the pan juices. seasoned to taste. Try plum (see page 271) or grape jelly (see page 272) with the partridge.

Quail

The *quail* was originally the *common quail* of the Old World, which was not successfully transplanted here. Our best-known quail today is the bobwhite (*Colinus virginianus*), which is found in all of the Eastern United States, west through the Great Lakes region, and south to New Mexico and Texas. Other varieties are Gambel's quail and the blue or scaled quail. Quail of one kind or another are now found in forty states.

Being so small, the bird makes a difficult target, but the size of the coveys compensates somewhat. Being seed eaters, quail are found in open fields, feeding and roosting on the ground.

Use a dog to work the fields over and flush the birds in the early morning or at dusk. They fly swiftly, going as fast as thirty to forty miles an hour when making for a nearby forest edge or thicket.

Quail and Cabbage

1 per person

4 quail, plucked and cleaned,   1 bay leaf
   cut into pieces   Salt and freshly ground pepper
1 onion   1 new cabbage, cut in wedges
2 carrots   2 cups stock
2 cloves

1. Place quail in a kettle, cover with water, and the onion, carrots, cloves, bay leaf, salt, and pepper, and simmer until the birds are tender.

2. Remove quail and arrange in a casserole. Surround with small cabbage wedges. Pour in the strained stock.

3. Bake, covered, in a 350° oven for 30 minutes, or until cabbage is done.

Quail Aux Shallots

1 per person

6 quail   4 mushrooms, sliced
4 tablespoons butter   1 cup chicken broth
1 teaspoon olive oil   ½ cup red wine
4 shallots, chopped   Few sprigs each, parsley and
                            thyme, chopped

1. Cut up the quail. Season with salt and pepper and brown in a skillet in the butter and olive oil. Transfer to baking dish. Sauté the shallots and mushrooms for a few minutes in the butter and oil, then add the broth, wine, parsley, and thyme, and season with salt and pepper to taste. Pour sauce over the quail.

2. Bake in a 350° oven for 45 minutes.

Broiled Quail

1 per person

Quail, plucked and cleaned   Salt and freshly ground pepper
Butter   Chopped parsley

1. Prepare the quail for cooking by splitting in half.

2. Melt butter in a skillet and brown the bird well on both

sides. (They should be fairly tender by this time.) Season with salt and pepper.

3. Place the birds in a broiler and broil until nice and brown, brushing frequently with butter from the pan as they cook.

4. Remove to a hot platter and sprinkle with parsley. Pass Bread Sauce (see page 143).

Roast Quail—I

1 per person

4 quail
4 tablespoons butter
Seasoned flour
1 onion, sliced paper thin
1 bay leaf

4 mushrooms, sliced
1 cup red wine
2 tablespoons flour
2 tablespoons butter

1. Dust the quail with seasoned flour and brown in melted butter.

2. Transfer to baking dish. Cook onion in the butter until transparent but not brown, add the bay leaf and mushrooms, and cook for a minute or two more. Remove the bay leaf. Add the wine, stir sauce and pour over the quail.

3. Roast the birds, covered, in a 375° oven for 45 or 50 minutes.

4. Remove to a serving platter and thicken the pan juice with a roux of flour and butter. Pass the gravy in a sauce boat. Serve cranberry jelly, (see page 268).

Roast Quail—II

1 per person

6 quails, plucked and cleaned
6 salt pork slices
1 tablespoon flour

1 tablespoon butter
1 teaspoon black cherry jelly
Freshly ground pepper

1. Place the birds in a roaster, breast side up, and cover each with a slice of salt pork.

2. Roast in a 350° oven for 30 minutes. Transfer to a hot platter.

3. Thicken the pan juices with a roux of flour and butter. Stir in the jelly. Add a little pepper. Serve sauce in a sauce boat.

Pheasant

The *ringneck pheasant* is probably the best-known upland game bird, since it is found in large numbers in the northern and central part of the country, from coast to coast.

The pheasant feeds mostly on grains and seeds and hides in the farmer's hedgerows or in wastelands that have gone over to sumac and goldenrod. When alarmed, he either crouches quietly in his hiding place or runs swiftly and silently close to the ground.

Hunting pheasant in groups is advantageous, as the field can be worked by men spaced at intervals and the pheasants flushed and driven so that they do not have a chance to hide. A good hunting dog is of great help. The best hunting is at sunrise on a clear day.

Braised Pheasant

Serves 6

2 pheasants, plucked and
   cleaned
Butter
1 cup dry Vermouth
1 cup chicken stock
1 clove garlic, crushed
1 onion, sliced thin

2 carrots, sliced thin
1 or 2 sprigs thyme
1 sprig rosemary
6 thin slices salt pork
6 mushrooms, sliced and sautéd
   in butter
Few sprigs parsley, minced

1. Split the pheasants, brown in a skillet in butter, and transfer to a large casserole.

2. To the butter in which the birds browned, add the vermouth, chicken stock, garlic, onion, carrots, thyme, and rosemary. Heat the sauce and pour over the pheasants. Top birds with salt pork.

3. Bake, covered, in a 325° oven for 1½ hours. Transfer pheasants to a serving platter and keep hot.

4. Thicken gravy to taste, add the mushrooms and parsley, and stir well. Pass in a sauce boat. Serve cranberry conserve (see page 261).

Pheasant à la King

Serves 4

This is actually made in the same way as chicken à la king, and is very good made of any game bird. We use pheasant because they are so plentiful here.

2 cups cooked, cubed pheasant
    meat
2 tablespoons butter
2 tablespoons flour
1 cup chicken broth

½ cup heavy cream
1 egg yolk, beaten
2 tablespoons sherry
Salt and freshly ground pepper
Buttered toast points

1. Melt the butter and stir in the flour. Cook for a minute or two, add chicken broth and cream, and stir until smooth. Heat through and pour slowly into the beaten egg yolk. Add sherry, salt and pepper.

2. Put the pheasant in the sauce, heat but do not boil, and serve on buttered toast points.

Pheasant-Ham Rolls

Serves 6

This is a good dish if you have leftover pheasant and wild rice.

1 cup chopped cooked
    pheasant
1 cup cooked wild rice
4 tablespoons melted butter
12 slices ham

3 or 4 large mushrooms,
    chopped
4 tablespoons butter
4 tablespoons flour
2 cups chicken broth

1. Combine the pheasant meat, wild rice, and butter. Spoon mixture onto the ham slices. Roll up, tie or fasten with skewers, and arrange in a baking dish.

2. Make a sauce as follows: Sauté the mushrooms in butter, stir in the flour, add the chicken broth and blend until smooth. (Better still, use pheasant broth made by simmering scraps and bones in water to extract the flavor.) Stir until thick and hot, check the seasoning, and pour over the rolls.

3. Bake in 325° oven for 25 minutes.

Roast Pheasant

Serves 2 to 4

Pheasant, plucked and cleaned
Wild rice stuffing
Salt pork slices
Flour and butter

1 tablespoon sherry
Buttered toast triangles
Parsley
Tomato wedges

1. Prepare the pheasant for cooking, using stuffing of your choice. We like a wild rice stuffing (see page 109). Truss the bird and lay salt pork slices on breast.

2. Roast, uncovered, in a 350° oven for 1 hour.

3. Make a sauce from the pan juices, thicken with a roux of flour, and butter, and add the sherry.

4. Serve on a hot platter surrounded by toast triangles and garnished with parsley and tomato wedges. Pass the sauce in a sauceboat.

Savory Pheasant

Serves 6

2 pheasants, plucked and
    cleaned
Seasoned flour
Butter
2 onions, chopped fine
½ cup sweet vermouth
1 teaspoon tomato paste

⅛ teaspoon cinnamon
1 teaspoon salt
A dash or two freshly ground
    pepper
Soft butter
Buttered toast

1. Cut pheasants into serving pieces. Dust with seasoned flour and brown in butter. Transfer to roasting pan.

2. To the butter in the skillet, add the onion and cook until transparent but not brown. Add the vermouth, tomato paste, cinnamon, salt, and pepper. Cook for a few minutes, then pour around the pheasants. Spread the pieces of bird with soft butter.

3. Roast in a 350° oven for an hour, or until meat is tender.

4. Arrange pieces of buttered toast on a hot platter, pour a spoonful of the sauce from the roaster over each piece, and lay the pheasant pieces on top. Garnish with water cress.

Pheasant with Cherries

Serves 4 to 6

2 pheasants, plucked and   ½ cup sweet vermouth
    cleaned   2 cups wild black cherries
Soft butter   Few sprigs thyme, chopped
Salt and freshly ground pepper   Fried bread triangles

1. Prepare pheasants for cooking, arrange in a roasting pan, and spread the breasts with soft butter. Season lightly.
2. Combine the vermouth, pitted cherries, and thyme, and pour around the birds.
3. Roast in a 350° oven for 45 minutes, basting with the pan juices. Transfer to a hot platter and garnish with fried bread triangles.
4. Serve the pan juices in a sauceboat.

Roast Pheasant Breasts

Serves 4

If you have a generous supply of pheasant, try this delicious but simple recipe. The rest of the pheasant may be used for pot pie (see page 102) or for an aspic (see page 104).

4 pheasant breasts   Buttered toast
4 slices salt pork   Lemon wedges
Melted butter

1. Arrange pheasant breasts in buttered baking dish and cover each with a slice of salt pork.
2. Bake in a 350° oven for 30 or 40 minutes, or until tender, brushing 2 or 3 times with melted butter.
3. Place each breast on a piece of buttered toast and pour the pan juices over them.
4. Serve with lemon wedges to bring out the flavor. Pass Bread Sauce (see page 143).

Pheasant Aspic

Serves 4

If you have used the breasts of four pheasants, use the remaining parts for aspic.

Pheasant bones, skin, and
    scraps
¼ pound soup meat, preferably
    veal
1 piece salt pork
Cold water
Salt
1 bay leaf
3 or 4 sprigs each, parsley,
    marjoram and thyme

2 or 3 cloves
3 peppercorns
Celery leaves
1 carrot
1 onion
¼ cup dry white wine
2 cups broth
2 tablespoons unflavored
    gelatin
Thinly sliced cooked ham

1. Put pheasant bones, skin, and scraps in a kettle together with soup meat and the salt pork, cover with water and add salt, bay leaf, parsley, marjoram, cloves, peppercorns, celery leaves, thyme, carrot, and onion. Simmer for 2 or 3 hours.

2. Strain the liquid, remove all the pheasant meat from the bones and cut into pieces.

3. Add the wine to the broth, and stir in gelatin dissolved in a little cold water to make aspic. Correct the seasoning.

4. Pour a layer of aspic in the bottom of a mold and chill to set. Arrange pieces of the pheasant on top, followed by a layer of ham, and cover with aspic. Chill again until set. Repeat until the mold is filled. Return to the refrigerator. When firm, unmold on a bed of water cress.

Wild Turkey

Wild turkey, as you know, was the *pièce de résistance* of many a Pilgrim meal. The turkeys were so plentiful there was no thought of the supply ever coming to an end, yet for almost a century this grand upland bird was virtually extinct.

A few years ago, however, turkeys began to appear in areas where reforestation had taken place. Subsequently the Pennsylvania State Game Commission developed a strain of wild turkeys, and thousands of them have been released in that state and in New York. Today a trap-and-transfer program is being carried out to even up the turkey population. It is hoped that these activities, and the strict enforcement of game laws, will soon result in a plentiful supply of this bird, and there will again be wild turkeys on many of our tables.

Turkey à la King

Follow the recipe for Pheasant à la King (see page 91).

Turkey Fricassée

Serves 6 to 10

This is a fine recipe to use if you suspect that your bird might be a little ancient. Size of bird governs number of servings.

1 turkey, plucked and cleaned	Bay leaf
Seasoned flour	Celery tops
Butter or chicken fat	Water
4 or 5 onions	Flour
Few sprigs parsley	Cream

1. Cut up the turkey and roll pieces in seasoned flour. Brown well in butter or chicken fat.

2. Place in a kettle with 4 or 5 onions, parsley, a bay leaf, celery tops, and water to cover. Simmer for an hour or two, or until turkey is tender.

3. To thicken the stock, add flour and cream and turn up the fire until the stew bubbles. Serve this with buttered noodles.

Braised Wild Turkey

Allow 1 pound per person

1 wild turkey, plucked and cleaned	Few sprigs each, parsley and thyme
Soft butter	4 cups chicken broth
1 onion	Salt and freshly ground pepper
1 carrot	

1. Prepare the bird for the oven, season with salt and pepper, and place in a roaster that has a cover. Spread soft butter liberally on the breast and roast uncovered in a 400° oven until brown.

2. Turn the oven down to 350°, add the onion, carrot, parsley and thyme, pour in the chicken broth, cover roaster and continue to cook for 3 to 5 hours, depending on weight, until tender. Transfer to hot platter.

3. Thicken the pan juice with a mixture of flour and water, add salt and pepper if necessary, and pass in a sauce boat. Serve with Cranberry Sauce.

Turkey Divan

Serves 6

This is an easy supper dish made of leftover turkey. I save some of the white meat especially for this.

2 boxes frozen broccoli	1 cup mayonnaise, preferably home made
Turkey slices to serve 6	
Salt and freshly ground pepper	1 cup cream, whipped

1. Cook the frozen broccoli (or its equivalent in fresh broccoli) until just tender and arrange in shallow buttered baking dish. Cover with slices of hot turkey and season with salt and pepper.

2. Combine the mayonnaise and whipped cream. Spread mixture over turkey, and brown under the broiler. The topping will brown and puff slightly. Or you may top your broccoli and turkey with a freshly made Hollandaise Sauce.

Wild Turkey Casserole

Serves 4 or 5

3 cups leftover turkey, sliced or cubed
3 tablespoons butter
2 tablespoons flour
1 cup turkey broth

1 cup cream
2 tablespoons sherry
Salt and freshly ground pepper
2 egg yolks, beaten
Buttered bread crumbs

1. In a skillet, melt the butter and stir in the flour. Slowly add Turkey broth, or, if this is not on hand, open a can of chicken consommé. Stir until smooth, thick and hot. Add cream, sherry, and salt and pepper. Gradually stir hot sauce into egg yolks.

2. Place layer of turkey meat in buttered casserole. Cover with sauce. Repeat, ending with sauce. Sprinkle with bread crumbs.

3. Bake in a 350° oven for 20 minutes or until bread crumbs brown and the casserole bubbles.

Turkey Cutlets

Follow the recipe for Partridge Cutlets on page 85.

Turkey-Oyster Pie

Serves 6

2 cups turkey
1 pint small oysters
4 tablespoons each butter and flour
1 cup each, cream and milk
Liquor from the oysters

Salt and freshly ground pepper
2 tablespoons chopped parsley
Powdered mace
Prepared poultry stuffing
Butter

1. Make a rich cream sauce using the butter, flour, cream, milk, liquor from the oysters, and salt and pepper to taste. Add the parsley, and a dash of powdered mace.

2. In a buttered casserole, place a layer of turkey, a layer of oysters, and a layer of prepared poultry stuffing. Cover with the sauce. Repeat, finishing with a layer of stuffing. Dot with butter.

3. Bake in a 350° oven for about 20 minutes.

Hot Turkey Mousse

Serves 4

1½ cups leftover turkey
3 tablespoons butter
1 teaspoon fresh rosemary
1 tablespoon flour
1 cup rich milk

Salt and freshly ground black
  pepper
2 eggs, lightly beaten
½ cup soft bread crumbs

1. Melt butter, add rosemary. Allow to stand. Butter a casserole.
2. Put the turkey through grinder, using the fine blade.
3. Remove rosemary from butter, stir in the flour and milk, and season with salt and pepper to taste. Slowly add sauce to beaten eggs, stir in bread crumbs and turkey, and pour mixture into the baking dish. Set dish in a saucepan of hot water.
4. Bake in a 350° oven for 45 minutes. This is good served with Mushroom Sauce (see page 156).

Roast Turkey

Allow about 1 pound per person

1 turkey, prepared for oven
Chestnut stuffing (page 106)

Soft butter or salt pork slices

1. Stuff turkey with chestnut stuffing. Spread soft butter liberally over the breast and legs, or cover with salt pork slices.
2. Roast in a 350° oven for 3 to 5 hours, depending on the size and age of the bird.
3. Make gravy from the pan juices and pass it in a sauce boat. Serve with Cranberry Conserve (see page 261).

Woodcock

The woodcock is a bird fascinating to the hunter as well as to the epicure. The best shooting is during the fall migration, when the flight birds come through on their way South and swell the ranks of those who have nested in our woods and swamps. The woodcock's presence can be detected by the holes his long bill has left in the soft ground where he has probed for food. The bird is a past master at quick disappearance, so when one is jumped, the hunter's aim must be swift and sure.

Woodcock Flambée

1 per person

Woodcock, cleaned and split
Seasoned flour
Butter

Bacon strips
Brandy

1. Dust the birds lightly with seasoned flour and brown in hot butter.
2. Transfer to a baking dish, and lay a strip of bacon over each one. Bake, uncovered, in a 350° oven for 20 to 30 minutes.
3. Transfer to hot serving dish, pour brandy over the birds, light and serve. Serve blackberry jam with beach plums (see page 278).

Baked Woodcock

This is a recipe for one woodcock; increase it to suit your needs. Allow one bird per person.

1 woodcock, cleaned and
    singed
Orange peel
Salt and freshly ground pepper
Celery leaves, chopped
2 sprigs thyme
1 small onion
Pinch of mace
1 juniper berry

The woodcock's liver
1 small carrot, chopped
2 tablespoons chopped onion
1 bay leaf
½ cup chicken stock
½ cup port wine
Soft butter
1 cup cream

1. Rub the bird inside and out with grated orange peel, then with salt and pepper. In the cavity place a few celery leaves, one sprig of thyme, the onion, mace, a juniper berry, and the liver. Sew up the opening.

Continued on next page

2. In a baking dish, combine the carrot, chopped onion, the rest of the celery leaves, a sprig of thyme, and the bay leaf. Place the woodcock on top and pour chicken stock and wine around it. Spread the butter over bird.

3. Bake in a 400° oven for 20 minutes. If you like your woodcock well done, which is considered a sacrilege among connoisseurs, leave it in the oven for 30 minutes.

4. Transfer the bird to a hot platter. Strain the pan juices into a saucepan and bring to a boil. Slowly add the cream, and reheat. Pass the gravy in a sauce boat.

Broiled Woodcock

1 per person

Woodcock, cleaned and split   Marinade (see page 130)
   down the back   Salt and freshly ground pepper

1. Marinate birds for an hour or two. Drain and pat dry.

2. Broil under broiler or even charcoal if possible, turning frequently, for about 15 minutes. This will produce a rare bird.

3. Season with salt and pepper. If you prefer not to marinate, spread the birds with soft butter. In either case, serve on buttered toast. Pass elderberry jelly. (See page 270.)

Braised Woodcock

This is a recipe for one bird. Adjust it to the number you are going to cook. This gives you a very delicately flavored dish.

1 woodcock, prepared for   1 sprig thyme
   cooking   Salt and freshly ground pepper
3 tablespoons butter   Buttered toast
1 juniper berry

1. Melt 2 tablespoons of the butter in a skillet and brown the bird well. When meat is tender, remove from bones and set it aside.

2. Melt the rest of the butter, add the juniper berry, thyme, and salt and pepper. Cook and stir for a minute or two. Remove the thyme and juniper. Add the woodcock meat, heat through, and serve on buttered toast. Serve with barberry jelly. (See page 268.)

Roast Woodcock

1 per person

Woodcock, plucked and cleaned
Soft butter
Sliced salt pork

Salt and freshly ground pepper
Buttered toast

1. Prepare, spread the birds with soft butter and cover each with a slice of salt pork. Season with salt and pepper.
2. Roast the woodcock in a 450° oven for 15 minutes, or 20 minutes if you prefer them well done. Serve on buttered toast, and pass spiced crab apple jelly (see page 269).

Woodcock in Cream

1 per person

Woodcock, plucked and cleaned
Woodcock livers

1 tablespoon butter per bird
Cream, 1 tablespoon per bird
Fried bread triangles

1. Prepare the woodcock for cooking, putting the liver and butter inside. Sew up the cavity. Fasten with skewers. Arrange in a baking dish and pour cream over them. Salt and pepper.
2. Bake in a 350° oven, basting with the cream, for about 25 minutes.
3. Transfer to a hot platter and surround with triangles of fried bread. Pour the pan juices into a sauce boat. Serve with black cherry jelly.

GAME BIRDS

GENERAL RECIPES

Game Bird Cutlets

Serves 4

Use any leftover meat from partridge, grouse, pheasant, or quail.

2 cups game meat, ground
2 tablespoons butter
2 tablespoons flour
1 cup chicken or game stock
Salt and freshly ground pepper

½ cup heavy cream
2 egg yolks
1 whole egg, lightly beaten
Bread crumbs

1. Melt the butter, stir in the flour and cook a few minutes. Stir in the stock, then the cream beaten with the egg yolks. Season with salt and pepper. Stir until smooth, thick and hot. Blend with the meat, and put mixture in the refrigerator to chill.

2. When firm, shape into cutlets, roll in beaten egg and bread crumbs, and fry in deep fat. Drain. Serve with Cranberry Conserve (see page 261).

Pot Pie

Serves 4

This is delicious made of any game bird—duck, pheasant, quail, and so on.

2 cups game bird meat
1 onion, cut up
A few celery leaves
1 sprig rosemary
2 or 3 slices salt pork or
    bacon, smoky-flavored
Water

1 cup mushrooms
Butter
1 can *petits pois*
1 stick pastry mix
Salt and freshly ground pepper
½ cup red wine, dry

1. Prepare the birds for cooking, cut into quarters and put them in a kettle. Add the onion, celery leaves, rosemary, salt pork or bacon, barely cover with water and simmer until birds are tender.

2. Remove all meat from the bones. Butter an oven dish.

3. Cook the mushrooms for a few minutes in butter. Open can of *petits pois* and add the juice to the broth.

4. Make pastry triangles, using a pastry mix or your favorite recipe for piecrust.

5. Arrange a layer of meat in the baking dish. Add a layer of peas and mushrooms. Season with salt and pepper. Arrange pastry triangles on top. Repeat the layers of meat, mushrooms, and peas. Pour the wine in the dish, fill up with hot stock to the level of the vegetables, and cover with the remaining pastry triangles.

6. Bake the pie in a 400° oven for 50 minutes, or until the crust is brown and the pie bubbles.

Game Bird Pie—I

Serves 6 to 8

This recipe comes from an old cookbook and is very good. It can be made with woodcock, quail, or other small birds.

1 dozen small birds, cleaned
   and singed
Chicken broth
Salt and freshly ground pepper
Dash of ground mace
Pinch of ground cloves
1 bay leaf
¼ pound salt pork, cut up

2 carrots, sliced
1 onion, sliced
½ cup butter
2 tablespoons flour
3 cups broth
2 cups diced boiled potatoes
Pastry crust (Use any standard
   recipe or prepared mix.)

1. Split each bird in half and arrange in a saucepan with enough chicken broth to just cover. Bring to a boil and skim. Add the salt and pepper, mace, cloves, bay leaf, salt pork, carrots, and onion. Simmer until birds and vegetables are tender, keeping the game covered with broth.

2. In another saucepan, melt the butter, stir in flour, and add broth from first saucepan to make a thin sauce.

3. Arrange the meat, vegetables, potatoes, in a deep baking dish, cover with sauce, and cover with a pastry crust.

4. Bake in a 350° oven for 1 hour. Serve with elderberry jelly (see page 270).

Game Bird Pie—II

Serves 6 to 8

3 cups meat from pheasant,
    partridge or other game
    birds
¾ pound lean veal
¼ pound fresh pork
Salt and freshly ground pepper
Few sprigs each, parsley and
    thyme, chopped fine

Dash of nutmeg
Truffles, chopped, optional
Bacon slices
½ cup stock
Pastry crust

1. Start by making a forcemeat of veal and pork, as follows: Grind it (or have your butcher do it) very fine. Season with salt and pepper, add the parsley, thyme and just a suggestion of nutmeg. If you have truffles on hand, add them.

2. Line a baking dish with some of the forcemeat, arrange pieces of meat over it and cover with a few slices of bacon. Continue these layers until dish is filled. Add the stock and cover with pastry crust.

3. Bake the pie in a 350° oven for 1¼ hours. Serve hot or cold.

Game Birds in Aspic

Serves 4

Game bird bones and scraps
1 carrot
1 onion
Celery leaves
1 tablespoon tarragon vinegar
1 teaspoon salt
6 peppercorns
Water

2 tablespoons plain gelatin
    soaked in ¼ cup water
Ham strips
Hard-cooked egg slices
2 cups cooked game bird, diced
Watercress
Cherry tomatoes

1. Make the aspic as follows: Put bones and scraps in a kettle with carrot, onion, celery leaves, tarragon vinegar, salt, and peppercorns; cover with water, bring to a boil, and simmer for an hour or two. Strain. You should have 2 pints of liquid.

2. Add the gelatin. Stir to dissolve.

3. Rinse a mold with cold water and cover bottom with a thin layer of aspic. When it begins to set, arrange the ham and egg slices in the aspic. When it is set, arrange pieces of game on top, cover with more aspic and again allow to set. Repeat layers of game, ham, eggs, and aspic. Refrigerate.

4. When set, unmold and garnish with watercress and cherry tomatoes.

STUFFINGS FOR GAME BIRDS

Olive Herb Stuffing for Wild Duck

Will stuff 4 ducks

This stuffing, though it is a little trouble to prepare, is especially delicious.

Duck livers	½ cup chopped ripe olives
½ pound salt pork, sliced	½ cup chopped mushrooms
1 onion, chopped	Salt and freshly ground pepper
1 clove garlic, crushed	3 egg yolks, lightly beaten
¼ cup chopped parsley	3 tablespoons brandy
¼ cup chopped celery leaves	4 tablespoons butter
3 tablespoons chopped chives	1 teaspoon olive oil
2 shallots, chopped	

1. Cook the duck livers until tender and press through a sieve or run through blender. If the livers are missing, having been shot up too badly for use or mislaid at the butcher's, I substitute chicken livers.

2. Cover the salt pork with boiling water and simmer for 10 minutes. Drain and put through the food chopper, using the coarse blade.

3. Combine the livers, salt pork, onion, garlic, parsley, celery, chives, shallots, ripe olives, mushrooms, and salt and pepper. Combine the egg yolks and brandy, and mix into stuffing. Allow to cool.

4. Stuff the birds lightly, truss them, and brown in the butter and olive oil before placing in roasting pan.

Apple Stuffing for Goose—I

12 tart apples, peeled, cored, cut up
⅔ cup water
4 cups dry bread crumbs

2 tablespoons sugar
4 tablespoons melted butter
Salt to taste

1. Simmer the apples gently in water until soft but not cooked to pieces. Cool.
2. Add other ingredients and mix lightly.

Apple Stuffing for Goose—II

1 loaf stale bread, cubed and dried
6 tart apples, peeled, cored, and cubed

1 lemon, rind and juice
Salt and freshly ground pepper

Combine bread and apple cubes in a bowl, add the lemon rind and juice, and season with salt and pepper. Mix lightly. This makes an interesting, tart stuffing which goes well with goose.

Chestnut Stuffing for Wild Goose or Turkey

Cut the recipe down for smaller game birds.

2 quarts chestnuts, shelled
Chicken bouillon
2 tablespoons butter
3 shallots, chopped
½ pound sausage meat
2 teaspoons minced parsley

1 teaspoon each, chopped chives, oregano and thyme
Salt and freshly ground pepper
1 cup soft bread crumbs
½ cup brandy

1. Boil chestnuts in bouillon to cover until tender. Chop coarsely.
2. Melt the butter, add the shallots, and simmer until tender but not brown. Add sausage meat and herbs, and cook for a few more minutes, mixing with a fork. Season with salt and pepper, add bread crumbs, brandy, and chestnuts, and toss together to mix.
3. Stuff the bird lightly.

Black Walnut Stuffing—I

Will stuff 2 or 3 small game birds. Superlative with pheasant.

2 cups soft bread crumbs
1 cup black walnut meats
4 tablespoons butter

½ onion, chopped
2 tablespoons milk
Salt

1. Stale homemade bread makes the best stuffing. Use center of the loaf.
2. Melt the butter and sauté the onion in it for a few minutes. Add the milk, nuts, and salt to taste.
3. Stuff the bird loosely.

Black Walnut Stuffing—II

Will stuff a goose or turkey.

1 cup black walnut meats
2 cups stale bread cubes
Butter

2 cups mashed potatoes
1 cup diced celery
Salt and freshly ground pepper

1. Brown bread in the butter and mix with potatoes. Add the celery and nut meats. (The amount of celery may be decreased and the nuts increased if you are as fond of the flavor of black walnuts as we are.) Mix all ingredients together and season with salt and pepper.
2. Stuff the bird loosely.

Celery Stuffing

This will stuff a brace of pheasants or grouse.

1 small garlic clove, put
    through a press
2 tablespoons minced onion
4 tablespoons melted butter
2 cups soft bread crumbs

2 tablespoons each chopped
    chervil and thyme
4 stalks celery, tops and all
4 tablespoons blanched, toasted
    almonds, chopped
Salt and freshly ground pepper

1. Sauté the onion and garlic in butter.
2. Combine all the ingredients, mix well and let the stuffing cool.

Liver Stuffing for Wild Duck

Will stuff 2 ducks

2 duck livers, chopped
2 scallions, tops and all,
   chopped
3 stalks celery, diced
2 cups soft bread crumbs
½ cup chopped almonds

2 tablespoons minced parsley
¼ cup butter, melted
1 egg, beaten lightly
Salt and freshly ground pepper

1. Combine the liver, scallions, celery, and bread crumbs and mix thoroughly. Add the almonds, parsley, melted butter, and finally the egg. Season to taste, toss together lightly, and stuff the ducks.

Pecan Stuffing

Use this for any game bird. For a large bird, such as turkey, double or triple the recipe.

2 cups soft bread crumbs
4 tablespoons butter
1 onion, minced
1 cup pecan meats

Salt and freshly ground pepper
1 egg, lightly beaten
Giblets, cooked and cut up

1. Melt butter in a saucepan, add the onion, and cook a minute or two. Mix with the bread crumbs, add the nuts, salt, and pepper, and finally the egg.

2. Add giblets to the stuffing; if you prefer, put them in the gravy.

3. Spoon stuffing in lightly, sew up or skewer the cavity. Truss the bird for roasting.

Stuffings for Roast Wild Duck

1. Bread crumbs, onions, parsley, celery, salt and pepper.
2. Duck livers, mushrooms, thyme, parsley, salt and pepper.
3. Apple and celery, shallots, salt and pepper.
4. Wild rice and mushrooms, salt and pepper.

Wild Rice Stuffing for Game Birds

Will stuff a brace of ducks

For stuffing a turkey or a goose, increase the amount proportionately.

Livers of the game birds,
chopped
Butter
4 shallots, sliced

2 scallions, white part only,
chopped
4 tablespoons chicken stock
1 cup cooked wild rice

In a frying pan, cook the livers in butter. Add the shallots and scallions, cook for a minute or two, and moisten with chicken stock. Add the rice, mix, and stuff the birds loosely.

Sage and Onion Stuffing

This will stuff a goose or a turkey

4 onions, chopped
¼ cup butter
4 cups soft bread crumbs

6 to 10 sage leaves, chopped
1 egg, lightly beaten
Salt and freshly ground pepper

1. Melt the butter, add the onions, and simmer a few minutes until transparent but not brown.
2. In a bowl combine the bread crumbs, onions, and butter, sage leaves, and egg. Toss until well mixed. Season with salt and pepper to taste. Stuff the birds lightly.

Potato Stuffing for Goose or Turkey

¼ pound salt pork, cut up fine
1 cup minced onion
2 cups hot mashed potatoes
1½ cups soft bread crumbs
1 egg

⅓ cup butter
1½ teaspoons salt
3 teaspoons fresh sage, cut fine
2 tablespoons chopped parsley

1. Try out the salt pork in a skillet. When crisp, remove the pieces and sauté the onion in the fat until transparent but not brown.
2. Combine all the ingredients and mix lightly. Allow to cool before stuffing the bird.

Oyster Corn Bread Stuffing for Game Birds

This amount will stuff a turkey or other bird of like size. Cut down the amount for smaller birds.

¼ cup butter
2 tablespoons minced onions
4 cups corn bread crumbs
2 eggs, lightly beaten

1 pint small oysters with liquid
2 tablespoons minced parsley
Salt and freshly ground pepper
A dash of mace

1. Sauté the onion in melted butter until transparent but not brown.
2. Stir into the corn bread crumbs, add the eggs, then the oysters, parsley, and seasoning.
3. Toss lightly to mix. Allow to cool before stuffing the bird.

Rice Stuffing for Game Birds

Enough to stuff 4 small birds or 1 large one

This is not wild rice, but the ordinary kind. You will find, however, that the stuffing is not ordinary.

1½ cups raw rice
4 slices bacon, cut into pieces
1 onion, sliced paper thin
4 mushrooms, sliced
1 cup chicken or game bird
    stock

½ cup dry white wine
6 sage leaves
Salt and freshly ground
    pepper
1 egg, beaten lightly

1. Cook the bacon until crisp, remove from skillet and use the fat for cooking the onion and mushrooms until onion is transparent but not brown. Add the rice and cook until it is golden. The stock goes in next. So far this has a familiar sound, but the next ingredients—the wine and sage leaves—add a different twist. Put these in, add salt and pepper, and simmer gently until the rice is tender and the liquid absorbed.
2. Add the egg, mix lightly, and stuff your birds.

CHAPTER 4

Small Game

Many of us tend to shun the unfamiliar, especially as far as food is concerned. I would not recommend munching on live grasshoppers as Japanese children do, but we could be more openminded in our approach to the unusual. By preparing in delicious ways the small game that exists at our very doorstep we can turn out many tasty meals, provided we can overcome the repugnance many of us feel when served an unaccustomed dish.

Small mammals such as muskrat, possum, rabbit, raccoon, squirrel, and woodchuck, are not only a fine source of protein, but serve to tantalize our taste buds with different and delectable flavors.

Muskrat

The muskrat is generally regarded as of interest for its fur only, as people are unaware that its dark-red meat is tender and rich in flavor. It is a clean little animal, living on water lily roots, cattails and the like, and occasionally raiding a nearby orchard or garden.

In some Eastern markets muskrat is sold under the name "marsh rabbit" and in restaurants is served as "musquash." Under any name, it is good eating.

Braised Muskrat

Serves 4 to 6

2 muskrats, cut up in pieces   Rosemary to taste
Seasoned flour   1 onion, cut up
2 tablespoons butter   Salt and freshly ground pepper
Few sprigs parsley   1 cup chicken stock

1. Dust the muskrat with the seasoned flour and brown in butter.
2. Add the parsley and rosemary, the onion, salt and pepper, and the stock.
3. Simmer until meat is tender and the liquid has been absorbed. It will be beautifully brown and deliciously fragrant.

Fried Muskrat

Serves 4 to 6

2 muskrats, cut up   Fine bread crumbs
1 cup flour   4 tablespoons bacon fat or salt
½ teaspoon salt   pork drippings
¼ teaspoon paprika   1 cup milk
1 egg   Salt and freshly ground pepper

1. Wash and dry the muskrat pieces.
2. Combine the flour, salt, and paprika in a paper bag and shake the muskrat in it until well coated.
3. Dip the pieces in egg beaten with a little water, then in the bread crumbs.
4. Melt the fat in the skillet over a hot fire, and brown the meat on all sides. Cover, lower the heat, and cook very slowly for 1 hour, or until tender. Transfer to a platter and keep hot while making the gravy.
5. Pour off all but 2 tablespoons of fat. Stir in 2 tablespoons of flour and stir until smooth. Slowly add the milk, stirring until thick and hot, add salt and pepper to taste, and pour over the muskrat.

Muskrat Stew

Serves 4

1 muskrat, cut up, washed and dried
1 cup flour
½ teaspoon salt
⅛ teaspoon pepper

2 tablespoons bacon fat
1 bay leaf
1 sprig parsley
6 small onions
6 carrots, sliced

1. Combine the flour, salt and pepper in a paper bag and shake the muskrat in it.
2. Melt bacon fat in a Dutch oven or a large heavy sauce pan, and brown the meat well.
3. Pour on boiling water to cover, add the bay leaf and parsley, and simmer until meat is almost done. It will take about an hour.
4. Add the onions and the carrots and simmer until they are tender. Remove the bay leaf.
5. Transfer meat and vegetables to a deep serving dish. Keep hot.
6. Thicken the stock with flour and water mixed together until smooth, bring to a boil, correct the seasoning, and pour gravy over the muskrat. Serve with dumplings (see page 283).

Opossum

Opossum, or 'possum, is a traditionally Southern dish and can be prepared in many different ways. Persimmons are the customary accompaniment, but apples may be substituted. Equal amounts of applesauce, chestnuts, and bread crumbs make a good stuffing.

I have been told that sassafrass twigs baked in the 'possum lend a delicious flavor to the meat.

Roasted 'Possum

Serves 4

1 'possum, skinned and cleaned   Dash of allspice
Persimmons   Beef bouillon
Mashed sweet potatoes.   Salt and freshly ground pepper
Bread crumbs   Melted butter
2 tablespoons minced parsley   2 cups boiling water
Rosemary and thyme to taste,   Heavy cream
   chopped

1. Make a savory stuffing of the persimmons, sweet potatoes, and bread crumbs in equal amounts. Add the parsley, a little rosemary and thyme and allspice. Moisten the stuffing with bouillon.

2. Stuff the 'possum and sew up or skewer the cavity. Gash it 3 or 4 times on either side of the backbone. Season with salt and pepper, brush generously with melted butter, cover with foil, and pour the boiling water around it.

3. Bake at 475° for 20 minutes, then reduce heat to 300°, basting as it cooks, until meat is tender, or about 25 minutes per pound.

4. At the end of 2 hours, remove the foil and brush heavy cream over the meat. Continue roasting until delicately browned. Serve the 'possum with sweet potatoes and stewed persimmons.

'Possum and Sweet Potatoes

Serves 4

1 'possum, skinned and cleaned   Salt and freshly ground pepper
1 bay leaf   1 teaspoon paprika
2 or 3 sage leaves, chopped   Salt pork
1 clove garlic, crushed   Sweet potatoes, parboiled

1. Crumble the bay leaf, and combine with the sage, garlic, salt, pepper, and paprika to taste.

2. Arrange the 'possum in a roasting pan, spread the herbs and spices on top, and cover with slices of salt pork.

3. Roast in a 300° oven for 1½ hours, or until tender, basting as it cooks.

4. For the last hour of baking, surround with the sweet potatoes. Bake until crusty and brown. Serve johnny cake with it.

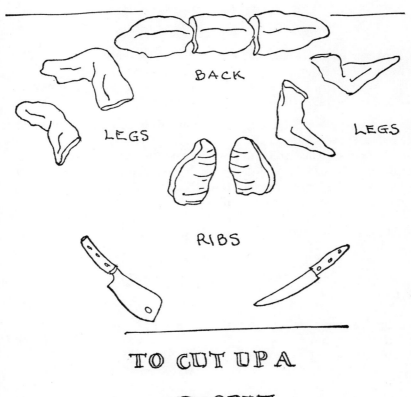

BACK

LEGS   LEGS

RIBS

TO CUT UP A

RABBIT

Rabbit

For these recipes you may use rabbit from the supermarket, jack rabbits from the woods, or the common garden variety of cottontail. Better to have him gracing your table delectably than eating your petunias.

As you know, rabbit should be cleaned immediately after it is shot. (See above chart of how a rabbit is cut up and also instruction matter at end of book, pages 307-308.)

Baked Rabbit

Serves 2 or 3

1 plump young rabbit, cut up   A dash of mace
Melted bacon fat   4 egg yolks, beaten
1 cup raw rice   1 or 2 tablespoons chutney
Chicken bouillon

1. Cook the rabbit gently in melted bacon fat until lightly browned and tender.
2. Cook rice according to directions on the package, using chicken bouillon instead of water. (A dash of mace adds an interesting flavor.) When rice is tender and all the liquid absorbed, allow to cool, then stir in the egg yolks.
3. Transfer rabbit to a buttered baking dish, and spread with chutney. Cover with the rice and bake at 350° for 20 to 25 minutes.

Rabbit, Country Style

Serves 2 or 3

1 tender young rabbit, cut up   1 bay leaf
Butter or bacon fat   ½ cup each, chicken broth and
1 onion and 1 carrot, sliced   dry white wine
    paper thin   A few mushrooms, sliced
1 sprig thyme   2 tablespoons each, flour and
Few leaves rosemary   butter

1. Brown the rabbit in butter or bacon fat, and transfer to baking dish.
2. To the skillet in which meat has browned, add the onion and carrot, thyme, rosemary, and bay leaf. Sauté a minute or two, then add the chicken broth and wine. Stir to remove any bits of crusty flavor from the bottom of the dish, and pour over the meat.
3. Cover and bake in a 325° oven for 1 hour, or until rabbit is tender. Transfer to a hot serving dish and keep hot.
4. Add mushrooms to the sauce and simmer until they are done. Thicken the sauce with a roux of the flour and butter. Serve gravy in a sauce boat.

German Hare

Serves 6

1 hare or 2 rabbits, cut up
Seasoned flour
2 tablespoons bacon fat
6 small onions

½ pound dried prunes, soaked
1 bay leaf
Salt and freshly ground pepper
1 bottle ale

1. Shake the rabbit pieces in a bag of seasoned flour and brown in bacon fat.
2. In a casserole combine the meat with the onions, prunes and bay leaf, season with salt and pepper, and pour the ale around it.
3. Roast, covered, in a 325° oven for 1½ to 2 hours, or until meat is tender. Remove the bay leaf. Serve with buttered noodles. Serve pan juices in a sauce boat.

Jugged Hare

Serves 4 to 6

If you are not familiar with this dish, at least it may have a familiar sound. It has been a favorite for many years and appears on the menus of fine restaurants in London and elsewhere.

Some recipes for jugged hare use the blood of the rabbit; we do not happen to care for this, but it is a matter of taste. My English cookbooks do not mention it.

First of all, let us get the business of forcemeat clear. Forcemeat is, according to the *Oxford Dictionary*, "meat, chopped fine, highly seasoned, and used for a stuffing or a garnish." The old English recipes say that jugged hare should be garnished with *balls of veal forcemeat*. If you are a purist (I have such tendencies myself), here you go:

Continued on next page

Veal Forcemeat

½ pound lean veal
6 strips bacon
¼ pound finely chopped beef
    suet
2 tablespoons bread crumbs
2 teaspoons parsley, minced

2 teaspoons onion, minced
Salt and freshly ground pepper
A dash each of mace, and
    nutmeg
2 eggs, beaten
Butter

1. Put the veal and bacon through the grinder, using the fine blade. Add the suet, bread crumbs, seasonings, herbs, spices, and finally the eggs. Mix well.

2. Shape the forcemeat into balls, roll in flour, and sauté in butter to a golden brown. Use as a garnish.

Now for the rabbit:

1 large rabbit, cut in walnut-
    size pieces
4 tablespoons olive oil
4 tablespoons port wine
A few peppercorns, crushed
1 bay leaf
1 onion, stuck with 3 or 4
    cloves
Lemon rind
Seasoned flour

Butter
3 tablespoons parsley, chopped
1 tablespoon thyme, chopped
Beef or chicken bouillon
Salt and freshly ground
    pepper
Rabbit blood (optional)
2 tablespoons soft butter
2 tablespoons flour
3 tablespoons port wine

1. Marinate rabbit meat in a stone jar or crock (hence the "jug"), in a mixture of the oil, wine, peppercorns, bay leaf, onion and cloves, and lemon rind. Allow to stand for 24 hours.

2. Dry the meat, roll in seasoned flour, and brown well in butter. Transfer to heat-proof jar (I use a pottery casserole), strain the marinade on top, add the thyme and parsley, and if the meat is not covered, add enough bouillon to do so. Add salt and pepper to taste.

3. Bake, covered, in a 300° oven for 3 to 4 hours, or until meat is tender. Transfer to a hot platter and keep hot while making the sauce.

4. If you have saved the blood, slowly stir it into the pan in which rabbit baked. Make a roux of the butter and flour. Add this. Stir in the port wine, correct the seasoning, and pour sauce over the rabbit.

5. Surround with the forcemeat balls, garnish the platter with sprigs of thyme and pass wild blackberry jelly.

Hassenpfeffer

Serves 6

No culinary consideration of rabbit or hare is complete without this traditional dish. It is usually served with buttered noodles or potato dumplings.

1 large hare or 2 rabbits, about 4 pounds in all, cut up	2 teaspoons salt
1½ cups vinegar	1 teaspoon freshly ground pepper
1½ cups water	1 sprig parsley
1 cup claret	3 sprigs thyme
1 tablespoon sugar	Seasoned flour
3 onions, sliced	Butter
12 whole cloves	1 cup thick sour cream
1 bay leaf	

1. Wash and dry the hare, put in a glass dish, and cover with marinade of water, vinegar, wine, sugar, onions, herbs, and seasonings. Let stand in the refrigerator for 24 hours, turning the meat occasionally.

2. Drain and pat the hare dry, and shake the pieces in a bag of seasoned flour. Brown well in butter in an iron skillet. Strain the marinade over the meat, cover the skillet, and simmer for about 1 hour, or until tender. If the hare is old, cooking may take nearer to 2 hours.

3. Transfer hare to a hot platter. Thicken gravy with ¼ cup of the seasoned flour, stirred with water until smooth. Bring to a boil and let simmer a few minutes. Stir in the cream. Heat thoroughly, but do not allow it to boil. Serve garnished with watercress, and pass the gravy in a sauce boat.

Roast Rabbit

Serves 2 to 4

Since rabbit somewhat resembles chicken in flavor, it is not surprising that sage and onions are a happy addition to any rabbit dish. Here is one that you will like.

1 tender young rabbit, cut up	1 cup cracker or bread crumbs
Seasoned flour	Salt and freshly ground pepper
Butter	8 to 10 sage leaves, chopped or
¼ pound salt pork	1 teaspoon dried sage
1 small onion	1 egg, beaten
	Butter or salt pork cubes

1. Shake the rabbit pieces in a bag of seasoned flour, brown in butter, and set aside.

2. Run the salt pork and the onion through the food chopper. Add the bread crumbs, salt and pepper, and the sage. Stir in the egg and spread the mixture in a baking dish. Arrange the rabbit meat on top, and dot with butter or salt pork cubes.

3. Bake in a 350° oven for about 45 minutes, or until tender.

Rabbit Pie—I

Serves 2 to 4

1 tender young rabbit, cut up	Salt and freshly ground pepper
Water	1 tablespoon flour to each cup
Bacon slices	liquid
3 or 4 hard-boiled eggs, sliced	Rich pastry

1. Cover the rabbit with water and simmer until tender. Remove all meat from bones.

2. Butter a shallow baking dish and lay several slices of bacon on the bottom. Cover with a layer of meat, then a layer of hard-boiled egg. Repeat, seasoning each layer, until the meat is used up, finishing with the bacon.

3. Mix flour with a little water and thicken the broth. Pour over the pie, filling the dish to the top with gravy. Cover with a rich pastry (see page 214), making slits in the top to allow steam to escape. Bake at 400° for about 1 hour.

Rabbit Pie—II

Serves 6

If you have 2 or 3 tender young rabbits, try dealing with them in this fashion:

2 or 3 rabbits, cut up	1 tablespoon chopped parsley
Seasoned flour	1 or 2 leaves rosemary
Butter, or bacon or salt pork fat	3 tablespoons flour
1 or 2 carrots, sliced	2 cups chicken broth
2 or 3 scallions, green parts	¼ cup dry white wine
included, sliced	Pastry triangles

1. Shake the rabbits in a bag of seasoned flour. Brown in butter, or bacon fat or rendered salt pork. If young enough, the rabbit will be quite tender by the time it is browned.

2. Transfer the pieces to a casserole. Combine the carrots, scallions, chopped parsley, and rosemary, and spread over the meat.

3. To the fat in the pan, add the flour and stir over a slow flame until smooth. Add the chicken broth and white wine, and simmer until sauce is thick and hot. Pour over the rabbit in the casserole, and top with rich pastry triangles.

4. Bake in a 350° oven for about 1 hour. The rabbit will be meltingly tender, the sauce fragrant, the pastry a delicate brown.

Smothered Rabbit

Serves 2 to 4

This is a recipe which comes from the Caribbean, but after all, a rabbit is a rabbit, so why not try it?

1 tender young rabbit, cut up	1 cup olive oil
1 cup tomato purée	¼ cup white wine vinegar
1 teaspoon salt	¼ cup green olives, sliced
1 garlic clove, crushed	5 or 6 potatoes, peeled and
1 small onion, sliced paper	diced
thin	1 cup sherry

Continued on next page

1. Place the rabbit in a saucepan with the tomato purée, salt, garlic, onion, olive oil, wine vinegar, and olives. Simmer gently for 1 hour.

2. Add the potatoes and the sherry, and simmer for 30 minutes more. The potatoes should be soft but not mushy, and the rabbit delectably tender.

Raccoon

The raccoon is a voracious eater. Since in the fall he must store up fat to last through a long winter's hibernation, he may raid a vegetable patch or a cornfield. He relishes frogs and fish.

The older raccoon will probably weigh 8 to 10 pounds and will be tough and stringy, but the meat of a young one is sweet and tender.

Roast Raccoon

Serves 2

1 raccoon, parboiled	1 teaspoon salt
2 onions	4 or 5 peppercorns
2 carrots	Water for stock
Celery leaves	Apples, cored, and filled with
1 bay leaf	Brown sugar

1. It is best to parboil the raccoon before roasting. To do this, put it in a kettle with the onions, carrots, celery leaves, the bay leaf, salt, peppercorns, and enough water to cover. When the water comes to a boil, simmer the coon until tender.

2. Remove from kettle and cut away all the fat you can. Reserve stock.

3. Place raccoon in a roasting pan, pour 1 cup of the stock over it, and surround with the apples.

4. Bake, uncovered, in a 300° oven until the meat is crusty brown and the apples cooked.

Squirrel

Squirrel can be cooked in the same way as rabbit. Red and grey squirrels are both common here, and the red are considered the more delicate meat.

Brunswick Stew

Serves 4

2 squirrels, cut up
2 tablespoons bacon fat
2 onions, sliced paper thin
Seasoned flour
2 cups chicken broth
½ cup sherry
1 tablespoon Worcestershire
    Sauce

Chopped parsley to taste
Salt and freshly ground pepper
2 or 3 ripe tomatoes, peeled
1 cup fresh lima beans
1 cup corn, cut from cob
½ cup okra
1 cup fine bread crumbs
2 tablespoons butter

1. In a skillet, melt bacon fat and cook the onions gently until slightly brown. Transfer to a flameproof casserole.

2. Roll the squirrel in seasoned flour and brown well in the bacon fat. Place on top of the onions in casserole.

3. To the bacon fat in the pan, add the chicken broth, sherry, Worcestershire Sauce, parsley, and salt and pepper. Heat and stir, and pour over the squirrel and onions. Cover and simmer gently for 30 minutes.

4. Add 2 or 3 ripe tomatoes, lima beans, corn, and okra. Again cover the dish and simmer 30 minutes more.

5. Add the bread crumbs and butter, and simmer for another 30 minutes. This delicious dish may be made of a combination of chicken and squirrel.

Dixie Squirrel

Serves 4

2 squirrels, cut up
Seasoned flour
2 tablespoons butter
¼ cup raw wild rice

4 stalks celery, cut up
3 tart apples, peeled, cored,
    diced

1. Wash and dry squirrels. Shake the pieces in a bag of seasoned flour, and brown in butter.

2. Arrange the meat in a buttered casserole, add the rice, celery, and apples, and pour on boiling water to cover.

3. Bake, covered, at 300° for 1 hour, or until meat is tender.

Stuffed Squirrel

1 squirrel serves 1 or 2

A squirrel may be stuffed and baked, as a chicken. The flavor of onions, mushrooms, and certain herbs seems to go well with it. We do not care for sage with this meat.

Squirrels, skinned and cleaned
Bread crumbs
Mushrooms
Onions
Celery
Oregano
Parsley
Salt and freshly ground pepper

1. Season and stuff the squirrels according to preference. The above ingredients make a tasty stuffing.
2. Roast squirrel in a 350° oven for 1¾ to 2 hours. A gravy may be made by thickening the juices in the pan.

Broiled Squirrel

Serves 1 or 2

Very young, tender squirrels may be broiled exactly as you would broil chicken.

1 squirrel, cut in serving pieces   Salt and freshly ground pepper
Melted bacon fat

1. Season squirrel with salt and pepper, arrange pieces on the broiler rack, brush with melted bacon fat, and broil about 35 or 40 minutes. Turn occasionally, and keep brushing meat with the fat. It will be crisp and brown when done.

Squirrel Fricassee

Serves 4

2 squirrels, cut in serving pieces   2 cups chicken broth
3 tablespoons bacon fat   Salt and freshly ground
Seasoned flour   pepper

Dust the meat with seasoned flour. Brown in a skillet in bacon fat over a low fire. Add the chicken broth and simmer until tender. Correct the seasoning, and serve as you would any stew, with biscuits or dumplings.

Squirrel Stew

Serves 4

2 squirrels, cut in pieces
2 tablespoons butter
1 large onion, sliced very thin
4 very ripe tomatoes, cut up, or

1 #2 can stewed tomatoes
Boiling water
Salt and freshly ground pepper
Flour and water

1. Melt the butter in a saucepan, add the onion, and cook until transparent. Add the tomatoes, and simmer for a few minutes with the onion. Add the meat and enough boiling water to cover, season with salt and pepper, and continue to cook until the meat is tender.
2. Thicken the broth with flour and water, and again bring to a boil.

Woodchuck

The woodchuck, or groundhog, is a rather engaging creature that we see occasionally waddling through the woods, or more often sitting up outside his hole, surveying the surrounding terrain. In spite of his indolent appearance, he can vanish like a flash if he senses danger.

The farmer takes a different view of this animal, as he is extremely fond of freshly sprouted garden stuff and has been known to ruin a corn patch when the ears are about ready to pick. He is also a menace to young fruit trees, so it is easy to see why he is found gracing farmhouse tables as a *pièce de résistance*.

Gastronomically speaking, woodchucks are at their best in the fall, when they have been busy building up a reserve supply of fat to carry them through a long winter.

Woodchuck à la King

Serves 6 to 8

1 woodchuck, cleaned and cut	2 tablespoons flour
2 onions	Salt to taste
2 tablespoons butter	1 cup cream
	2 tablespoons sherry

1. Prepare the woodchuck by using tenderizer, if you want to play it safe.

2. Place in a kettle, cover with boiling water, add the onions, and simmer until tender. Transfer meat to a hot serving platter and keep hot while making gravy.

3. Reduce the stock to about 2 cups of liquid, thicken with a roux made of flour and butter, add salt, and stir in the cream. Reheat, stir in sherry while the gravy is hot, and pour over the woodchuck.

Fried Woodchuck

Serves 6

1 woodchuck, cleaned and cut up	Few peppercorns
Weak brine	Salt
1 bay leaf	Fat (vegetable shortening and butter, or lard or bacon fat)
Few sprigs parsley	Seasoned flour
1 onion	2 cups stock
2 or 3 carrots	

1. Cut into serving pieces, soak overnight in a weak salt solution.

2. In a kettle, combine water and bay leaf, parsley, onion, carrots, peppercorns, and salt, and parboil meat by simmering until tender—about 1 hour. Drain and dry, reserving the stock.

3. Melt the fat in a skillet. Roll meat pieces in seasoned flour and brown well. Add the stock, cover and simmer for another hour or so, or until the meat is ready to fall off the bones. Remove cover and cook until the liquid is absorbed. Transfer to a serving dish.

4. Make a gravy, using the remaining stock, and pour over the woodchuck. Serve with mashed sweet potatoes.

Woodchuck Fricassee

Serves 6 to 8

This may sound like your grandmother's favorite chicken recipe. Anyway, it is good.

1 woodchuck, cleaned and cut up	2 tablespoons butter or bacon fat
Water	2 tablespoons flour
1 small onion	Salt and freshly ground pepper
Seasoned flour	1 cup stock
	1 cup milk or cream

1. Put the woodchuck in a saucepan, cover with water, add the onion, and simmer for 1 hour.

2. Drain and dry the meat. Reserve the stock. Dust the pieces with the seasoned flour. Melt the butter or bacon fat in a skillet and cook the meat gently until brown and tender. Transfer to a serving platter and keep hot.

3. Stir the flour into the fat in the skillet, cook for a minute or two, add salt and pepper, pour in the stock in which the woodchuck cooked, and finally the milk or cream. Stir until sauce is smooth, thick and hot, and pour over the woodchuck or serve separately in a gravy boat.

Woodchuck Patties

Serves 4 to 6

If your woodchuck seems rather ancient, and is therefore likely to be tough, you could make woodchuckburgers (to coin a phrase).

Meat of 1 woodchuck, ground	Onion, minced
Seasoning to taste	Thyme, chopped

1. Shape woodchuck meat into patties and season to taste, treating as you would beef. I suggest the addition of onion and chopped thyme.

Woodchuck Pie

Serves 6

1 woodchuck, cut into serving
    pieces
Bacon fat
Seasoned flour
Water

2 onions
3 carrots, sliced thin
2 or 3 tablespoons flour
Baking powder biscuits

1. Dust the meat with seasoned flour and brown thoroughly in melted bacon fat in a saucepan. Cover with water, add the onion, and simmer gently for about 1 hour. Add carrots, and simmer for 10 or 15 minutes more. Correct the seasoning.

2. Transfer meat and vegetables to a baking dish. Thicken the liquid in the pan with flour, stirring until smooth. Pour the hot gravy over the woodchuck and top with the biscuits.

3. Bake, uncovered, in a 400° oven until woodchuck is tender, and the biscuits lightly browned, or about 30 minutes.

Game Sausages

If you know a country butcher who makes his own sausages, take him your game scraps and trimmings. Half game and half pork make a good combination, and you can have him season it as he does his pork sausage.

We like a sausage flavored with herbs. Sage is especially good. Add a little thyme or a dash of rosemary and nutmeg.

Bones

Save these for soup or gravy.

CHAPTER 5

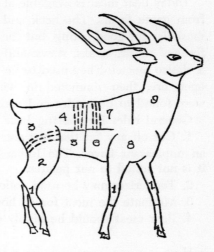

Big Game

Survival, for the early pioneers in this country, was often determined by the abundance of big game. They and the Indians relied heavily on the herds of bison, deer, elk, bear, and bighorn sheep which were found in the mountainous regions.

Today most hunters enjoy the sport of hunting deer, and occasionally bear. Both bear meat and venison are obtainable at game farms and markets.

Bear

There is a tale concerning a small band of pioneers in the early days of the West, who were near starvation when one of their members shot a grizzly. And so their lives were saved. Several persons in the group declared afterwards that "next time they'd rather starve." On the other hand, hunters and trappers have long enjoyed bear meat cooked over a campfire. It was an important item of the diet of the colonists who found black bear "tender and sweet." Bear meat does have a rather strong flavor, and for most of us may be considered a cultivated taste.

129

Today bear meat is available at city markets, where it is shipped from game farms. The neck and hindquarters are apt to be too muscular for good eating, but the rest of the animal is sold in the form of roasts, steaks, stews, and paws. The latter are considered a choice morsel. They used to be baked in clay in the ashes of an open fire, then simmered in wine and herbs, whereupon they were found to be tender and succulent.

General rules for cooking bear meat are:

1. Cut off any fat that has not been removed—it is apt to have an unpleasant flavor. The Indians used bear fat in cooking, but it is not suited to our palates.

2. Tenderizer may be used, following the directions on the label.

3. Marinate the meat for 48 hours, covered, in the refrigerator.

4. Bear meat should be highly spiced and well seasoned.

Here is a good marinade for a roast of bear: adjust the quantity to the amount of meat you are preparing.

Marinade #1

2 cups water	A dash of chili powder
1 tablespoon salt	Juice of 1 lemon
¼ cup vinegar	Juice of 1 orange
2 tablespoons pickling spices	Herbs to taste

1. Mix well and pour marinade over the meat. Turn occasionally during the 48-hour period. Burgundy or sauterne may be substituted for the water. Rosemary, sweet basil, sage or thyme are flavors that blend well with bear meat.

Marinade #2

1 cup salad oil	1 bay leaf
2 cups dry vermouth	2 tablespoons brown sugar
1 onion, sliced	6 crushed peppercorns
1 lemon, sliced	3 tablespoons chopped rosemary leaves

Follow directions given above.

BLACK BEAR

Roast Bear Paws

Serves 4

4 small bear paws or 2 large
   ones, skinned
Seasoned flour
3 tablespoons bacon fat
1 teaspoon cinnamon

1 teaspoon allspice
Salt and freshly ground pepper
2 onions, sliced very thin
4 slices salt pork
1 cup water

1. Dust paws with the seasoned flour, and brown well in a skillet in melted bacon fat. Transfer to a casserole and sprinkle with cinnamon, allspice, salt and pepper.

2. In the bacon fat in the skillet cook the onions until transparent but not brown. Arrange around the paws in the casserole and lay the salt pork on top. Pour the water around the paws.

3. Roast, covered, in a 350° oven for 4 hours, or until tender. Serve with sauerkraut and potatoes boiled in their jackets.

Bear Steak

Serves 4 to 6

Bear steak, 1½ to 2 inches
   thick
Sauterne marinade cover
   (see page 130)
1 tablespoon dry mustard
1 tablespoon horse radish

½ cup tomato juice or chili sauce
Juice of 1 lemon
Vegetable oil
Salt and freshly ground pepper
Butter
Minced parsley

1. Marinate the steak for 48 hours, turning occasionally. Remove from the marinade and pat dry.

2. Combine the mustard, horse radish, tomato juice, or chili sauce, and lemon juice, and spread over the steak on both sides. Allow to stand for an hour or so.

3. Heat the oil in a skillet, and sauté the steak over a hot fire for 5 to 7 minutes on each side, or longer if you like your steak well done.

4. Transfer to a hot platter, season with salt and pepper, pour melted butter over it, and sprinkle with minced parsley.

Bear Stew

Serves 6 to 8

3 pounds bear meat
Burgundy marinade to cover
(see page 130)
¼ pound salt pork, sliced thin
Seasoned flour
1 bay leaf

Few sprigs thyme
1 clove garlic
18 baby carrots
18 small onions
Salt and freshly ground pepper

1. Cube the bear meat and marinate for 48 hours, drain and pat it dry. Strain and reserve the marinade.
2. Try out the salt pork in a skillet. When crisp, skim out the bits of pork and set them aside.
3. Shake the bear meat in a bag of the seasoned flour, and brown it well in the pork fat.
4. Put the meat in a kettle, and add the bay leaf, thyme, and garlic. Pour the marinade over it and simmer for 3 or 4 hours, or until meat is tender. Replenish the liquid with water as needed.
5. Half an hour before the meat is done, remove the bay leaf, thyme and garlic. Add the carrots and onions, and continue cooking until vegetables are tender. Season with salt and pepper to taste. Thicken the broth, add the salt pork bits, and serve in a deep platter, surrounded with parsley dumplings (see page 283).

Roast Bear

Serves 6 to 8

4 pounds saddle of bear
Marinade cover (see page 130)
2 tablespoons soy sauce

1 tablespoon honey
1 teaspoon ground ginger
Salt and freshly ground pepper

1. Marinate the roast for 48 hours, turning occasionally. Remove from the marinade and pat dry, reserving the liquid.
2. Combine the soy sauce, honey, ginger, and salt and pepper. Spread the roast with this mixture and place in a roasting pan.
3. Roast, covered, in a 350° oven for 2½ hours if the bear is young, 3½ to 4 if aged. Baste frequently with the marinade as it cooks. Serve with spinach noodles, spooning the pan juices over them.

Venison

Technically this term includes not only deer but reindeer, moose, elk, caribou, and antelope. However, it is generally taken to refer to deer. The recipes could be applied to the other meats as well.

Venison à la Mode

Serves 4 to 6

If you have enjoyed *bouef à la mode,* you will like venison cooked this way. One of the less tender cuts may be used. The venison is marinated, and may be cut into pieces or left in one chunk, as circumstances seem to indicate.

3 pounds venison
Marinade to cover, made of:
    4 cups dry red wine;
    A few celery leaves;
    2 or 3 peppercorns;
    2 or 3 whole cloves;
    1 bay leaf;

Few sprigs each, thyme and
    parsley;
Salt to taste.
Flour
Bacon fat or olive oil
12 tiny peeled onions
12 baby carrots

1. Marinate the venison for at least 24 hours, turning occasionally. Three hours before meat is to be served, remove from the marinade, pat dry with a paper towel, and dust lightly with flour.
2. Using bacon fat or oil, brown the meat on all sides, then transfer to baking dish. Pour the marinade around it, and roast, covered, in a 350° oven for 2½ hours.
3. Add the vegetables during the last half hour.

Venison Hash

Serves 4

2 cups cooked venison, diced
2 tablespoons butter
½ onion, minced
2 cups boiled potatoes, diced

Few sprigs parsley, chopped
Salt and freshly ground pepper
½ cup milk
Pickled beets

1. Melt the butter in a pan, add onion and simmer until transparent but not brown.

2. Add the venison, potatoes, parsley, and salt and pepper. Mix well, add the milk, cover, and cook over a low fire until the hash is hot and the bottom crusty brown.

3. Turn out on a large round platter and surround with hot pickled beets.

Venison Liver

Serves 4

This is considered the choicest part of the deer. To cook it, I follow a recipe I have long used for calves' liver. You may use any liver recipe successfully.

4 average slices venison liver	2 tablespoons flour
2 tablespoons bacon fat	1 cup beef bouillon
2 onions, sliced very thin	1 tablespoon tomato catsup
Salt and freshly ground pepper	2 tablespoons sherry

1. Melt the bacon fat in a skillet, add the onions, and cook until transparent. Lay them aside.

2. Season liver with salt and pepper and cook in the fat over a slow fire for a few minutes. Transfer to a casserole.

3. Stir flour into the fat (adding a little more fat if necessary) and add the bouillon, catsup and sherry. Heat and stir well. Season with salt and pepper to taste.

4. Pour the sauce over the liver, cover with onions, and bake in a 350° oven for 30 minutes, or until thoroughly heated through. Serve with buttered noodles.

Venison Heart

Marinate the heart overnight, then slice and cook it as you would steak. Serve with buttered noodles.

Braised Venison

Serves 6

3 pounds sliced venison, shoulder,
   breast or flank
Marinade to cover, made of:
   ¼ cup olive oil;
   1 cup dry red wine;
   A few sprigs parsley;

1 clove garlic, crushed;
2 tablespoons brandy;
1 bay leaf.
½ pound salt pork, diced
1 tablespoon flour
Fried bread

1. Marinate the meat for several hours, or, better still, overnight in the refrigerator.

2. Try out salt pork in a skillet and set it aside. Drain the meat, pat dry, sauté in the pork fat, and arrange in a baking dish. Stir flour into the skillet and cook for a few minutes. Add the marinade, heat, and pour over venison.

3. Bake in a 350° oven for 40 minutes. Serve on a hot platter garnished with fried bread, the crisp bits of salt pork and parsley.

Venison Chops with Chestnuts

Serves 4

4 venison chops
Marinade (see page 130)
2 tablespoons butter
2 stalks celery, diced
2 scallions, chopped fine

2 ripe tomatoes, cut up
1 cup chestnuts, chopped (see
   page 152)
Pinch of sugar
Salt and freshly ground pepper

1. Marinate the chops in standard marinade (or use that for venison à la mode) for an hour or so.

2. Melt the butter in a skillet and sauté the celery and scallions. Add the tomatoes, and simmer for 5 or 6 minutes more.

3. Prepare the chestnuts, add to the sauce, and simmer until they are cooked. Stir in the sugar and salt and pepper to taste.

4. Drain the chops, pat dry, and sauté in butter for 5 minutes on each side. Serve on a hot platter surrounded with the chestnut sauce.

Venison Liver in Wine

Serves 4

4 slices venison liver
Seasoned flour
3 tablespoons butter
1 cup consommé

1 cup Burgundy
1 cup water
2 tablespoons chopped scallion
 tops
1 teaspoon salt

1. Shake the liver in seasoned flour and sauté lightly in melted butter. Transfer to baking dish.
2. Combine the consommé, wine, water, scallion tops, and salt, and pour over the liver.
3. Bake, covered, at 350° for 45 minutes.
4. The gravy in the pan may be thickened with flour and water and poured over the liver.

Roast Venison with Whortleberries

Allow 2 or 3 servings per pound

I came across this interesting-sounding recipe, but was baffled by the "whortleberries" of which I was sure there were none around here. Upon looking them up, I was relieved to find that they are the same thing as huckleberries.

1 venison roast
Marinade to cover, made of:
  1 cup olive oil;
  1 bottle dry white wine;
  2 cloves garlic, sliced;
  2 bay leaves;
  1 sprig thyme;

1 carrot, sliced;
2 onions, sliced;
2 shallots, sliced;
6 juniper berries.
4 tablespoons whortleberry jam
2 tablespoons lemon juice
1 tablespoon sweet butter

1. Marinate the meat for 24 hours, turning occasionally. Drain.
2. Allow 10 minutes to a pound, roast the venison in a 350° oven, basting with the marinade. Remove from the oven and allow to stand in a warm place.
3. Prepare sauce by straining the marinade and the juices in the roasting pan into a saucepan, then add the whortleberry jam, lemon juice, and sweet butter. Heat and serve in a sauce boat.

Roast Venison—I

The virtue of this dish lives in its excellent sauce. Use a tender cut of meat.

2 to 3 pound venison roast
Soft butter
Salt and freshly ground pepper
2 or 3 onions, sliced thin
3 or 4 carrots, sliced thin

1 bay leaf
Few sprigs each, parsley and
  thyme
½ cup sherry
Dash of powdered cloves
1 cup beef broth

1. Butter the top of the roast and season with salt and pepper. Arrange in a pan with the onions, carrots, bay leaf, parsley, and thyme.

2. Roast in a 350° oven, allowing 10 minutes per pound. When done, remove the roast from the pan and keep warm.

3. To the pan gravy, add sherry, powdered cloves and beef broth. Simmer until liquid is reduced to half its volume. Strain. Correct seasoning and serve in a sauce boat.

Roast Venison—II

Serves 4 to 6

1 leg venison, about 3 pounds
Thyme, basil, parsley, and
  lemon verbena to taste,
  chopped fine

2 teaspoons salt
Pinch garlic salt
Freshly ground pepper
Olive oil

1. If you suspect your leg of venison might be tough, use tenderizer according to directions on page 130.

2. Combine herbs, salt, garlic salt, and pepper. Mix thoroughly.

3. With a small sharp knife, make cuts about ¼ of an inch deep all over the venison. Rub the herb mixture well into the gashes. Spoon olive oil over the meat.

4. Roast in a 350° oven for 30 to 40 minutes.

Venison Stroganoff

Serves 4

I use leftover venison for this, following my own recipe for Beef Stroganoff.

Sliced cooked venison to serve 4   2 cups beef consommé
2 tablespoons butter   Salt and freshly ground pepper
1 small onion, sliced thin   1 tablespoon sour cream
2 tablespoons flour   1 tablespoon tomato paste

1. Melt the butter in a saucepan, add onion, and cook until transparent but not brown. Stir in the flour and cook until smooth. Pour the consommé in slowly while you stir. Salt and pepper. Cook until thick and hot.

2. Place the sauce over boiling water to keep hot, and add the venison.

3. Just before serving, slowly add the sour cream and tomato paste, being careful not to let the sauce curdle. Serve with rice, Indian style.

Venison Steak with Sour Cream

1 small steak per person

Venison steaks   Sour cream
Salt and Freshly ground pepper   Paprika
Butter

1. Season the steaks with salt and pepper, and sauté gently in butter for about 5 minutes on each side. Pour the sour cream over them. Cover the dish and allow to simmer for 5 minutes.

2. Remove to a heated platter, pour the sour cream sauce over them, and sprinkle generously with paprika. Serve surrounded with cooked noodles seasoned with parsley butter.

Venisonburgers

Venison, ground   Thyme, fresh-chopped or dried
Salt and freshly ground pepper   Dry red wine

1. Use the tougher parts and/or scraps of deer meat, season with salt, pepper and a bit of thyme. Pour the wine over the ground meat, and let stand overnight.
2. When ready to cook, shape the meat into patties and grill over a charcoal fire or an electric grill to the desired degree of doneness.

Moose

Our experience with moose is limited but when a friend gave us a piece of unidentified moosemeat of dubious origin, we made MOOSEBURGERS and found them delicious.

Mooseburgers

Moosemeat, ground twice   Salt and freshly ground pepper
Lemon juice

1. Combine meat with lemon juice, salt and pepper, and shape into patties.
2. Sauté in butter as you would beef patties.

CHAPTER 6

Butters, Sauces, and

Garnishes for Fish and Game

One reason for the reputation of French cooks is that they excel in the variety and quality of their sauces. They will go to no end of trouble to prepare a sauce which will enhance a certain dish to their satisfaction.

A good sauce is subtle and smooth. It complements the flavor of the dish but does not dominate it. Fish and game not only profit from fine sauces, but almost demand them.

Béchamel Sauce

I find myself using a variation of béchamel sauce a great deal. Here is my basic sauce:

2 tablespoons butter
2 tablespoons minced onion
2 tablespoons flour

1 cup milk
Salt and freshly ground pepper

Melt the butter, add the onion, and cook until transparent but not brown. Stir in the flour, cook a minute more, slowly add the milk, and season with salt and pepper to taste. When the sauce thickens, strain it.

Béchamel Sauce Variations

Béchamel Sauce with Herbs: To the milk, add a bay leaf and a sprig or two of thyme or a few rosemary leaves. Bring the milk just to a boil, let the herbs stand in it until it cools, remove them and proceed as above.

Béchamel Sauce with Stock: In place of the milk use beef stock or chicken bouillon, either canned or made from a cube.

Rich Béchamel Sauce: Use half cream and half milk, beating an egg yolk in at the last minute.

Béchamel Sauce with Wine: To any of the above sauces, a little sherry or dry white wine may be added.

Béchamel Sauce with Capers: (Excellent with fish.) Make the sauce with chicken or fish stock. Add 2 tablespoons of dry white wine (Chablis or Rhine Wine). Chop 2 tablespoons capers and 1 tablespoon fresh tarragon. Add and stir until hot. For an interesting variation, substitute the pickled nasturtium seed for the capers.

Béchamel Sauce with Eggs: Make the sauce either with milk and cream, or with fish stock. Add 2 chopped hard-boiled eggs and about 2 tablespoons of finely chopped parsley. Use on poached fish. For additional flavor, try a pinch of mustard or a drop of Worcestershire Sauce.

Béchamel Sauce with Curry: Make the sauce with chicken stock and add a teaspoon of curry powder. Excellent on hot stuffed deviled eggs, or on shrimp.

Arrowroot

This may be used as a thickening agent in place of flour, using 1 tablespoon to 1 cup of liquid. It makes a very smooth sauce or gravy.

Bread Sauce

Here is a delicious sauce for partridge, grouse, or quail. This sauce, as well as the one for Jelly Sauce on page 155, came from an old family cookbook published in 1875.

2 cups dry bread crumbs
1 pint milk
1 small onion, sliced
1 tablespoon butter
½ teaspoon salt

Dash of pepper
Nutmeg
1 tablespoon butter
Dash of paprika

1. Sift the dry bread crumbs, separating the fine from the coarse ones.
2. In a sauce pan, heat the milk and onion until the milk is scalded. Remove the onion and add enough fine crumbs to thicken sauce. Add butter and season with salt, pepper, and nutmeg.
3. In a separate pan, sauté the coarse crumbs with a tablespoon of butter until light brown, stirring all the time; add the paprika.
4. Serve the fried bread crumbs on the dish with the game; serve the sauce in a gravy boat.

Sauce Béarnaise

This is a delicious hot sauce for fish. It may be served with beef as well.

1 cup dry white wine
3 shallots, chopped
1 sprig each tarragon and
    parsley, minced
A few leaves chervil, minced

¼ cup soft butter
3 egg yolks, beaten
1 teaspoon lemon juice
Salt and freshly ground pepper

1. In a sauce pan, combine the white wine, shallots, chervil, tarragon, and parsley. Simmer until the liquid is reduced to about half its volume.
2. Alternately add the butter and egg yolk, a little at a time, stirring constantly. Add the lemon juice and season with salt and pepper.

Almond Sauce for Fish

¼ cup blanched almonds,
   chopped
2 tablespoons butter
2 tablespoons flour

1 cup fish stock
1 tablespoon pickled nasturtium
   seeds
Salt and freshly ground pepper

Melt the butter, brown the almonds, stir in the flour, and add the fish stock. Stir until sauce is thick and hot, season with salt and pepper to taste, then add the pickled nasturtium seeds. Serve with any hot fish.

Butter Sauce

This is good with pan-fried fish.

2 tablespoons butter
1 tablespoon flour
½ cup water

1 teaspoon white wine vinegar
Salt and freshly ground pepper

Melt the butter, add the flour, and cook for a minute or two. Stir in the water, white wine vinegar, and a little salt and pepper. Stir until thick and hot.

Herb Butter

Use any herb you like, such as tarragon, parsley, chervil, or a combination of them. Herb butter may be spread on fish or meat; it makes a good base for a sandwich or canapé as well.

Soft butter
Herbs, minced

Few drops lemon juice

Combine the herbs and butter, mix well, add the lemon juice, and serve on hot fish.

Onion Butter

¼ cup onion, chopped or sliced
   very thin

6 tablespoons butter
Minced parsley

Melt the butter, and cook the onion until slightly brown. Pour over fish. Sprinkle minced parsley on top.

Anchovy Butter

This will pep up a bland fish and is wonderful on steak too.

1 tablespoon anchovy paste   1 tablespoon minced parsley
4 tablespoons butter

Cream the butter, and combine with the anchovy paste and minced parsley. Spread on hot fish.

Anchovy Sauce

1 tablespoon anchovy paste   2 tablespoons flour
2 tablespoons butter   1 cup milk

Melt the butter, stir in the flour, add the milk, and stir sauce until thick and hot. Blend in the anchovy paste and serve.

Beurre Noir
or
Black Butter

This is merely butter melted over a slow fire and simmered until brown. It is excellent over fish or vegetables and can be varied by the addition of minced parsley, a little tarragon vinegar, or both.

Golden Butter

Serve this with fish.

4 tablespoons soft butter   Salt and freshly ground pepper
2 hard-cooked egg yolks   Lemon juice

Put the hard-boiled egg yolks through a sieve and blend with the butter. Season with salt and pepper to taste, and add a few drops of lemon juice.

Nasturtium Butter

2 tablespoons nasturtium leaves   2 tablespoons soft butter

Mix the chopped nasturtium leaves with the butter and spread on hot fish.

Curry Sauce

There are many different recipes for curry sauce but this is the one I generally use.

1 tablespoon curry powder	2 tablespoons flour
2 tablespoons butter	1 teaspoon brown sugar
1 small onion, chopped fine	3 cups milk
1 small piece ginger root, cut fine	Salt

Melt the butter in a skillet and add the onion, ginger root, and curry powder. Simmer and stir for a few minutes, then add the flour and brown sugar. Cook for a few minutes more, gradually pour in the milk, add salt to taste, and continue to cook and stir until the sauce thickens. Strain. More curry powder as well as more salt may be added—this is entirely a matter of taste.

For a cook in a hurry, I give these:

Quick Curry Sauce—I

Curry powder to taste	2 tablespoons flour
2 tablespoons butter	2 cups chicken or beef bouillon, canned or made with bouillon cube

Melt the butter and stir in the flour. Add the bouillon, put in the amount of curry powder that you like and stir until sauce is thick and hot.

Quick Curry Sauce—II

1 can condensed cream of chicken soup	Curry powder to taste

Add the curry powder to the soup, heat, and stir until smooth and well blended.

Cumberland Sauce

This is a well-known sauce served with game and cold meats.

1 lemon, rind and juice
1 orange, rind and juice
¼ cup water
¼ cup port wine
2 teaspoons red currant jelly

2 teaspoons vinegar
½ teaspoon prepared mustard
Salt and freshly ground pepper
A few glacé cherries, cut fine

1. Combine the grated lemon and orange rind and water and simmer for a few minutes. Add the port wine, red currant jelly, vinegar, mustard, salt and pepper, and the orange and lemon juice. Simmer 10 minutes longer.
2. Strain the sauce, add the glacé cherries, heat and serve.

Cucumber Sauce

This is good with cold fish of any kind.

3 cucumbers, sliced paper thin
Salt
½ cup sour cream
Several sprigs dill weed

1 tablespoon garlic chives
A little mustard
Few drops lemon juice

1. Select small cucumbers so that the seeds are not too coarse. Salt and let stand until water collects in the bottom of the dish.
2. Drain and add the sour cream, dill weed, garlic chives, mustard, and lemon juice. Mix in a blender until smooth. Correct the seasoning. Keep the sauce cold until you are ready to serve it.

Herb Sauce for Cold Fish

3 tablespoons olive oil
1 tablespoon tarragon vinegar
1 hard-cooked egg yolk, sieved
1 teaspoon capers
1 tablespoon chives

1 tablespoon each, chopped
  chervil, tarragon, and burnet
Salt and freshly ground pepper
Garlic to taste (optional)

Mix oil and vinegar; add egg yolk and herbs. Season to taste (garlic optional). Mix well and serve with cold poached fish.

Brown Sauce

Use this as a base for sauces and gravies.

2 tablespoons butter
Few slices onion (optional)
3 tablespoons flour
1 cup stock—game, veal,
    chicken or beef

Salt
Paprika
2 tablespoons sherry or Madiera

Melt the butter, stir in the flour, and cook over a low fire until the flour is thoroughly and evenly browned. Then stir in the stock, salt, and paprika. Bring to a boil. Add the wine. You may brown a little onion in the butter before browning the flour. Tomato sauce or tomato paste may be substituted for ¼ cup of the stock.

Sauce Aux Fines Herbes

You may vary the herbs to suit your taste. Use lemon verbena, chives, tarragon, chervil, lovage, parsley, or thyme, or any combination you like. This is very good over baked fish.

4 tablespoons herbs, chopped
    fine
4 tablespoons butter
2 shallots, chopped
½ cup mushrooms, chopped

1 clove garlic, crushed
2 tablespoons flour
2 cups milk or fish stock
Salt

1. Combine shallots, mushrooms, and garlic and cook gently in melted butter for 10 minutes. Lift out and set aside.
2. Stir the flour into the butter in the saucepan, slowly add the milk or fish stock, and stir until sauce is thick and hot. Add the herbs and salt to taste. Heat and serve.

Egg Sauce

2 hard-cooked eggs, chopped
2 tablespoons butter
2 tablespoons flour

1 cup fish stock or court bouil-
    lon
Salt and freshly ground pepper

Melt the butter, stir in the flour, slowly add the fish stock, and stir until sauce is thick and hot. Add the seasonings and eggs.

Game Fumet

This concentrated stock is considered indispensable in the making of game sauces. It gives a rich extract of which a teaspoonful, added to the sauce, lends a wonderful flavor.

Scraps, bones, and trimmings
   of any game
2 or 3 tablespoons minced ham
2 small onions, chopped
2 or 3 shallots, chopped
A few sprigs each, parsley,
   and thyme

1 bay leaf
2 tablespoons butter
1 cup brown veal or chicken
   sauce
2 tablespoons Madeira

1. In a kettle, combine the ham, onions, and shallots, a few sprigs of parsley and thyme, the bay leaf, and butter. Add the game scraps and cook very slowly, stirring frequently, until delicately browned. Add the brown sauce and the Madeira. Simmer for 30 minutes more.

2. Strain and cook again until liquid is thick like "Molasses in January." Bottle and store in the refrigerator.

Easy Hollandaise Sauce

2 egg yolks, lightly beaten
2 tablespoons lemon juice

½ cup cold butter
Salt

In a saucepan, combine egg yolks, lemon juice, and butter. Stir over a very slow fire until butter has melted and the sauce is blended. Season with salt to taste. If you like a very tart Hollandaise, add more lemon juice.

Dill Sauce for Cold Fish

This is a sharp, smooth sauce that complements any seafood.

2 tablespoons dill weed,
   chopped fine
1½ cups olive oil
½ cup white wine vinegar

Pinch of mustard
Pinch of salt
Dash of tobasco
¼ cup heavy cream, whipped

Combine all the ingredients except the cream. Mix well. Gently fold the dill mixture into the whipped cream.

Dill Sauce for Hot Fish

3 tablespoons dill weed
2 shallots, chopped
2 tablespoons butter
2 tablespoons flour

½ cup dry white wine
½ cup water, fish stock or
   court bouillon
Salt and freshly ground pepper

Sauté the shallots gently for a minute or two in the butter, stir in the flour and add the wine and other liquid. Season with salt and pepper and add the dill weed. Amounts may be varied to suit your taste. Stir until sauce is thick and hot.

Fennel Sauce

Serve with fish.

2 tablespoons butter
1 tablespoon onion, chopped
   fine
2 tablespoons flour

1 cup fish stock or water
Salt
1 tablespoon fennel leaves,
   chopped

Melt the butter and cook the onion until transparent but not brown. Add the flour, stir in the fish stock or water, and season with salt to taste. Strain, reheat, and add the fennel leaves.

Giblet Gravy for Wild Duck

Duck giblets, wing tips, neck
   and badly shot up pieces
1 sprig each, parsley, rosemary
   and thyme, chopped
1 small onion, chopped
2 tablespoons butter

2 tablespoons flour
¼ cup sherry
2 tablespoons grated orange
   rind
Salt and freshly ground pepper

1. Cover the pieces of duck with water, add the herbs and onion, and simmer for 1 hour. Strain the stock.

2. Melt the butter, stir in the flour, add 1 cup of the stock, the wine and the orange rind. Season to taste. Chop the giblets, return to the sauce, heat and serve.

Grape Sauce for Game Birds

4 cups wild grapes
Boiling water
4 tablespoons butter
¼ cup sherry

3 whole cloves
1 tablespoon lemon juice
½ cup chestnuts, chopped
 medium coarse

1. Wash the grapes, cover with boiling water and simmer for five minutes. Drain. Put through a sieve to remove seeds.

2. Melt the butter in a saucepan, add the sherry, cloves, and lemon juice, and simmer for 5 minutes. Remove cloves, add the chestnuts and the grape purée. Heat and serve in a sauce boat. If the sauce is too thick for your taste, thin out with a little of the water in which the grapes cooked.

Fish Fumet

For a rich flavor, use this concentrated fish stock in any fish sauce.

Raw fish scraps: heads, bones,
 and skin
4 tablespoons butter
1 onion, sliced
2 shallots, sliced

1 sprig each, thyme and parsley
4 cups water
4 tablespoons dry white wine

1. Melt the butter, add the onion, shallots, fish scraps, and herbs, and cook over a low fire until slightly browned. Add the water and wine and simmer for 30 minutes. Strain.

2. Return to saucepan and simmer until the liquid is reduced to about half. Store in a covered jar in the refrigerator.

Chestnuts

Due to the chestnut blight, sweet American chestnuts nearly belong to the past, but imported Italian chestnuts are adequate.

To Prepare Chestnuts

Using a sharp knife, cut a cross on the flat side of the chestnut. Then:

1. Simmer in water for about 10 minutes, or until the shells and skins can be removed.

or:

2. Bake in a shallow pan in a 350° oven until the shells and skins can be removed.

or:

3. In a skillet, heat in olive or salad oil over a hot fire for five minutes. Allow to cool so that nuts may be handled, then remove the shells and skins.

Chestnut Sauce for Game Birds

1 cup cooked chestnuts
3 tablespoons butter
3 tablespoons flour
1 cup milk

½ cup heavy cream
Salt and freshly ground pepper
Dash of nutmeg

1. Make a cream sauce using the butter, flour, milk, and heavy cream. Season with salt, pepper, and freshly grated nutmeg.

2. Put the cooked chestnuts through your blender or grate or chop them very fine. Combine the nuts and the sauce, and heat. Serve in a sauce boat.

Chestnut Purée

This is perfect with game birds.

Chestnuts
Boiling milk or chicken stock
Heavy cream

Butter
Salt and freshly ground pepper

1. Cook the chestnuts, which have been shelled and skinned according to directions given above, in milk, or stock. Sieve them.

2. Combine with the cream, butter, salt and pepper, and whip them until smooth. Return purée to the stove to heat, and serve.

Braised Chestnuts

Serve them with game. They are delicious.

1 pound chestnuts   Chicken broth to cover

1. Remove the shells and skins from the chestnuts according to directions on page 152, and place them in a buttered casserole.
2. Pour broth over them and bake in a 350° oven for 45 minutes.

Horseradish

We have an open spot in our woods where wild horseradish thrives. Its roots go down in the moist soil, sometimes for an amazing distance, and run underground to send shoots up to the surface again. Should you pull up a large root to grate, cut off the top with its curly leaf and plant it; it will grow another root. Thus you can have your horseradish and eat it too.

Scrub and peel the roots and grate or grind very fine, or chop them in your blender. You will find that grinding horseradish is worse then peeling onions; if at all possible, do it at an open window, or, better still, outdoors, so that your eyes will not suffer.

Mix your grated horseradish with vinegar and store it in a covered jar in your refrigerator.

We like horseradish with beef, pork, and tongue. It goes very well with corned beef and with beets.

To serve with duck or pork, mix with applesauce.

Horseradish Sauce—I

4 tablespoons freshly grated   Salt and freshly ground pepper
   horseradish   A few drops lemon juice
½ cup soft butter

Mix the horseradish with the butter. Add the seasonings and lemon juice. Blend well. Spread this sauce on hot broiled or poached fish, or serve with boiled beef.

Horseradish Sauce—II

4 tablespoons fresh grated   ½ teaspoon powdered sugar
  horseradish   ½ teaspoon salt
5 tablespoons wine vinegar   2 teaspoons prepared mustard

Blend all the ingredients and serve with cold meat or fish.

Horseradish Sauce—III

This is the simplest horseradish sauce to make.

Fresh grated horseradish   Salt and freshly ground pepper
Sour cream

Mix all the ingredients together. The proportion is strictly a personal thing and is determined by your taste.

I like to add a little lemon juice as it seems to smooth out the flavor.

Horseradish Bread Sauce

This is a sauce served in English homes and restuarants and to be found in any English cookbook. It takes a little longer than the ones already given but is worth the trouble.

1/3 cup fresh grated horseradish   3 tablespoons butter
1½ cups milk   Lemon juice to taste
3 tablespoons soft bread crumbs   Salt and freshly ground pepper

Combine the horseradish, milk, and bread crumbs in the top of a double boiler. Cook for 25 minutes, stirring frequently. Add the butter, and lemon juice, salt and pepper to taste. Heat and serve.

Hot Horseradish Sauce

4 tablespoons fresh grated   ¾ cup heavy cream
  horseradish   2 tablespoons sugar
3 tablespoons butter   1 tablespoon lemon juice
3 tablespoons flour

Melt the butter, stir in the flour and add the cream, sugar, and lemon juice. Stir until thick and hot. Add the horseradish and blend well.

Jelly Sauce for Venison

This recipe dates back to 1875 but it couldn't be better.

1 tumblerful grape or currant 1 tablespoon sherry or red wine
 jelly
1 tablespoon butter

1. Melt the jelly over a very slow fire, stirring carefully so that it does not scorch. Add the butter and boil for 1 minute. Remove from the fire and keep hot.
2. Just before serving, add the wine.

Sauce Meunière

4 tablespoons butter 2 tablespoons minced parsley
2 teaspoons lemon juice

Melt the butter, add the lemon juice and parsley, heat and pour over hot fish.

Mornay Sauce

2 tablespoons butter 2 cups milk
2 teaspoons minced onion 1 egg yolk, beaten with a
2 teaspoons minced parsley   little milk
2 tablespoons flour 1 tablespoon grated Parmesan
Salt and freshly ground pepper   cheese

1. Melt the butter and simmer the onion and parsley in it for a few minutes, stir in the flour, and cook for a few minutes. Slowly add the milk, and stir until sauce is thick and hot.
2. Pour some of the hot sauce over egg-yolk and milk mixture, stirring as you pour, add to the rest of the sauce, season with salt and pepper to taste, add the cheese, reheat and serve.

Maître D'Hôtel Sauce

1 cup Béchamel Sauce 2 tablespoons melted butter
Parsley to taste, minced 2 tablespoons lemon juice

Add the parsley, butter, and lemon juice to the Béchamel Sauce (see page 141) and mix well.

Mushroom Sauce—I

1 cup field mushrooms or
    morels, sliced
3 scallion tops, cut up fine
2 tablespoons butter
1 tablespoon flour
½ cup chicken broth

½ cup heavy cream
1 tablespoon each, chopped
    thyme, oregano, and
    parsley
Salt and freshly ground pepper
¼ cup sherry

Melt the butter, cook the mushrooms and scallion tops in it over a slow fire for 5 minutes, stir in the flour and cook 1 minute more. Slowly add the chicken broth and the cream, and stir until sauce is thick and hot. Add herbs, seasonings, and sherry.

Mushroom Sauce—II

12 large mushrooms, chopped
    fine
2 tablespoons butter
2 scallions
2 tablespoons flour

1 cup consommé
Parsley
Freshly grated nutmeg

Chop the mushrooms and cook them in the melted butter for a few minutes. Add the sliced scallions and cook these. Stir in the flour and add consommé. Cook, stirring until the sauce is thick and hot. Add minced parsley and a suggestion of nutmeg. Heat and serve.

Oyster Sauce for Fish

1 cup small oysters
1 tablespoon butter
1 tablespoon flour
1 cup milk

½ cup cream
Salt and freshly ground pepper
Mace to taste

1. Simmer the oysters in their own liquor until the edges curl. Drain and chop, reserving the liquor.

2. Melt the butter and stir in the flour. Slowly add the milk and cream, and stir until sauce is thick and hot. Add the oysters, the oyster liquor and salt and pepper to taste. Just a suggestion of mace is good, but don't overdo it. Check the seasoning and serve hot over any hot fish.

Port Wine Sauce for Wild Duck

1 cup port wine
2 shallots, sliced
1 or 2 sprigs thyme
½ cup orange juice
1 cup chicken stock

2 teaspoons cornstarch
Salt and freshly ground **pepper**
Orange sections
Grated orange rind

1. Simmer the shallots and thyme in the port wine and orange juice. When the liquid has been reduced to half, add the chicken stock.

2. Mix the cornstarch with a little orange juice or water. Stir into the liquid and cook sauce until thick and hot. Add the orange sections and rind, and season with salt and pepper to taste.

Orange Sauce for Wild Duck

1 cup orange juice
1 tablespoon grated orange rind
1 tablespoon cornstarch

3 tablespoons sugar
2 tablespoons of curaçao or
Grand Marnier

Mix the cornstarch to a paste with a little of the orange juice. Combine in a saucepan with the rest of the juice and the sugar, and cook until thick and clear, stirring as it cooks. Add the orange rind and the liqueur and serve hot.

Nasturtium Seed Sauce

This is excellent with seafood or lamb. The recipe for pickled nasturtium seeds is on page 261.

1 tablespoon nasturtium seeds
½ cup mayonnaise
½ cup sour cream
2 tablespoons nasturtium vinegar

1 teaspoon onion juice
½ teaspoon salt
1 teaspoon paprika

Combine the mayonnaise, sour cream, nasturtium seeds, and the vinegar in which the seeds have been pickled. Add the onion juice obtained by scraping an onion, the salt and the paprika. Blend well.

Hot Mustard Sauce

2 teaspoons dry mustard
1 teaspoon flour
Tarragon vinegar

½ cup chicken broth
1 tablespoon sherry
1 sprig each, tarragon and
  parsley

Mix the mustard and flour, then stir in the vinegar to make a paste. Add the broth, the sherry and the herbs. Cook until the sauce is hot.

Sour Cream Mushroom Sauce

1 pound mushrooms
2 cloves garlic, crushed
6 tablespoons butter
4 tablespoons flour

2 cups chicken broth
Salt and freshly ground pepper
1 cup sour cream

Cook the mushrooms and garlic in butter for a few minutes, add the flour, and cook a minute or two more. Stir in the broth, salt and pepper, and bring to a boil. Slowly add the cream. Heat but do not allow to boil.

Port Wine Sauce

Serve with game. It is a simple sauce, but delicious.

½ cup port wine
1 shallot, chopped

Juice of ½ lemon

Combine ingredients and simmer for a few minutes. Strain the sauce, reheat and serve.

Port Wine Sauce for Venison

½ cup game stock
2 whole cloves
½ cup wild cherry jelly

½ cup port wine
1 tablespoon lemon juice
Salt and freshly ground pepper

Simmer the stock and cloves for 15 or 20 minutes. Remove cloves. Add the jelly, wine, lemon juice, salt and pepper. Stir over low heat until jelly is melted and all ingredients well blended.

Vinaigrette Sauce

Here are the ingredients for three versions of this sauce. They are all good, so take your pick—or create your own. Serve with cold fish, or with cold vegetables such as asparagus, artichokes, or beans.

Sauce #1

½ cup olive oil
2 tablespoons wine vinegar
½ teaspoon prepared mustard
2 teaspoons chopped parsley

2 teaspoons chopped tarragon
1 tablespoon chopped chives
1 teaspoon chopped chervil
Salt and freshly ground peppei

Blend all ingredients and chill.

Sauce #2

½ cup olive oil
2 tablespoons wine vinegar
2 tablespoons minced shallots

2 hard-cooked eggs, chopped
2 tablespoons capers, chopped
1 tablespoon chopped pickle

Blend all the ingredients and chill. If you can get those wonder, ful tiny Kosher dill tomatoes, use them in place of the pickle.

Sauce #3

½ cup olive oil
2 tablespoons herb vinegar
2 teaspoons chopped chives

1 teaspoon minced pimento
3 green olives, chopped fine

Blend all the ingredients and chill.

Remoulade Sauce

You may use any combination of herbs you like. Serve with cold fish.

2 cups mayonnaise
1 tablespoon dry mustard
2 tablespoons Capers,
    chopped

1 teaspoon parsley, chopped
1 teaspoon tarragon, chopped

Blend the mayonnaise (see page 180) and mustard, add the herbs, and mix well.

Shallot Sauce

3 shallots, chopped
¾ cup dry white wine
4 tablespoons butter

2 tablespoons flour
1½ cups chicken broth
Salt and freshly ground pepper

1. Simmer the shallots in wine until liquid is reduced to ¼ cup.

2. Melt the butter, stir in the flour, add the broth, and stir until smooth and thick. Season with salt and pepper to taste, and combine with the shallots and wine. Serve with game birds or other poultry. To serve with fish, substitute fish stock or court bouillon in which fish has been poached for the chicken broth. To serve with steak or boiled beef, substitute consommé.

Velouté Sauce for Fish

2 tablespoons butter
1 tablespoon flour
1 cup fish stock

Salt and freshly ground pepper
Lemon juice, a few drops
Dill weed, chopped fine

Melt the butter and stir in the flour. Cook for a few minutes before adding the stock. Simmer until thick and hot, then add salt and pepper to taste, the lemon juice, and a little dill weed. For meats, substitute consommé for the fish stock and add a few mushrooms, chopped and sautéed in butter.

Piquante Fish Sauce

6 tablespoons butter
¼ cup white wine

½ teaspoon prepared mustard

Mix all the ingredients well. Heat, and pour over pan fried fish.

Tomato Sauce

1 cup tomato juice
2 tablespoons butter
¼ medium onion, chopped fine

2 tablespoons flour
Oregano, a few leaves, minced
Salt and freshly ground pepper

Melt the butter, add the onion, and simmer a few minutes, not allowing it to brown. Stir in the flour, then add the tomato juice, stirring while you pour. Add the oregano, and season to taste.

Tartar Sauce

To make this, use home-made mayonnaise (see page 180).

1 cup mayonnaise	1 teaspoon chopped thyme
1 tablespoon capers, chopped	1 tablespoon chopped chives
1 teaspoon minced parsley	1 teaspoon chopped chervil
1 tablespoon chopped sweet pickles	1 tablespoon dry sherry

Combine all the ingredients and mix well. The herbs may be varied to suit your taste.

Hot Tartar Sauce

Follow the above recipe, but start with 1 cup of Béchamel Sauce (see page 141) instead of the mayonnaise.

White Wine Sauce for Fish

2 tablespoons butter	4 tablespoons butter
1 tablespoon flour	2 egg yolks, beaten
1 cup fish stock	Lemon juice
3 tablespoons dry white wine	Salt and freshly ground pepper

1. Melt the butter, stir in the flour and cook for a few minutes. Add the fish stock and wine, and simmer 5 minutes more. Add the butter, a little at a time.

2. Slowly stir the sauce into the egg yolks, add a little lemon juice, and season with salt and pepper to taste. Heat and serve.

Wine Sauce

Serve this with any game.

1 small can crushed pineapple	1 tablespoon dry mustard
4 tablespoons butter	2 tablespoons lemon juice
¾ cup brown sugar	1½ cups dry sherry

Combine all the ingredients but the sherry, and bring to a boil. Add the sherry, reheat, and serve.

Wine Sauce for Duck or Venison

1/3 cup barberry jelly
2 tablespoons butter
2 tablespoons lemon juice

Grated orange rind to taste
½ cup port wine

Melt the jelly over a slow fire, watching carefully so that it does not scorch. Add the butter, lemon juice, and orange rind, and cook for a few minutes. Add the wine, reheat and serve.

Wild Duck Sauce—I

¼ cup red currant jelly
3 tablespoons butter
2 tablespoons sherry

Salt and freshly ground pepper
Lemon juice

Melt the jelly over a very slow fire, watching and stirring so that it does not scorch. Add the butter, sherry, salt and pepper, and enough lemon juice to make it tart enough to suit you. Blend and serve.

Wild Duck Sauce—II

This is a sauce we serve with cold duck. It is rich, smooth and delicious.

1 shallot, chopped
1 sprig thyme, chopped
1 sprig chervil, chopped
3 peppercorns, crushed
2 tablespoons white wine vinegar

3 egg yolks, beaten
1½ tablespoons tomato paste
3 tablespoons butter
¾ cup heavy cream
Salt and freshly ground pepper

1. In a pan, combine the shallot, thyme, chervil, peppercorns, and vinegar. Simmer until the liquid is almost gone.
2. Keeping the pan over a slow fire, add the egg yolks, a little at a time, alternating with the tomato paste. Slowly stir in the butter and hot cream, season with salt and pepper to taste, and blend thoroughly.

CHAPTER 7

Wild

Vegetable

Dishes

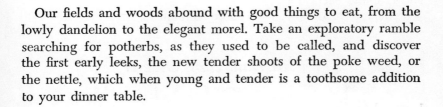

Our fields and woods abound with good things to eat, from the lowly dandelion to the elegant morel. Take an exploratory ramble searching for potherbs, as they used to be called, and discover the first early leeks, the new tender shoots of the poke weed, or the nettle, which when young and tender is a toothsome addition to your dinner table.

Dandelions

The young shoots picked in the spring while they are still white and tender add an enjoyable bitter tang to a salad. The cold cooked shoots may be served with a vinaigrette sauce.

When used as a potherb, I like to cover them with boiling water which is then poured off to remove the slightly bitter taste.

Dandelions may be raised in the cellar in the same way as chickory (see page 181).

Dandelion Scallop

Serves 6

2 quarts dandelion greens   2 cups milk
1 quart boiling water   Salt and freshly ground pepper
1 bouillon cube   Buttered bread crumbs
2 tablespoons butter   Sliced bacon, cooked crisp
2 tablespoons flour

1. Wash the greens thoroughly several times in lukewarm water. Drain.

2. Dissolve the bouillon cube in the boiling water and add the greens. Boil for 30 minutes. Drain the greens and chop them.

3. Melt the butter, add the flour and stir, and cook for a few minutes. Add the milk, and cook until the sauce is thick and hot. Season with salt and pepper to taste.

4. Butter a baking dish and place a layer of the greens in it. Spoon the sauce over them. Repeat until all the greens and sauce are used up, finishing with the sauce. Sprinkle with bread crumbs, and crumble bacon on top.

5. Bake in a 350° oven for 20 or 25 minutes.

Wilted Dandelion Greens

Serves 4

1 pound greens   ¼ teaspoon salt
6 slices bacon, cut in strips   Chives
⅓ cup wine vinegar   Pinch of sugar, optional

1. Wash the greens thoroughly several times in lukewarm water. Drain.

2. Cook bacon strips until crisp. Remove the bacon, and add the dandelion greens to the fat in the skillet together with the wine vinegar and salt. Simmer gently until the greens are wilted. Correct the seasoning. You may find you need more vinegar, or perhaps a pinch of sugar.

3. Transfer to a serving dish, and sprinkle with chopped chives and bacon.

Boiled Dandelion Greens

Serves 6

2 quarts greens   ¼ pound salt pork, cubed
4 quarts water   8 small potatoes, peeled

1. Wash the greens thoroughly several times in lukewarm water. Drain.
2. Cube the salt pork, and add to the greens and water. Simmer in a kettle for 1½ hours.
3. Add the potatoes and simmer for another 30 minutes.

Dog-Tooth Violet, Trout-Lily, or Adder's Tongue

If these charming little flowers abound in your woods as they do in ours in the early spring, try cooking the leaves as a pot-herb. As the tiny bulbs are deep in the soil, cutting the leaves at the surface will not destroy your flowers for the following spring.

Fiddleheads

The fiddlehead, or cinnamon fern, grows along streams in shady places. The succulent, soft budding stems are cut when they are not more than 2 inches above ground, and have an unusual flavor which has been described as being "between asparagus and mush-rooms," and "very much like artichokes." Cut the fiddleheads in May or the first part of June as the crosiers will become bitter as they develop. The fiddleheads are available in cans, and the fresh ones sometimes appear on the market in large cities.

I am including a recipe in case you are familiar with them or would like to try them.

There is also a brake or bracken, to be found in pastures (*Pteridium aquilinum*) which can be creamed or served with butter. Pick 6-inch stalks and boil them until tender.

The Ostrich Fern (*Pteretis nodulosa*) is good scalloped, topped with crumbs.

Fiddlehead Sauté

Serves 4

These are good served with a roast. Pour some of the pan gravy over them.

20 fiddleheads   Butter
Salted water   Salt and freshly ground pepper

1. Wash the fiddleheads several times, as they are apt to be sandy. Drain.
2. Boil in salted water until tender. Drain.
3. Sauté them in butter and season with salt and pepper to taste.

Leeks

We find that wild leeks grow in great abundance in our woods. They start appearing in early May and in a week or two are ready to dig. The white part, which is what we eat, is delicate in flavor but quite small. As they grow, they become quite strong so spring is the time to use them. By late June or early July the tops will have disappeared and you must wait until the following spring to make that divine Vichyssoise.

Leek Soufflé

Serves 4

12 to 14 leeks, white part only,   ¾ cup beef consommé
    sliced thin   Salt and freshly ground pepper
3 tablespoons butter   4 eggs, separated
1 tablespoon flour

1. Melt the butter in a sauce pan and add the leeks. Simmer gently until golden but not brown, stir in the flour, and cook for a minute or two. Pour in the consommé and stir until thick. Season with salt and pepper to taste. Cool the sauce a little, then gradually stir it into the slightly beaten egg yolks. Fold in at

least 4 egg whites, beaten until stiff but not dry. (If you have an extra egg white or two, it will do your soufflé no harm.)

2. Pour the soufflé into a buttered soufflé dish, and bake in a preheated 400° oven for 25 to 35 minutes. Serve at once.

Milkweed

The young seed pods, cooked and served like asparagus, are tender and pleasant in flavor.

Mushrooms

In the fall we find that which is most prized by the epicure. Our woods are filled with eager pickers of these delicate fungi who seem, thank goodness, to know what they are gathering.

If you are fortunate enough to know a mycologist, as we do, he can teach you to identify a few of the edible varieties. While not many mushrooms are poisonous, if you are not absolutely certain of their identification, it is best to patronize a grocery store. You may raise mushrooms in your own cellar by purchasing trays that need only to be watered and watched.

The following mushrooms are found around here, and are easily recognized by the experts:

The Common Field Mushroom (Agaricus campestris) from which the commercially grown mushroom has been evolved. This is found in the fields in the fall, and on golf courses during late summer.

The Morel (Morchella esculenta) is native to France but is found on this side of the ocean. They appear in the damp woods and ditches in early spring, and if you are fortunate enough to have them growing nearby, do not overlook them as they are considered a great gastronomic treat. The French consider them to be a perfect accompaniment to fresh-water fish. Use them in any mushroom recipe.

The Giant Puffball (Calvatia gigantea) is the easiest of all to identify. Its characteristic round shape is unmistakable. There is also a poisonous puffball, but its center is black, while the center of the edible one is white when fresh, turning yellowish when too old to be used.

The Oyster Mushroom (Pleurotus ostreatus) is found growing on fallen logs and has a slightly fishy flavor, as you might expect from its name.

The Chantarelle (Cantharellus cibarius) which grows summer and autumn in coniferous woods is said to be most delicious. I have not found any here though they are native to this region.

The Velvet Stemmed Agarie (Collybia velutipes), a delicate and tasty mushroom, is found in late autumn and in winter under the snow. It grows on tree trunks and stumps. Use this mushroom immediately after gathering as it does not keep well. It is good for drying.

The Fairy Ring (Coprinus micaceous) is a fragile little fungus that is sometimes to be found on your lawn in damp weather. They can be cooked in any way but are especially good raw. (See Appetizers, page 5).

The Shaggy Mane (Coprinus comatus) is a similar mushroom.

The Parasol Mushroom (Lepiota procera) grows on the edge of the woods, often in the grass. It is excellent dipped in egg and bread crumbs and fried.

You may find different mushrooms in the same locality in different years, as they may appear only once in a while. This is because of varying weather conditions.

Of course there is no reason not to mix various kinds of mushrooms in any mushroom dish. Add any of them to soups and stews, to vegetables, gravies, and spaghetti sauce.

To Dry Mushrooms

Method #1

Cut off the tips of the stems and, using a needle and heavy thread, string the mushrooms as children used to string popcorn. Hang the strings in the kitchen, up out of the way, and in a few weeks they will be dry. You can leave them there, or store them in a jar on your shelf to prevent them from catching dust.

Method #2

String the mushrooms as above and hang them in the sun for a few days. Then put them in a very slow oven to complete the drying.

Method #3

Mushrooms stored loosely in the refrigerator will dry to some extent; as long as they are kept refrigerated they will keep for a long time.

To use dried mushrooms, soak them in lukewarm water before cooking. Use the water in a sauce or gravy.

Broiled Mushrooms

Serves 4

16 field mushrooms, caps only   Chopped chives
Butter   Grated cheddar cheese
Salt and freshly ground pepper

1. Wash mushrooms, saving stems to use later for soup.
2. Butter a shallow baking dish or cookie sheet and place the caps on it, gill side up. Season with salt and pepper and put a pinch of chives on each one, topped by a spoonful of cheese.
3. Slide under the broiler for 8 to 10 minutes, testing with a fork for doneness. They should be tender, but neither too soft nor completely raw in the center.
4. Serve mushrooms on toast generously brushed with lemon butter.

Brandied Mushrooms

Serves 6

2 cups mushrooms, washed   2 tablespoons brandy
    and sliced   1 cup heavy cream
½ cup butter   Salt and freshly ground pepper
2 shallots, chopped

1. Melt the butter in a skillet, add the shallots, and cook for a minute or two, not allowing them to brown.

2. Add the mushrooms, and cook gently for a few minutes more. Add the brandy, pour in the cream, and simmer, stirring, until sauce is hot. Season to taste.

Mushroom Pancakes

Makes about 20 small pancakes

Pancakes

2 eggs   1 cup milk
2 egg yolks   ⅞ cup flour
1 tablespoon sugar   2 tablespoons melted butter
Pinch of salt   1 teaspoon brandy or rum

1. Combine and beat the eggs and egg yolks. Add the sugar and salt, beat in the milk, then the flour. When batter is smooth, add the butter and brandy or rum. Let stand an hour before using.

2. Cook the pancakes in a 6-inch buttered skillet, spreading the batter *very* thin, or use an electric skillet, setting the temperature as recommended by the manufacturers. Fill with mushroom filling below and roll each pancake up as it is done. Keep warm.

Filling

2 cups mushrooms, chopped   1 tablespoon sherry
2 tablespoons butter   ¼ cup minced parsley
2 tablespoons flour   Freshly grated nutmeg
1 cup cream   Melted butter
Salt and freshly ground pepper   Grated Parmesan cheese

1. Melt the butter and simmer the mushrooms for 4 to 5 minutes. Add the flour, stir, slowly pour in the cream, and stir until thick

and hot. Add salt and pepper to taste. Add the sherry, parsley, and nutmeg.

2. Unroll the pancakes. Spread with the filling, roll up again and arrange close together in a shallow buttered baking dish. Brush the tops with melted butter and sprinkle with a little cheese.

3. Put in a hot oven to heat and brown, or slide under the broiler for a minute or two.

The pancakes may be made ahead of time and kept in the refrigerator until needed.

Mashed Potato-Mushroom Casserole

Serves 6

5 or 6 potatoes, cooked and
    mashed
4 or 5 rosemary leaves
¼ cup cream
8 tablespoons butter
Salt and freshly ground pepper

1 dozen large mushrooms,
    sliced
2 tablespoons flour
1½ cups milk
Chives

1. Combine the rosemary leaves and cream in a saucepan and bring to a boil. Set aside.

2. To the potatoes, add 4 tablespoons of the butter, the cream from which the rosemary has been removed, and salt and pepper to taste. Beat the mixture until light and creamy and place in either end of an oven dish.

3. Melt the rest of the butter, add the mushrooms, and simmer for a few minutes. Stir in the flour and cook for a few minutes. Slowly add the milk, stir until sauce is thick and hot, and add salt and pepper to taste. Add the chopped chives, stir, and pour the creamed mushrooms in the center of the dish between the potatoes.

4. Bake in a 450° oven until the dish is hot and the potatoes browned a little or about 15 minutes.

Puffballs

These must be picked when they are not too old, and used immediately. Peel, slice, and store them in the refrigerator briefly.

Puffball Sauté

Sauté sliced puffballs in butter. Add salt and freshly ground black pepper to taste.

Puffballs in Cream

Sauté diced puffballs, add cream, and salt and pepper to taste. Heat and serve.

Creamed Puffballs

Make a rich cream sauce, adding a little sherry. Add sautéed puffballs. Serve on toast.

Puffball Salad

Dice puffballs and add them raw to a salad.

Spinach-Mushroom Casserole Supreme

Serves 6

Spinach and mushrooms always seem to be a happy combination, and here they are again.

2 boxes frozen chopped spinach	2 tablespoons flour
2 tablespoons butter	2 cups cream or milk
1 cup mushrooms,chopped	Buttered bread crumbs

1. Cook the frozen spinach, according to directions on package, or its equivalent in fresh spinach. Drain thoroughly.

2. Melt the butter in a saucepan, and cook the mushrooms for a few minutes. Shake flour over them and stir, cooking gently. Add the cream or milk (I use half of each.) Cook and stir until sauce is thick and hot.

3. In a buttered casserole, place a layer of spinach, cover with sauce, and repeat, topping with buttered bread crumbs.

4. Bake in a 350° oven until the dish is hot and the bread crumbs brown. Instead of the bread crumbs, you may use a can of French fried onions for topping.

Mushrooms and Rice

Serves 4

Serve this with any game or game bird.

1 cup cooked rice
½ pound mushrooms, sliced
2 tablespoons butter
½ onion, minced

Salt and freshly ground pepper
Chopped parsley
Freshly grated nutmeg

1. Melt the butter and cook the onion for a minute or two. Add the mushrooms. Simmer over a low fire until mushrooms are cooked. Add the rice and cook until rice begins to brown. Season with salt and pepper to taste, then add the parsley and a dash of nutmeg.

Sicilian Mushrooms

Serves 4

1 pound mushrooms, sliced if
    large, whole if small
3 tablespoons olive oil
1 clove garlic, crushed

Salt and freshly ground pepper
3 very ripe tomatoes, mashed
1 sprig each, basil and parsley,
    chopped

1. Heat the oil in a skillet, add the garlic and mushrooms, and sauté until tender. Add the tomatoes. (You may substitute canned tomatoes in winter.) Season with salt and pepper to taste, and cook for 10 or 15 minutes. Add the basil and parsley and serve.

Poke Weed

In the spring the round pink shoots of poke weed may be cooked like asparagus and served hot with Hollandaise Sauce, or cold with a Vinaigrette Sauce.

Some people recommend adding a pinch of soda to water in which the sprouts are boiled.

Try boiling them with cubed salt pork. Serve johnny cake with it.

As the bush grows during the summer, it is of no further value to us as food, but the berries it produces feed the birds.

Nettle Greens

You will find this a pleasant change from spinach. This is a recipe which requires you to wear gloves—at least to start with. The stinging nettle, which grows in moist spots along the edge of the woods, leaves a painful sting on the skin of anyone careless enough to touch it. It has an intriguing flavor, although I often wonder who ever had the curiosity and the temerity to find this out. The nettle is best gathered in the spring, when the leaves are young and tender.

Nettle Greens

Serves 4

4 quarts nettles
2 tablespoons butter
2 tablespoons flour
2 cups milk

Salt and freshly ground pepper
Buttered bread crumbs, or
Grated cheese

1. Put on your gloves, take a 6-quart basket and a pair of shears and pick your greens. If you fill the basket, by the time the leaves are removed from the stems you will have 4 quarts.
2. Pour boiling water over them and drain. This removes the sting. Chop and put them in a buttered casserole.
3. Melt the butter in a saucepan, stir in the flour and cook for one minute. Slowly add the milk, stir until the sauce thickens, and season with salt and pepper.
4. Pour the sauce over the greens, mixing lightly, and top with buttered bread crumbs or grated cheese.
5. Bake in a 350° oven 20 to 30 minutes.

Wild Rice or Canada Rice

This rice grows in the shallow water along the edges of lakes and ponds in Southern Canada and the Great Lakes. It was an important food for the Indians of that region. Today it provides food and shelter for fish and water fowl, and is valued for that reason as well as for its appeal as an epicurean dish.

The wild rice must be harvested as soon as it is ripe, otherwise the grains drop and are lost. The difficulties of harvesting the crop, as well as the increasing demand for it in food markets, have raised the price incredibly. However, there is no other accompaniment to wild duck or goose that serves its purpose. We buy and cook it in small quantities, preferring to have a little of that rather than a lot of some substitute.

Wild Rice
Serves 6

There are different theories about cooking wild rice. Generally speaking, if you follow the directions on the box you won't go wrong. Here is one method that I like:

1 cup rice	¼ cup butter
2 quarts water	Freshly ground black pepper
2 teaspoons salt	

1. Wash the rice thoroughly. This means washing it in several waters, and then finally running water from the tap over it in the sieve in which you have put it to drain.

2. Bring water and salt to a boil. Add the rice and simmer for about 40 minutes: it should be thoroughly cooked but not mushy.

3. Drain the rice. Melt the butter in a skillet, add rice and brown lightly over a brisk fire. Check the salt and add a little pepper.

Wild Rice Curry
Serves 6

2½ cups cooked wild rice	2 egg yolks, beaten with
6 slices bacon, cut up	1 cup light cream
½ cup minced onion	½ teaspoon salt
½ cup grated raw carrot	1 tablespoon curry powder

1. Fry the bacon until crisp, remove from skillet and set aside.

2. Sauté the onion and carrot in the bacon fat for a few minutes. Add the rice, the egg yolks and cream, the salt, and the curry powder. Adjust seasoning to your taste. We like a strong curry flavor; you may not. Mix well and transfer to a buttered casserole.

3. Set the casserole in a pan of hot water and bake in a 300° oven until curry is set.

Wild Rice and Mushrooms

Cook wild rice in the usual way, adding a few mushrooms first sautéed in butter.

Stuffed Grape Leaves with Rice

Serves 4

8 grape leaves
½ cup rice
1 pound ground beef
Salt and freshly ground pepper
3 tablespoons olive oil
1 onion, minced
½ green pepper, chopped fine

1 cup tomatoes, fresh or canned
½ cup chicken broth
1 tablespoon sugar
1 tablespoon vinegar
1 bay leaf
A few sprigs thyme

1. Pick young, tender grape leaves. (In winter you may buy them in cans).

2. Blanch in boiling water for a minute or two. This keeps them from breaking when you stuff them. Drain, and make the filling as follows:

3. Cook the rice until tender. Drain it.

4. Season the beef and combine with the onion, green pepper, and tomatoes. In a skillet, heat the olive oil and sauté the vegetables and meat for a few minutes. Add the drained rice and mix well.

5. Lay each grape leaf flat, put a spoonful of filling in the center, and fold over the sides, then the top and bottom, to form little envelopes. Fasten with toothpicks and arrange in a buttered oven dish.

6. Mix the broth, sugar, vinegar, and herbs, and pour over the leaves.

7. Bake for 30 minutes in a 350° oven. Serve with a tossed salad and French bread.

CHAPTER 8

Salads and Salad Dressings

All vegetables and flowers were once known as herbs. They were used for flavor and aroma as well as medicinally. Now we classify the leafy vegetables as salad greens, and their variety may be pleasantly added to by the use of wild greens such as dandelion, chickory, sorrel, and leeks. Freshly picked raw mushrooms, as well as nasturtium leaves from your flower garden, give an interesting piquancy to your salads. The selection of fresh herbs as ingredients to compound the perfect dressing is a challenge to your imagination and ingenuity.

French Dressing

French dressing may be varied endlessly by the addition of herbs—try tarragon and lovage; chives and dill; garlic, chives and thyme. Chopped scallions are good; chervil adds a distinctive flavor; watercress may be whipped in with your blender.

Did you ever try adding a *little* anchovy paste, or fresh tomato juice, or a spoonful or two of sour cream to your olive oil when making a salad? Another interesting variation is the use of half lemon juice and half lime juice instead of vinegar.

1 cup olive oil	1 teaspoon salt
⅓ cup red or white wine vinegar	A dash freshly ground pepper
	½ teaspoon dry mustard

Blend the oil, vinegar, salt and pepper (most recipes say "white" pepper, but we prefer the black), and mustard. Shake well.

Stuffed Grape Leaves

Serves 6 to 8

The recipe for this delicacy comes from the Near East. It makes a delicious and unusual appetizer, or may be served as a salad.

2 dozen large grape leaves
Lightly salted water
1 cup oil
2 cups onions, chopped or sliced
½ cup raw rice
½ cup minced parsley
¼ cup seedless raisins
¼ cup chopped nuts
¼ cup tomato sauce

¼ cup water
¼ teaspoon allspice
¼ teaspoon cinnamon
¼ teaspoon freshly ground pepper
½ teaspoon salt
A few slices onions.
Grape leaves
Water

1. Use tender young grape leaves. Wash them well, and cook in salted water for 5 minutes, drain, and let them cool.

2. In the meantime, prepare the filling: In a skillet, heat the oil—this may be a salad oil or olive oil. (We use a peanut oil which is used a great deal in Near Eastern cooking.) Add onions and cook until slightly golden but not brown. Add the rice, cover the pan tightly and simmer about 30 minutes, or until the rice is done. Add the parsley, raisins, nuts, tomato sauce, water, allspice, cinnamon, pepper and salt, and cook for 5 minutes more.

3. Cool the filling, place a teaspoonful on each grape leaf and fold into neat little squares. Secure with toothpicks.

4. Cover the bottom of a saucepan with the onion and grape leaves, and lay the stuffed grape leaves on top. Cover with a plate to weigh them down, then pour on water to come up over the plate. Simmer slowly for 1 hour. Cool the leaves in the saucepan.

5. When cold, place in the refrigerator until ready to serve.

Puffball Salad

Try adding diced raw puffballs to your salad. They may be marinated first.

Dandelion Salad

Amounts vary according to your taste and the number of people you wish to serve.

Dandelion greens

Water cress or garden cress

Salad burnet

Lemon balm

Chives

Pickled nasturtium seeds

Olive oil

Tarragon vinegar

Salt and freshly ground pepper

Garlic, optional

1. Pick tender, young dandelion greens. Cut the greens and herbs into whatever size pieces you like. Combine in a salad bowl, adding a few nasturtium seeds.

2. Add oil and vinegar, salt and pepper to taste, toss and serve. You may add garlic but this is a salad so full of flavor that we prefer it without.

Hot Dandelion Salad

Serves 4 to 6

1 pound dandelion greens

4 slices bacon, cut in strips

2 tablespoons butter

2 eggs, beaten with

½ cup cream

1 teaspoon salt

Freshly ground pepper

1 teaspoon sugar

½ teaspoon paprika

4 tablespoons wine vinegar

1. Pick young, tender dandelion greens, wash carefully in lukewarm water, and dry. Put them in serving bowl.

2. Fry the bacon until crisp and pour, together with the hot fat, over the greens.

3. Melt the butter, add the eggs and cream mixture, the salt, pepper, sugar, paprika, and vinegar. Cook over a low fire, stirring constantly, until sauce is thick and hot. Pour over the greens and toss lightly.

Marinated Fiddleheads

Listed as an appetizer (see page 3), these may be added to a salad, for a "different" touch.

Elderflower Vinegar

This adds an exotic flavor if used to make a salad dressing for a fruit salad.

Elder flowers   White wine vinegar

1. Dry the elder flowers on trays outdoors if the weather is fine, or in a slow oven with an open door. Weigh the blossoms and pack into jars.
2. Heat white wine vinegar, using 1 pint to each pound of blossoms. Pour the hot vinegar over the flowers, cover, and let stand for about ten days.
3. Drain through cheesecloth and pour into sterilized bottles.

Mayonnaise

2 egg yolks or 1 whole egg   Paprika
1 pint oil, olive, or salad   2 tablespoons white wine
1 teaspoon sugar   vinegar or your favorite
1 teaspoon mustard   herb vinegar
½ teaspoon salt   1 tablespoon hot water
Freshly ground pepper

1. Beat the egg in your mixer. Add 1 tablespoon oil. Beat until egg and oil are blended. Add 2 more tablespoons of oil and beat again. Then add 3 tablespoons oil. At this point the mayonnaise should begin to thicken, and you can begin to add the oil more rapidly. Continue until all the oil has been added.
2. Add the sugar, seasonings, and vinegar. Check the seasoning. If you prefer a more tart dressing, add more vinegar.
3. The hot water added at the last will help to keep the dressing from separating in the refrigerator. Most recipes call for white pepper in a mayonnaise, but we prefer the flavor of the black.

Mayonnaise Variations

Ginger Salad Dressing for a fruit salad.

Mayonnaise   Heavy cream, whipped
Preserved ginger, finely
    chopped

Green Mayonnaise for cold fish and seafood.

Mayonnaise	Water cress put through your blender with enough oil to blend it

Horseradish Dressing

Mayonnaise	Prepared mustard
Horseradish	

Roquefort Mayonnaise

Mayonnaise	Sherry
Roquefort cheese	

A Winter Garden in the Cellar

Chicory

This often-despised "weed" can produce delectable little shoots, to be picked and enjoyed all winter in your salads.

Dig the chicory in the fall, cutting off the long roots so the plant will fit in a deep box. Plant them in garden soil with the crowns just showing, cover with 18 inches of sawdust, and put them in a dark place in your cellar where the temperature is as near 55° as possible. Water them, and in about 5 weeks you should see the sprouts appearing. Cut them for tossed salads when about 3 inches high.

This chicory is related to the Witloof chicory or *barbe de capucin* which is raised commercially and sold as French endive.

Dandelions

In the fall, dig dandelions and plant them in boxes of garden soil. Leave them outside until you have had a hard freeze, then bring one box into the cellar. A temperature of 50° to 55° is ideal. Put in a dark place and keep them watered. Tender white sprouts will appear, to be picked for your winter salads. When one box stops producing, bring in another.

Poke Weed

Dig the roots in the fall. Like chicory, this plant has a long tap root which will have to be cut off to fit your box. Plant the roots in garden soil and bring them into the cellar after the first hard freeze. Put the box in a dark, warm place—55° is ideal—and keep watered. Cut the sprouts when they are 6 to 8 inches high. Another crop will spring up, and you can cut a crop once a week for about 3 months. Cook these tender shoots like asparagus.

Mushrooms

Mushroom trays will produce a delectable supply all winter (see page 167). Proper temperature and adequate moisture will keep them coming in abundant quantities.

CHAPTER 9

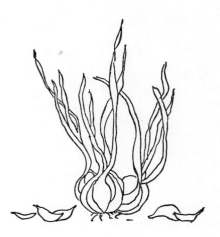

Herbs

Our interest in culinary herbs is constantly increasing. Could it be that since we no longer serve meals of many courses, we feel that the few dishes we serve should be as delectable as possible?

On the other hand, if you look in old cookbooks, you will find herbs not only mentioned in many recipes but used in generous quantities. Our forebears had a limited quantity of foodstuffs and relied heavily upon herbs to add interest to their meals.

Herbs crop up all through history. Words such as cassia, chicory, cumin, hyssop myrrh, and saffron are all borrowed from Mesopotamia, where they first appeared in cuneiform records developed in that country. So you see, the use of herbs is as old as the hills. A convenient chart showing the uses of herbs appears on pages 192-195.

The Herb Garden

I could write many books on the subject of my herb garden, its rewards and pleasures—the uses of herbs, culinary, medicinal, aromatic. Consequently, I really had difficulty deciding which recipes to select for this chapter. My final decision has been to include primarily the herbs I have found easiest to cultivate and those most useful in the kitchen, with recipes for some of my favorite dishes that depend on these herbs for their distinctive character.

How dull my family's food must have been back in the days when I knew nothing about herbs! I believe that the only seasoning on my shelf, other than salt and pepper, was a box of poultry seasoning, and this I used with such caution I might have left it out altogether. When I learned to put parsley in food, not around it, I felt that I had reached the height of culinary sophistication.

The dreary state of affairs improved with the disappearance of domestic help from our kitchen. If I was to do my own cooking, I decided, I refused to be bored to death. This course I recommend to every housewife in a similar predicament.

If you must buy herbs, buy the best. Make sure they have not been on the store shelf very long. Do not let them sit on your pantry shelf indefinitely either; renew them often. Some herbs, such as sage, rosemary, and thyme, retain their flavor well and I have used them even after eighteen months. Those that will hold up for about a year, but might well be renewed often include basil, lovage, marjoram, and dill weed. Tarragon, summer savory, chervil, parsley, and chives seem to lose their flavor after about six months.

Actually there really is no substitute for fresh herbs, so even if you are not a gardener at heart I hope your interest in food will lead you to cultivate a few favorites. If you have a small, sunny space in your yard, start with one or two herbs you are accustomed to use. Most people use parsley, chives, and sage. Chives are found in pots on every vegetable counter in the spring and parsley plants may be bought from a market or nurseryman. Sage seeds, obtainable wherever seeds are sold, germinate easily and grow quickly.

While there is no substitute for herbs picked fresh from your garden, the next best thing is to freeze them. Pick them, wash them, and pat them dry. They can then be put into small freezer bags or in small glass jars, and placed in your freezer. When you cook, just chip off what you need, returning the rest to your freezer. This gives you the delightful flavor of fresh herbs all winter.

Herbs from your garden may also be dried. You may cut most of them twice during the summer. They should be washed after picking, dried gently in a towel, and either spread on coarse screening to dry in the shade, or hung in bunches in some hot place such as an attic, with, however, circulation of air going through.

The idea is to dry them quickly. This will depend on the weather. One year I lost my entire crop of tarragon because there was so much humidity in the air that by the time the leaves had lost their moisture the flavor had disappeared as well.

After the herb is thoroughly dry, remove the leaves from the stems, crush them lightly with a rolling pin, and store in clean, dry jars. If kept in a dark place, they retain their flavor longer.

I keep my dried herbs in a rack on the kitchen wall where I can reach them easily while cooking. I have made my own labels for each jar, and by making the labels large enough to cover the glass, I am able to keep the light from reaching the herbs, yet have them easily accessible.

When cooking with fresh herbs, you will need about three times the amount of dried herbs called for.

Herbs in my Garden

Balm, Lemon

While this is generally thought of as an aromatic herb only, its leaves add an interesting tang to salads. The dried leaves may be added to a potpourri. Pick the stalks of yellow-green leaves for a fragrant addition to a bouquet.

Lemon balm is a perennial whose leaves die down to the ground each winter. The plant reappears each spring, growing to about 18 inches.

Basil

There are several varieties of this delicious herb, but we prefer the ordinary sweet basil. As it is annual, the seeds must be planted each spring. Pinch the seedlings back so that the plant will be bushy, then keep the tops cut off so that no blossoms will develop. In this way you will be able to pick basil all summer and still have plenty to dry or freeze.

Use basil to make herb vinegar; use it in salads. It has a special affinity for tomatoes. Basil butter is excellent on broiled fish. Try some in tomato soup or juice. A leaf adds to boiled potatoes, too.

Borage

This herb has a rough, grey-green leaf, and develops into a plant 2 or 3 feet high, with graceful hanging stems on which charming blue or pinkish-blue star-shaped flowers are suspended.

This annual seeds itself prolifically so that once you have a plant in your garden, you will never be without it.

The young leaves are good added sparingly to salad, giving it a cucumber flavor, and the flowers may be candied and used to decorate a festive dessert.

Burnet, Salad

The unnusual leaves of this herb are an attractive addition to your garden as well as to your salad.

Salad burnet is a perennial, and once established, is a most satisfactory and dependable plant. The leaves are still to be picked late in the fall, when more tender herbs such as basil have long since disappeared.

Chervil

Chervil is a dainty little herb of the parsley family; and while it is an annual, it self-sows so freely that you can be assured of two crops each year if you allow it its eccentricities.

First of all, chervil does not care for too much sun and must be partially shaded. It must also be kept well watered. The tiny white flowers which appear early and profusely should be removed to insure the production of the lacy green leaves all summer. Chervil can be picked until late in the fall unless you deliberately allow it to go to seed.

Chervil is a most delicious herb, notably with fish or potatoes. Try it instead of the usual parsley with new boiled potatoes. Sprinkle it chopped on vichyssoise.

Chives

This well-known but important herb is one that fortunately grows easily in the garden and can be brought into the house in a pot in the fall. It also appears in most markets early in the spring.

I do not recommend dried chives. When I am without the fresh ones, I substitute the tops of green onions, cut very fine. Frozen chives are excellent.

The lavender blossoms of chives add an attractive color to your border; but keep them picked if you wish to go on cutting.

Garlic chives are an interesting variety and are eaten with relish by people who cannot tolerate garlic. Furthermore, the odor does not linger on one's breath.

Chives have many uses in the kitchen. Put them in salads, in cottage or cream cheese, in scrambled eggs, in omelettes, or in anything else you can think of.

Cress

Garden cress, or pepper grass, is a spicy-tasting green that is good added to a salad in limited quantities.

Upland cress is another kind that will grow in your herb garden.

Dill

This herb is generally thought of in connection with pickles, but there are other delightful uses for it.

It is an annual that grows readily from seed. In my garden it seems to be of short duration, so I pick the feathery leaves when I can, to dry or freeze. The seeds will drop and germinate the following spring, so that you will have a perpetual crop of dill. Use the dill leaves, or dill weed as it is generally called, with fish, boiled potatoes, cucumbers, shrimp, and in salads. It also improves the flavor of cabbage, turnips, and cauliflower.

Garlic

If you are as fond of cooking with garlic as I am, plant a few cloves in a sunny corner of your garden. Each one will grow and multiply. When the green tops fade, your garlic is ready to harvest. You will find it crisp, juicy, and of a delicate flavor that cannot be matched by the dried garlic one buys.

I feel that garlic is a "must" in salad, and a necessary ingredient of the court bouillon in which seafood is poached. If used correctly, its flavor is so subtle that "garlic-haters" will enjoy it, for they will be unaware of what the flavor is and will only know that it is delicious. Always add the garlic to a dish by crushing the cloves through a garlic press, unless you wish to put in a whole clove during the cooking period, to be removed later.

Lovage

This is a hardy perennial which grows as tall as six feet. My own lovage plant is only three feet tall but it produces enough leaves for our use.

The leaves impart a bitter, celery-like flavor, but are good in soups and salads if used sparingly. The stalk of lovage can be candied like angelica.

Wild Marjoram

For many years I tried unsuccessfully to raise sweet marjoram. It is an annual, and each year I would sow seeds with discouraging results. I have therefore settled on wild marjoram, or origanum, and am very happy with it. It is a hardy perennial and thrives in any soil; in fact, you may think it does too well, as little plants come up all over the place.

We like this herb in salads. It also goes especially well with cheese and tomatoes and is a "must" in a spaghetti sauce.

Nasturtiums

Each spring I plant a package of nasturtium seeds in one corner of my herb garden.

We like a few of the leaves cut up in salad, and we like to pickle the seeds, being sure to pick them before they are hard. You will find a recipe on page 261.

The flowers may be put in a salad as well, but while this adds an interesting note of color, we feel that they really belong in a vase in the center of the table.

Parsley

This herb is easy to cultivate once you get it started. Germination of the seeds is slow, but when it gets going you can pick freely all summer.

As it is a biennial, the plant will supply you generously the second summer as well, provided that you keep the blossoms cut off as they appear.

It is said that a plant or two can be dug in the fall and kept on the window sill in the kitchen to snip all winter. This is for those with greener thumbs than mine. I have tried it both with parsley and other herbs, always with little success; but I do know it works for others.

No doubt good growing weather in your kitchen should include sunshine and humidity, and perhaps there should be no gas fire. I never did determine the exact cause of my failure—I merely resort to buying parsley in the winter.

I discussed elsewhere the freezing of parsley, which I recommend.

If the winter is fairly mild, place a piece of coarse-meshed wire, such as hardware cloth, over your parsley in the garden, to prevent it from being crushed by the ice and snow. You will find that it stands up nicely during the winter and that you can reach underneath the wire and clip off bits whenever you need them.

We like parsley in practically everything. It has a quiet unassuming flavor that blends with other herbs. Use it in meat and poultry dishes; add it to stuffings and soups; put it in biscuits and omelettes; in fish and cheese.

Rosemary

This is a delightful herb of many uses. It is well to remember, however, that a little goes a long way, and can easily be overdone if you have not had experience in using it.

Rosemary is treated as a perennial in the south. But in our cold climate winter kills it, and so it must be taken indoors, or renewed each spring.

Use rosemary with chicken or duck, lamb or pork. It goes well with seafood, especially salmon. As it has a distinctive flavor, I do not like to combine it with other herbs but depend on the rosemary alone to flavor any dish in which I use it.

Sage

This is an herb everyone knows, which is surprising, inasmuch as its uses are more limited than most.

Sage is raised easily from seed; and if the plant becomes woody after a few years, it should be renewed. I usually cut the plants down to the ground in the spring to get a growth of fresh young leaves to pick.

The old plants can be dug up in the fall; the woody parts cut off and discarded. Then plant the newer shoots, but make sure they have a good root system.

Sage is used in stuffing for poultry and pork.

It dries well, or can be frozen.

Shallots

The shallot resembles garlic in form, since it is made up of cloves; but the flavor is a delicate and mild version of the flavor of an onion.

Shallots are not easy to come by even though they are repeatedly called for in recipes.

When I can get a few, I store them in the refrigerator in a loosely covered dish and plant them in the spring. Each clove will then result in a bulb, and my supply for the winter is assured.

Shallots can be used in anything that will be improved by a

subtle onion flavor. The French use them extensively in their sauces. Shallot butter on a charcoal-broiled steak is heavenly. Kidneys and liver are improved by their addition.

Tarragon

This herb I have found difficult to establish, but once that has been accomplished, it seems to thrive with little attention.

As tarragon does not set seed, you must buy plants. In my case, I had to send for them at some distance, which is not ideal, as any plant is bound to suffer in the shipping. After the third attempt, however, I got a plant going, and now have plenty for myself and my friends.

The herb books say that as tarragon grows, the roots become so tangled as to "choke the plant," and to avoid this it must be dug up and separated every 3 years, which I have done.

If you are not a tarragon user, you are missing a great flavor treat.

I use it with almost everything. The leaves are put in salads and made into herb vinegar. It enhances chicken, fish, lamb, pork, eggs, cucumbers, and beets.

Thyme

It is interesting to try different varieties of thyme. The ordinary broad-leaved thyme, or *Thymus Vulgaris,* is easy to cultivate and the most satisfactory for general use.

There is a lemon thyme, a small-leaved or French thyme, a carpeting thyme for paths and for planting between flagstones.

Thyme is a perennial and can generally be picked all winter, being practically an evergreen. The old plants become woody, but as it is easily increased by layering or by root division, that presents no problem.

The blossoms may be added to your potpourri.

The leaves may be used to complement the flavor of lamb, poultry, or fish, and can be put in stuffing for pork or chicken. Use it in soups or stews or in fish or clam chowder.

HERB	SOUPS HORS D'OEUVRES	POULTRY MEAT	SEAFOOD
BASIL	Tomato Vegetable	Lamb Pork Stews	
BAY LEAF		Game Beef Marinade Meat Loaf Pot roast Stews	Court bouillon
CHERVIL	Chicken Cheese dip Leek Potato Seafood bisque	Game Poultry	Any
CHIVES	Any Chopped as garnish on soup Dips and spreads	Any	Any
DILL WEED	Dips Fish chowder Potato	Lamb Pork Veal	Any Salmon and shrimp especially
GARLIC	Dips and spreads	Beef Chinese dishes Chicken Lamb Marinade	Court bouillon Lobster Shrimp

VEGETABLES	SALADS SAUCES	EGGS & CHEESE
Cabbage Eggplant Beans Onions Tomatoes	Tomato Tossed Green	Spaghetti sauce Any cheese dish or sauce
	Tomato aspic	Spaghetti sauce
Asparagus Potatoes Tomatoes	Cucumber Tomato Tossed green Seafood	Eggs of any kind Sauces for fish Vinaigrette Sauce
Beans Mushrooms Potatoes Tomatoes	Any	Omelets, Scrambled eggs etc. Vinaigrette sauce
Beets Cabbage Potatoes Tomatoes Turnip Zucchini	Cabbage Cucumber Potato Tossed green	Cheese dishes Sour cream salad dressing
	Tomato aspic Any other	Tomato sauce Spaghetti sauce

HERB	SOUPS HORS D'OUVRES	MEAT POULTRY	SEAFOOD
LOVAGE	Any soup stock Vegetable	Beef Veal Stuffings	Court bouillon
OREGANO	Any Tomato Vegetable	Pork Beef Chicken Veal	
PARSLEY	Any Chopped for garnish	Any	Any
ROSEMARY	Chicken Vegetable	Chicken Lamb Pork Stews Sweetbreads Veal	Shrimp Salmon
SAGE	Cheese spread with other herbs	Chicken Pork Poultry stuffing Sausage	
SHALLOTS	Chowders	Beef Lamb Poultry Veal	Any
TARRAGON	Chicken Dips and spreads Mushrooms Tomato Vegetable	Chicken Lamb Pork Veal	Any
THYME	Clam chowder Clam dip	Chicken Lamb Pork Veal Marinades Stews	Any

VEGETABLES	SALADS SAUCES	EGGS & CHEESE
Potatoes	Any Salad Tomato Sauce	Stuffed eggs
Eggplant Mushrooms Zucchini	Any Salad Tomato Sauce Spaghetti Sauce	Cheese dishes
Carrots Peas Potatoes Tomatoes	Any	Any
Beans Spinach	Barbecue Sauce	Egg dishes
Onions		
Beans Cabbage Turnips	Many Sauces	Cheese & egg dishes
Beans Beets Carrots Cabbage Mushrooms Peas Tomatoes	Any Many Sauces	Cheese dishes
Beans Beets Mushrooms Peas Potatoes	Chicken Seafood Many Sauces	Cheese dishes

CHAPTER 10

Recipes Depending on Herbs

APPETIZERS

Basil Canapes

1 tablespoon minced sweet
   basil
½ teaspoon minced chives

½ cup sweet butter
½ teaspoon toasted sesame seeds

Mix all the above together and spread on thinly sliced dark rye bread.

Cauliflower Dip

1 small, raw cauliflower
1 cup sour cream
Minced parsley

Minced dill
Minced lovage
Salt

1. Divide cauliflower into bite-size flowerets.
2. Combine the sour cream and herbs, season with salt to taste, mix well and pour into a small bowl.
3. Surround with the cauliflower and serve with cocktails.

Herb Cheese Spread

This may be put into small jars or pots, covered with paraffin and kept until needed.

If made with cream cheese instead of cheddar, omit the butter. Use immediately, as a cream-cheese spread will not keep.

2 tablespoons butter
3 tablespoons cream
4 tablespoons sherry
2 cups grated cheese, cheddar

2 teaspoons each, parsley, chives
1 teaspoon each, chervil, tarragon thyme

1. Run the parsley, chives, chervil, tarragon, and thyme through blender with the sherry.
2. In the top of a double boiler, melt the butter, add the cream and grated cheese. (We like an old, sharp cheese but that is a matter of taste.) Add the herbs and heat, stirring while mixture melts. Cool and spread.

Cream Puffs with Shrimp

About 3 dozen small puffs

Puffs

1 cup water
½ cup butter
⅛ teaspoon salt

1 cup flour
4 eggs

Filling

Tiny cocktail shrimps
Mayonnaise
Dill weed, minced

Garlic, used sparingly
Lemon juice, a few drops

1. In a saucepan, combine water and butter and boil until butter melts. Add the salt and then the flour all at once. Cook over a very low heat, stirring vigorously until the flour forms a ball. Remove from fire.
2. Add 1 egg at a time, beating until it is completely blended in before breaking the next. Stir until mixture is smooth.

Continued on next page

3. Drop about ½ teaspoonful at a time on an ungreased baking sheet.

4. Bake at 375° for about 20 minutes, or until the puffs are brown and dry on top. Cool.

5. To make filling, combine mayonnaise, dill weed, garlic, and lemon juice. Fold in the shrimp, being careful not to mash them, and fill the puffs with the mixture. Chill until serving time.

Stuffed Eggs

(*See page 207*)

Raw Mushrooms

(*See page 5*)

Tomato Appetizers

Cherry tomatoes, cut in halves   Sweet basil, minced
Salt

Sprinkle a little salt on the cut surfaces of the tomatoes, then sprinkle with basil.

SOUPS

Jellied Herb Bouillon

Serves 6

3 cans beef bouillon
1 or 2 sprigs parsley
2 tablespoons tarragon leaves
2 tablespoons chives

⅓ cup sherry
3 tablespoons unflavored gelatin
4 tablespoons water
Tarragon for garnish

1. In a blender, combine the bouillon, parsley, tarragon leaves and chives. Add the sherry.

2. Heat the broth. Soften the gelatin with cold water, add to broth, and stir to dissolve thoroughly. Pour the soup into a pan to chill.

3. When firm, cut into cubes. Serve in bouillon cups, garnished with tarragon.

Chervil-Cucumber Soup

Serves 4

This is indeed a treat to serve to your favorite guests.

2 scallions, sliced very thin
Butter
3 small cucumbers, sliced
1 cup water
3 tablespoons cornstarch
3 tablespoons cold water

2 cups chicken broth
1 cup cream
Salt and freshly ground pepper
Cucumber slices, rind left on
Minced chervil
A few sorrel leaves, optional

1. Simmer scallions in a little butter until soft, add cucumbers and water, and simmer until the cucumbers are soft. Add the cornstarch mixed with cold water, and add the broth, heat the soup and strain it. Return to stove, pour in the cream, and season with salt and pepper.

2. Serve hot, topped with thin slices of cucumber and chervil. A few sorrel leaves add a distinctive flavor, although one must be careful not to overdo, as the cucumber-chervil flavor is most delicate.

Jellied Herb Consommé

Serves 6

This recipe may be varied by using chicken broth and rosemary, chives and parsley. Use Madeira with this and add a touch of curry powder to the whipped cream.

6 cups consommé
Parsley, chives and chervil
   to taste, chopped

3 tablespoons plain gelatin
3 tablespoons sherry
Salted whipped cream

1. Heat the consommé with the herbs. (The ones listed make a good combination. Add the gelatin softened in a little cold water, stir to dissolve it, and add the sherry. Strain soup and place in the refrigerator to set.

2. Spoon the jellied consommé into cups and top with the whipped cream.

MEATS

Calves' Liver Sauté
Serves 6

6 slices calves' liver
Butter
4 shallots, chopped
1 tablespoon flour
1 cup beef bouillon

2 tablespoons chopped garlic chives
1 tablespoon minced parsley
2 tablespoons dry red wine

1. Brown the liver quickly in butter and transfer to a hot plate.
2. Cook the shallots for a few minutes in the butter, stir in the flour, and cook a minute or two more. Stir in the bouillon and simmer until the sauce thickens. Add the chives, parsley, and wine and return the liver to the sauce.
3. Simmer for about 10 minutes and serve.

Calves' Liver in Red Wine Sauce
Serves 6

If you can depend on your butcher to give you fresh, young beef liver you will like it as well as calves' liver. If you are not sure of its tenderness, sprinkle a tenderizer on the liver one half hour before cooking.

6 slices liver
6 slices bacon
Seasoned flour
2 whole scallions, chopped fine
2 tablespoons bacon fat

1 tablespoon flour
1 cup dry red wine
2 tablespoons chopped parsley
1 tablespoon chopped thyme
1 tablespoon chopped marjoram

1. Sauté the bacon until crisp. Set aside and keep hot.
2. Dust the liver with flour and sauté for 5 to 8 minutes on each side. Overcooking will toughen it. Transfer to hot serving dish.
3. Simmer the scallions in the bacon fat until transparent, add the flour, stir in the wine, and add the parsley, thyme, and marjoram. Heat the sauce and pour over the liver.
4. Top with the bacon and serve.

Charcoal-Broiled Lamb Chops

Serves 4

Have your lamb chops cut 2 inches thick. You may use loin chops or shoulder chops if your butcher can give you meaty ones. We prefer the latter.

4 lamb chops
¾ cup olive oil
⅓ cup dry red wine
1 clove garlic
2 tablespoons chopped parsley

1 or 2 sprigs rosemary
1 sprig thyme
3 whole cloves, crushed
3 peppercorns
½ teaspoon salt

1. Mix a marinade of olive oil, wine (Burgundy or claret), garlic, parsley, rosemary, thyme, cloves, peppercorns, and salt. Pour over chops and let stand for an hour or two, turning occasionally.

2. Broil over a charcoal fire, basting with the marinade as chops cook. If you like them pink inside, allow about 15 or 20 minutes.

Lamb Shanks with Herbs

Serves 4

For a different flavor, the thyme and rosemary may be omitted and a dill sauce (see page 150) served.

4 lambs' shanks
Seasoned flour
Butter
1 sprig thyme
A few rosemary leaves

Salt and freshly ground pepper
2 cups hot water
3 or 4 carrots, cut in strips
2 potatoes, peeled and cubed
1 onion, sliced thin

1. Shake the shanks in a bag of flour and brown them in butter in a skillet.

2. Add the thyme, rosemary, salt and pepper, pour the water over the lamb meat, and simmer for 1½ hours. Add the carrots, potatoes, and onion, and continue cooking for 30 minutes.

3. Serve surrounded with vegetables. Thicken the gravy and pour over the meat.

Leg of Lamb with Herbs

Serves 6 to 8

The garlic will emit an alarming odor while cooking but the lamb will have a heavenly flavor.

1 leg lamb	1 teaspoon salt
1 clove garlic, crushed	A dash or two of pepper
½ bay leaf, crumbled	Olive oil
1 tablespoon rosemary, minced	

1. Combine the garlic, bay leaf, and rosemary, and add salt and pepper.
2. Using a small sharp knife, make little cuts about ¼ of an inch long all over the meat. Rub the herb mixture into the cuts and brush the roast with olive oil.
3. Roast the lamb in the usual way. For a 5-pound roast, I allow about 3 hours in a 325° oven.

Shepherds' Pie

Serves 6

This is most delicious. If you have ever had reservations about lamb stew, cast them aside and proceed.

2 pounds shoulder of lamb, cut up	4 large carrots, slivered
3 tablespoons butter	1 tablespoon fresh dill, minced
Chicken broth	8 or 10 lemon balm leaves, minced
1 large clove garlic, crushed	Rich baking powder biscuits

1. Brown the lamb well in butter, cover with broth, and add the garlic. Simmer for an hour or so, or until meat is almost tender. Add the carrots, dill and lemon balm. Simmer for 10 minutes, and pour the mixture into a baking dish.
2. Bake in a 400° oven for 15 minutes.
3. In the meantime, make biscuits and place them on top of the hot stew. If you have sour cream available, use it in the biscuits.

4. Bake the pie for about 15 minutes more, or until biscuits are brown.

For a Game Pie

Parsley   Thyme
Shallots   Rosemary
Mushrooms

Chop and mix. Add to a game pie.

POULTRY

Tarragon Chicken

Serves 6

For this you may use either roasting or frying chicken. If you use a roaster, roast in the usual way after treating it with herbs as I describe. For fryers, follow this method:

Have small frying chickens cut in half allowing one-half chicken per person.

3 2-pound frying chickens   1½ cups minced parsley
½ cup soft butter   ⅓ cup chopped chives
1 tablespoon fresh tarragon   1 teaspoon salt
  leaves   Soft butter

1. Combine the tarragon, parsley, chives, and salt with the butter. Gently separate the skin from the breast of the chickens and push the herb butter underneath to cover as much of the meat as you can. Any that is left over may be spread in the cavity.

2. Place chickens in a roasting pan, skin side up. Spread with butter and bake in a 400° oven for 50 to 60 minutes, basting occasionally with the herb-flavored juices in the bottom of the pan. The chickens will be tender, brown, and delightful in flavor.

Charcoal Broiled Chicken
Serves 8

Rather than using broilers, we use frying chickens weighing from 3 to 4 pounds each and have them cut in quarters. How many you buy to serve your guests depends on the size of the chickens and the appetites of your guests. One large fryer can serve 4 people but we prefer to prepare more. Any left-over chicken is delicious in a lunch salad or used to make a curry the next evening, stretching it with a few mushrooms.

2 to 3 frying chickens
¾ cup olive oil
⅓ cup wine, red or white
3 or 4 sage leaves, chopped
1 sprig rosemary
1 sprig tarragon

3 peppercorns, crushed
3 tablespoons chopped parsley
2 tablespoons finely chopped chives
Crushed garlic, used sparingly

1. Prepare a marinade of the olive oil and wine combined with the rest of the ingredients. Mix and pour over the chicken, and let stand in the refrigerator for one or two hours, turning once or twice and spooning the marinade over the pieces. Standing all day does no harm.

2. Broil the chicken over a charcoal fire, allowing about 40 to 45 minutes, turning and moving the chicken around so that it is evenly cooked. Brush occasionally with the marinade and you will find your bird tender and juicy—the crust crisp and the flavor heavenly.

SEAFOOD
Shrimp with Herbs
Serves 4

1 pound shrimp, shelled and deveined
1 cup water
2 tablespoons white wine
Parsley
Thyme
Bay leaf

Celery leaves
2 peppercorns
½ teaspoon salt
2 whole cloves
Melted butter
Lemon juice

1. In a saucepan, combine the water and a bouquet garni of parsley, thyme, bay leaf, and celery leaves. Add peppercorns, salt, and cloves, and bring to a boil. Add the shrimp and simmer for 10 minutes.

2. Remove shrimp, and serve with butter to which a few drops of lemon juice have been added.

CHEESE, EGGS, AND PASTA

Eggs in Black Butter

Serves 2

This is a welcome change from scrambled, fried, or poached eggs for breakfast. It is an old French recipe and has been enjoyed by many people for a long time. I recommend it.

4 eggs
3 tablespoons butter

1 teaspoon tarragon wine vinegar

1. In a skillet, cook the butter until brown—do not be misled by the word "black."

2. Drop in the eggs and cook until they are as you like them. Transfer to a hot platter.

3. Stir the vinegar into the butter, pour over the eggs and serve immediately.

Tarragon Eggs

Serves 4

8 eggs, hard-cooked
2 tablespoons butter
2 tablespoons flour
1 cup chicken broth, canned or made with cubes
2 tablespoons heavy cream

Salt and freshly ground pepper
1 tablespoon each, chopped parsley and tarragon
Buttered whole wheat toast rounds

1. Melt the butter and stir in the flour. Cook for a minute or two, add the broth, stir until thick, and add the cream, parsley, tarragon, and salt and pepper to taste. Add the sliced eggs.

2. Serve hot on rounds of toast.

Vegetable Omelet

Serves 8 to 10

Although this is an excellent way to use up odds and ends of vegetables, it is so delicious that I do not depend on leftovers but actually prepare extra vegetables for it. We enjoy this treat for lunch, or as an accompaniment to ham for a buffet supper. It should be served piping hot. If you bake it in a square dish, it can be served cold the next day, cut in squares, with a cold buffet.

5 tablespoons butter
1 onion, chopped fine
8 eggs, beaten
Salt and freshly ground pepper

1 cup cream
Chopped herbs, to taste.
2 cups cooked vegetables

1. In a skillet melt the butter, add the onion, and cook over a low fire until onion is transparent but not brown.

2. Combine the eggs, salt and pepper to taste, and the cream. Add herbs such as chives, sage, parsley, chervil or tarragon. Add vegetables, which can include practically anything: corn, asparagus, zucchini, peas, string beans. Add the sautéed onion, mix well, and pour into a buttered casserole.

3. Bake the omelet in a 300° oven for about 30 minutes, or until it sets.

Cappelletti with Basil

Serves 4

This is an unusual way to serve pasta. In an Italian food store I buy cappelletti, which is pasta formed into little hat-like shapes. They come in a box green and white mixed. The green ones, which are made with spinach, not only have the advantage of containing fewer calories (so it is claimed), but add color interest to the dish.

Spinach noodles can be substituted. If you are unable to buy them, why not try your hand at making them (see page 285)?

Cook your pasta "al dente," which means that it is cooked but still firm when you pinch it. Some people prefer it slightly uncooked in the center, but everyone agrees that it should never be soft. The choice is in the degree of firmness.

One pound will serve 6 to 8 people. The cappelletti I speak of come in a 12-ounce box and that serves 4 nicely.

1 box cappelletti
4 quarts water
1 teaspoon olive oil
Salt
Sweet butter

1 clove garlic
6 to 8 leaves sweet basil,
   minced
Freshly ground pepper
Grated Parmesan cheese

1. Bring the water to a boil, add the oil, salt, and the cappelletti. The oil keeps the pasta from sticking together. When done, drain and transfer to a hot serving dish.

2. While the pasta is cooking, melt a generous amount of sweet butter, add the garlic, basil, and a little pepper. Mix well and pour over the pasta. Turn pasta gently so that the herb butter goes all through the dish. Shake the cheese on top.

3. Serve with a green salad and red wine. If your casserole has to stand a bit, use an ovenware dish and keep it hot. A slight wait will do no harm.

Stuffed Eggs

Serves 3 for lunch

These may be served as hors d'oeuvres or placed in a casserole, covered with a cheese sauce, baked in the oven, and served hot on toast.

6 eggs, hard cooked
2 tablespoons mayonnaise
1 tablespoon sherry
¼ teaspoon mustard

Salt and freshly ground pepper
1 tablespoon each, parsley and
   sweet basil, minced
Tarragon vinegar

1. Cool the eggs, shell, and cut them in half.

2. Mash the yolks in a bowl, and combine with mayonnaise, herbs, and dry ingredients. Thin to the right consistency with a little vinegar, and return yolk mixture to the halves of the whites.

Lasagne

Serves 8 to 10

This is a favorite supper dish and one that can be prepared ahead of time and slipped into the oven at the last minute.

You can bake this in one large square baking dish, to be cut into squares for serving, or if you have small French pottery dishes, individual servings can be made and placed in front of each guest, steaming and fragrant.

Tiny meat balls can be substituted for the sausage.

Use the wide, or lasagne, noodles. They come in 1-pound boxes.

1 pound lasagne noodles	4 cups spaghetti sauce
1 pound cooked sausage	Parmesan cheese, grated
1 pound ricotta	1 cup dry red wine
1 pound Mozzarella cheese	Sweet basil leaves, chopped

1. Cook the noodles according to the directions on the box. Drain. Have ready the sausage, ricotta (which is the Italian cottage cheese), and Mozzarella cheese. I use the canned variety of spaghetti sauce.

2. Arrange layers of noodles, meat, sprinkled with sweet basil, cheese, and sauce, repeating until ingredients are used up. Shake grated cheese generously over the top. Add the wine last.

3. Bake in a 375° oven for 20 minutes.

VEGETABLES

Baked Beets

Serves 4

Baking time varies greatly with the size and age of the beets.

4 medium beets	Melted butter, lemon juice, and
Sour cream and dill, or	lemon balm

1. Scrub beets and bake in a 325° oven for 1 to 2 hours, or until soft. Peel and slice.

2. Serve with either of the above combinations. In either case chop the herb fine.

Herb Mushrooms
Serves 4

1 pound mushrooms
4 tablespoons butter
1 clove garlic, crushed
2 tablespoons oregano, chopped

1 sprig parsley, chopped
Salt and freshly ground pepper
Lemon juice

1. In a saucepan, melt the butter, add the garlic, and cook for a minute or two. Add the mushrooms. If large, remove the stems and use only the caps; if small, use them whole. Sprinkle with oregano and parsley and season lightly with salt and pepper.

2. Cook gently until tender, sprinkle with lemon juice, and serve.

Peas Neopolitan
Serves 4

This is a new way to cook fresh garden peas when you are tired of them cooked in the French manner, if that is possible.

2 cups freshly shelled peas
½ cup tomato juice
Salt and freshly ground pepper
2 or 3 sprigs chervil
1 sprig parsley

1 sprig thyme
1 leaf oregano
2 cups potato balls
Butter

1. In a saucepan, combine the tomato juice (fresh is best, but canned will do), a little salt and pepper, the chervil, parsley, thyme, and oregano. Add the peas and potato balls. Simmer for about 15 minutes.

2. Remove the herbs, add butter generously and serve.

Baked Potatoes with Dill
Serves 6

6 Idaho potatoes
Salt and freshly ground pepper

6 teaspoons sour cream
Dill weed, chopped

1. Bake the potatoes in the usual way.

2. Remove a slice of the skin from each and mash the potatoes slightly with a fork. Season with salt and pepper.

3. Spoon the sour cream on top and sprinkle with dill weed.

Potato Casserole

Serves 4 to 6

This may be prepared in the morning and baked at dinner time.

2 dozen tiny new potatoes
1 large or 2 small onions, sliced
4 tablespoons butter
2 tablespoons flour
½ cup beef bouillon

½ cup cream
2 tablespoons chopped parsley
2 teaspoons chopped chervil
Salt and freshly ground pepper
Grated cheddar cheese

1. Boil the potatoes, drain, peel and place them in a shallow buttered casserole. In a skillet, brown the onions in the butter, add flour, stir, and cook a few minutes. Slowly add the bouillon and the cream, stir until thick, and add the parsley and chervil. Season with salt and pepper to taste. Pour over the potatoes and top with cheese.

2. Bake in a 450° oven for 15 minutes, or until the casserole is thoroughly hot and the cheese melts and browns.

Herb Tomatoes with Cheese

Serves 6

This is equally good as a luncheon dish and as an accompaniment to a meat course at dinner. Do not prepare it too far ahead of time, since the juice from the tomatoes will collect in the bottom of the dish and dilute the cheese.

6 tomatoes, sliced
3 tablespoons fresh basil,
   chopped

Salt and freshly ground pepper
½ cup soft cheddar cheese
   spread

1. Place the tomatoes in a shallow greased casserole. Sprinkle with basil, season with salt and pepper, and spoon the cheese on top.

2. Bake only long enough to heat through, or until the cheese is a little bubbly. You may like to slip the dish under the broiler for a second or two to brown. Over-cooking will make the tomatoes runny.

Chervil Potatoes

Serves 6

This is really an adaptation of that delicious traditional potato dish, *Potatoes Anna*.

5 or 6 potatoes	Chopped chervil
Salt and freshly ground pepper	¼ pound butter

1. Peel the potatoes and slice them as thin as you can, keeping covered with water as you slice to prevent them from turning brown. Drain and dry well with a towel.

2. Butter a casserole generously and arrange a layer of potatoes on the bottom and around the sides. Add salt, pepper, chervil, and butter. Repeat these layers, using all of the butter.

3. Bake in a 400° oven for about 50 minutes. Turn out on a heated serving dish. Potatoes will retain the shape of the casserole and will be crisp and brown on the outside and meltingly tender and buttery inside.

Potatoes Maître D'Hôtel

Serves 4

This, actually, is a variation of the classic dish. I use the tiny new potatoes, either red or white, and leave the skins on. You may peel them if you like, but the skins add to the flavor.

20 tiny new potatoes.	3 tablespoons lemon juice
4 tablespoons butter	Salt and freshly ground pepper
6 lemon verbena leaves, chopped	

1. Boil the potatoes. Season with salt and pepper.

2. Melt the butter, add the lemon verbena leaves and the lemon juice, and pour over potatoes.

Tomatoes with Basil

Fresh tomatoes	Fresh basil, chopped

There is no better way to serve tomatoes than to slice them and sprinkle with chopped fresh basil.

HERB MARINADE AND VINEGARS

Marinade

A good marinade is the cook's best friend. We marinate in order to add flavor and to tenderize. Use marinade on meat, fish, and salad ingredients (except greens). Here is a basic marinade which may be varied according to the purpose for which you intend to use it. You may add garlic cloves, chopped green olives, and herbs such as tarragon or chives, Tabasco Sauce, Soy Sauce, and so on, selecting the flavor that seems to go best with what you are preparing.

¾ cup olive oil
1/3 cup dry wine, red or white
1 small bay leaf
2 teaspoons minced parsley

Other herbs to taste.
¼ teaspoon salt and freshly ground pepper

1. Combine the ingredients, and marinate the fish or meat for an hour or two, or even overnight.

2. Remove from marinade and place on the broiler under the prepared fire, or over it if you are using charcoal. Have the marinade at hand to brush over the meat as it cooks.

Herb Vinegar

This is a recipe which may be used with any herb you like, with possibly the exception of sage. I have made herb vinegar with much the same combination of herbs I might put in a salad: tarragon, salad burnet, garlic, marjoram, thyme, basil. This gives a very pleasant flavor though no one herb can be identified.

1 cup herb leaves   Hot wine vinegar, red or white

1. Gather the leaves of whatever herb you prefer, wash and put them into a quart jar. Fill the jar with vinegar, cover tightly, and let stand for 2 weeks.

2. Strain vinegar, bring to a boil, and pour into sterilized jars or bottles. Seal or cork tightly. Do not use a jar with a metal cap. Allow only glass or cork to touch the vinegar.

Tarragon Wine Vinegar

½ gallon dry red wine
6 cups cider vinegar
3 or 4 whole cloves

1 cup fresh tarragon leaves
4 medium cloves garlic, cut up

1. Buy an inexpensive wine. Combine with the vinegar, cloves, tarragon leaves, and garlic. Let stand for an hour or so, then simmer for 15 minutes.

2. Strain through cheesecloth, pour into sterilized bottles, and cork tightly.

Nasturtium Vinegar

In the summertime we like nasturtium leaves added to the greens in our salads. In the winter we compensate for the lack of fresh leaves by using nasturtium vinegar. This is made of the blossoms, but has the same characteristic nasturtium flavor.

We also pickle the seeds (see page 261).

1 quart nasturtium flowers
1 shallot, finely chopped
1 medium clove garlic, cut up

A sliver of red pepper
Red wine vinegar, hot
⅛ teaspoon salt

1. Wash the nasturtium flowers and drain quite dry. In a quart jar, combine them with the shallot, garlic, and red peppers. Fill the jar with vinegar, cover tightly, and let stand for 2 months.

2. Strain the vinegar, add salt, pour into sterilized bottles and cork tightly.

Spicy Herb Vinegar

2 tablespoons tarragon leaves
4 tablespoons rosemary leaves
8 tablespoons mint leaves
2 tablespoons sage leaves
1 tablespoon rue
1 bay leaf

2 garlic cloves, cut up
½ ounce each, cloves, allspice,
  cinnamon, mustard seed,
  and pepper
2 teaspoons salt
1 quart red wine vinegar, hot

1. Combine all the herbs and spices in a large glass or crockery container. Add the vinegar. Cover tightly and shake or stir daily for 2 weeks.

2. Strain the vinegar into sterilized bottles. Cork tightly.

CHAPTER 11

Desserts

Oh the heavenly scents that emerged from my grandmother's kitchen in those days when calories didn't count!

There might be a spicy gingerbread in the oven, into the batter of which she had stirred a generous handful of the wild huckleberries that grew in the back pasture. Or it might be a wild strawberry pie, just out of the oven, its scarlet fruit still bubbling between the delicate flakiness of its lattice crust, filling the air with mouth-watering fragrance. There might be blueberry grunt, or a hearty steamed cranberry pudding, sending forth tantalizing aromas which drew hungry children from all around to her kitchen door.

Here are a few of the most unforgettable recipes to tempt you.

PIES AND TARTS

The pastry mixes on the market are a wonderful convenience for the cook in a hurry, as well as excellent for certain recipes such as Pot Pie, where a less rich crust is desirable. Sometimes, if I am using a mix which calls for cold water, I substitute cream for the water, which, I think, improves it.

Personally, I like a rich crust, and ignore all recipes in cookbooks, (except my own), and make it the following way:

Rich Pastry for Pies and Tarts

Makes 1 2-crust pie, or 2 pastry shells, or 24 2-inch tarts.

2 cups of flour
¾ teaspoon of salt
1 cup of shortening

2 or 3 tablespoons of cold
water

1. Mix the flour and salt, and, adding half of the shortening, cut it in with a pastry blender (old-fashioned cooks used to use their fingers) until the mixture resembles a fine meal. Then blend in the rest of the shortening, less thoroughly.

2. Sprinkle the water over the mixture gradually, mixing it lightly with a fork, until you have added just enough water to hold it together. If you add too little water it will be difficult to roll out; too much water will give you a tough crust.

3. Roll out each half lightly on a floured board, and proceed according to the recipe you are using.

4. Brushing the crust before baking with milk, or cream, or egg yolk and water, will brown it beautifully.

Blackberry Roll

Serves 8

Rich pastry (see above)
4 cups blackberries
Flour
Butter

1 cup sugar
Grated nutmeg
1 tablespoon flour

1. Make rich pastry and roll into a rectangle. Shake a little flour over it and dot with butter.

2. Wash and drain the blackberries. Combine the sugar, a little grated nutmeg and the flour. Toss the berries in this lightly and spoon them evenly over the crust. Roll as you would a jelly roll and put into a baking dish.

3. Bake in a 350° oven for 30 to 40 minutes. Serve warm, with heavy cream.

Blackberry Deep Dish Tart
Serves 8

4 cups blackberries
1 cup sugar

Butter
Rich pastry crust (see page 214)

1. Mix the blackberries and sugar, adjusting proportions according to the sweetness of your fruit. Put the fruit in a deep baking dish, dot with butter and cover with pastry crust. Slit the top to allow steam to escape.

2. Bake in a 425° oven for 45 minutes, or until crust is nicely browned. Serve warm with heavy cream or ice cream.

Blackberry Pie
Serves 6 to 8

Pick wild blackberries and proceed as for blueberry pie immediately below.

Blueberry Pie
Serves 6 to 8

There is nothing more delicious, but do plan to have it after a rather light meal so that your family and guests can do it justice.

1 quart blueberries, washed and drained
½ cup water
1 cup sugar
2 tablespoons cornstarch

Pinch salt
3 tablespoons water
Grated lemon rind, optional
Pastry (see page 214)

1. Cook berries over a slow fire with half cup of water and sugar adding a little lemon rind for flavor until berries are soft. Combine the cornstarch and salt with 3 tablespoons of water; stir slowly into the berry mixture, and cook for 5 minutes. Cool.

2. In the meantime make the pastry shell. Fill with the cool berries. Top with a lattice crust.

3. Bake in a 450° oven for 10 minutes, then continue baking in a 375° oven for 30 minutes longer, or until the crust is brown. Serve warm with a scoop of French vanilla ice cream on the top.

Blueberry Deep Dish Pie

Serves 6 to 8

Use a deep pan with straight up-and-down sides.

Rich pastry for a two-crust pie   1½ cups sugar
   (see page 214)   Butter
3 cups blueberries, washed
   and drained

1. Line a pie tin with pastry. Roll the rest out and cut it into thin diamond-shaped pieces.
2. Combine blueberries and sugar, spoon half into the pie tin, and dot with butter. Place pastry triangles on top. Repeat, using the rest of the berries and pastry triangles.
3. Bake pie in a 400° oven until pastry is brown and the fruit bubbly. Serve warm with scoops of vanilla ice cream.

Blueberry Deep Dish Tart

Follow directions for BLACKBERRY DEEP DISH TART (see page 216). Serve warm with heavy cream or custard sauce (see page 244).

Elderberry Pie

Serves 6

Pastry (see page 214)   3 tablespoons flour
4 cups freshly picked   Pinch salt
   elderberries   Butter
1 cup sugar   Few drops lemon juice

1. Line a pie tin with pastry
2. Wash and drain the berries. Mix the sugar, flour, and salt, stir berries in lightly, and fill the pie shell. Dot generously with butter. Sprinkle lemon juice over the berries, and top with a lattice crust.
3. Bake in a 425° oven for 35 minutes, or until crust is golden brown. Serve warm, topped with vanilla ice cream.

Elderberry Sandwich Tarts

6 to 8 tarts

Rich pastry (see page 214)   2 cups hot milk
½ cup sugar   4 egg yolks, lightly beaten
1/3 cup flour   1 tablespoon rum
½ teaspoon salt   Elderberry jelly

1. Roll pastry out and cut into squares with a knife, or use a fancy square cookie cutter. Place squares on a cookie sheet and prick with a fork.
2. Bake in a 475° oven for 5 to 8 minutes.
3. Make a cream filling as follows: In the top of a double boiler, combine the sugar, flour, and salt and pour in the hot milk. Stir until thick and hot, this time cooking directly over the fire. Slowly stir the hot sauce into the beaten egg yolk, return to the double boiler, and cook over hot water, stirring until mixture thickens. Cool and add rum.
4. To put the tarts together, spread one pastry square with elderberry jelly, cover this with custard filling, and put the other square on top.

Wild Strawberry Tart

Serves 6

Pastry (see page 214)   1 tablespoon flour
3 tablespoons butter   1 tablespoon fine bread
3 tablespoons sugar   crumbs
1 egg   Sour cream
3 tablespoons wild straw-
    berry preserve

1. Line a pie tin with pastry.
2. Cream the butter and sugar, add the egg and beat well. Stir in the strawberry preserve, flour and bread crumbs. Spread this filling on the pastry.
3. Bake at 350° for 30 minutes, cool and spread with sour cream. You will find that the sour cream and strawberries blend delightfully together.

Wild Plum Pie

Serves 6

Wild plums have a delightful flavor. Although they are apt to be rather small, your patience will be rewarded if you pick them and convert them into this pie.

Pastry shell (see page 214)
2 pounds plums, pitted
1 to 1½ cup sugar
1 cup water
4 tablespoons cornstarch

3 tablespoons cold water
2 tablespoons butter
1 teaspoon grated orange rind
Heavy sour cream
Nutmeg

1. Make a pastry shell, sift flour lightly over the bottom and put into the refrigerator to chill while making the filling.

2. Weigh the plums after the pits have been removed. Add sugar depending on the sweetness of the fruit, then add the water. Simmer until fruit is tender.

3. Mix the cornstarch with cold water and stir into the fruit. Cook, stirring until liquid is clear and thick, then add butter and grated orange rind. Stir thoroughly, pour into the crust, and top with a lattice crust.

4. Bake the pie in a 450° oven for 10 minutes, then at 375° for another 20 minutes. The crust will be golden brown and the filling delightfully fragrant. We like this served cold with heavy sour cream to which just a touch of nutmeg has been added. If you serve it warm, top with whipped cream or ice cream.

Wild Plum Tarts

Serves 6

1 jar wild plum jam
12 rounds rich pastry

1 cup whipped cream
Crystallized ginger

1. Make a rich pastry, using your favorite recipe. Cut rounds, with a 3-inch cookie cutter, prick them with a fork, and bake in a 475° oven for 5 to 8 minutes. Cool.

2. Place a spoonful of wild plum jam on the top of each one, then a spoonful of whipped cream, and last a little finely chopped crystallized ginger.

Wild Strawberry Rhubarb Pie

Serves 6

If your supply of wild strawberries is limited, you can make a delicious pie by combining them with rhubarb.

Rich pastry (see page 214)   1¼ cups sugar
1 cup strawberries, hulled   1 tablespoon cornstarch
2 cups rhubarb, cut small   1 egg, beaten

    1. Line a pie tin with pastry.
    2. Combine the berries and rhubarb.
    3. Mix the sugar and cornstarch, add the egg, fold in the fruit, and spoon mixture into the pie shell. Top with a lattice crust.
    4. Bake in a 400° oven for 35 minutes.

Wild Strawberry Pie

Serves 6

Pie shell   2 cups wild strawberries
1 small pkg. cream cheese   Strawberry glaze
Cream

    1. Bake a pie shell, using your favorite recipe. Let it cool.
    2. Spread the shell with cream cheese mixed with enough cream to soften it. Spoon on the berries, and cover with strawberry glaze (see page 280). Serve with scoops of vanilla ice cream.

Strawberry Pineapple Pie

Serves 6

Pastry shell (see page 214)   1½ cups heavy cream
1 cup wild strawberries, hulled   2 tablespoons confectioners'
1 cup pineapple bits, drained   sugar
                                   3 tablespoons Benedictine

    1. Make a pastry shell, bake and set it aside to cool.
    2. Combine berries and pineapple and fill the shell.
    3. Whip the cream, fold in the sugar and the liqueur. Spoon into the pastry shell and decorate the top with strawberry leaves.

Black Walnut Pie

Serves 6

We make this pie as we do SOUTHERN PECAN PIE.

Pastry shell (see page 214)	½ cup melted butter
3 eggs	1 cup corn syrup
2/3 cup sugar	1 teaspoon vanilla
Salt	1 cup black walnuts

1. Line a pie tin with pastry and chill while you are making the filling.
2. Beat the eggs with the sugar and a pinch of salt. Add the melted butter and corn syrup. (Some recipes specify "dark," others "light" syrup—take your choice.) Add the vanilla and walnuts. Pour mixture into the pie shell.
3. Bake in a 375° oven for 40 to 50 minutes. The center of the pie should be set. Serve cold or slightly warm.

CAKES

Blackberry Shortcake

Follow directions for Strawberry Shortcake on page 227. The blackberries, however, should be sugared ahead of time and be allowed to stand to draw the juice.

Ginger Blueberry Cake

Serves 6 to 8

This is a new twist to a gingerbread. This dessert is hearty but deliciously different.

1 cup blueberries	Blueberry Sauce
1 box gingerbread mix	

1. Follow directions on the box. Fold in the berries. Bake as directed.
2. Serve warm topped with a scoop of vanilla ice cream and Blueberry Sauce (see page 242).

Rose Geranium Cake

Makes 2 layers

This is a cake worthy of being served on the most festive occasions.

Cake

Large rose geranium leaves,   ½ cup soft butter
  washed and dried   1 teaspoon rose flavoring
2¼ cups sifted flour   1 cup milk
1½ cups sugar   4 egg whites
3½ teaspoons baking powder   Butter and flour
1 teaspoon salt

1. Sift the flour, sugar, baking powder, and salt into a bowl. Add the butter and flavoring and two thirds of the milk. Beat until well mixed. Add the rest of the milk and beat for 2 minutes. Put in egg whites and beat another 2 minutes.

2. Butter and flour 2 layer cake tins. Line the pans with rose geranium leaves. Pour the batter on top.

3. Bake in a 350° oven for 30 to 35 minutes, or until cake is springy and has begun to shrink away from the sides.

4. Turn the cakes upside down on cake racks to cool. When cold, carefully pull the geranium leaves off.

Filling

1 cup milk   1 tablespoon cornstarch
6 rose geranium leaves   ¼ teaspoon salt
¼ cup sugar   1 tablespoon butter

1. In a saucepan, combine the milk and geranium leaves, and bring to a boil. Cool the milk and remove the leaves.

2. Combine the sugar, cornstarch, and salt, gradually stir in the milk, and cook over a low fire, stirring until mixture is thick. Cook for 2 more minutes, remove from the fire, add the butter and set aside.

3. When filling is cool, spread it between the layers of the cake and frost.

Frosting

2 tablespoons butter
2 cups confectioner's sugar

1½ tablespoons cream
1 teaspoon rose flavoring

1. Melt the butter, add the sugar, and stir in enough cream to make the icing of proper consistency to spread. Let this stand over hot water for 10 minutes. Remove and add the flavoring. Spread on the top and sides of the cake.
2. Decorate with candied rose petals.

Strawberry Cream Roll

Serves 6 to 8

The roll

3 eggs
1 cup sugar
⅓ cup hot water
1 teaspoon vanilla

1 cup sifted flour
1 teaspoon baking powder
¼ teaspoon salt
Confectioner's sugar

1. Butter a jelly roll tin and line it with foil or buttered white paper.
2. Beat the eggs until thick and lemon-colored. Gradually add sugar, beating constantly. Add the water and vanilla. Fold in flour, baking powder and salt and pour batter into the tin.
3. Bake at 375° for about 15 minutes, or until it is springy to the touch and begins to shrink away from the sides of the pan.
4. Lay out a tea towel and sprinkle with confectioner's sugar. Turn the jelly roll out on the towel. Take off the paper or foil. Cut away the crusty edges, roll the cake up in a towel, and leave it to cool.

The filling

1 cup wild strawberries
1 cup cream, whipped

1 teaspoon plain gelatin
1 tablespoon sugar

1. Wash the berries if necessary and drain them.
2. Whip the cream, add gelatin and sugar, and fold in berries.
3. Unroll the cake, spread with the strawberry cream, and roll up again. Chill. Cover the top with more whipped cream and decorate with crystallized violets. A few fresh violet leaves on top of and around the dish add to its attractiveness.

Strawberry Shortcake Pie
Serves 6

2 cups wild strawberries
Sugar
1 cup flour
1½ teaspoons baking powder
½ teaspoon salt

4 teaspoons butter or vegetable
   shortening
⅓ cup cream
Butter

1. Hull the strawberries and sugar them lightly.
2. Sift the flour, baking powder, and salt. Cut in the shortening and stir in the cream. Blend thoroughly. Pat the dough out so that it will more than cover an 8-inch baking dish.
3. Fill the center with the sugared berries. Dot with butter generously. Fold the extra dough over the fruit.
4. Bake in a 425° oven for 25 minutes. The berries will be juicy and the crust crisp around the edges. Cut the pie in wedges and serve warm with heavy cream or vanilla ice cream.

Strawberry Biscuit Tarts
About 1 dozen

1¾ cups flour
2½ teaspoons baking powder
1 teaspoon salt
1 tablespoon sugar

4 tablespoons butter
¾ cup rich milk
Wild strawberries
Cinnamon sugar

1. Sift the flour, baking powder, salt and sugar together.
2. Cut in the butter with a pastry blender. Mix in the milk.
3. Turn the dough on a floured board and knead for a few minutes. Pat or roll out to ¼ inch thickness and cut into 2-inch rounds.
4. Place a spoonful of berries in the center of each. Sprinkle a little sugar on top if you think it necessary. Cover with a second pastry round and press the edges together with a fork. Prick the top in several places. Place on a cookie sheet.
5. Bake in a 400° oven for 20 minutes.
6. Shake cinnamon-sugar over tarts and serve warm. A Strawberry Sauce (see page 243) may be served with the tarts. In that case omit the cinnamon-sugar.

Old Fashioned Jam Cake

Makes 3 layers

This makes a rich, very moist cake that keeps exceptionally well.

1 cup seedless blackberry jam
1 box Spice Cake Mix
2/3 cup milk
2 eggs

¼ cup butter, melted and
cooled
Whipped cream

1. In a bowl, combine the Spice Cake Mix and the milk. Beat for about 2 minutes, add the eggs, and beat for 1 minute more. Pour in the butter, mix, add the blackberry jam, and beat for 1 minute. Pour the batter into 3 buttered and floured layer cake tins.

2. Bake in 350° oven for about 20 to 25 minutes, or until a toothpick comes out clean when cake is tested. (I find that the consistency of the jam that you use makes a slight difference in the timing.)

3. Spread whipped cream between the layers and on top. See page 317 for how to keep whipped cream from separating.

Black Walnut Torte

Serves 6 to 8

6 egg yolks
1½ cups black walnuts, ground
fine or chopped in blender
Pinch of salt
1 teaspoon vanilla
1 tablespoon dark rum
6 egg whites, stiffly beaten

⅓ cup fine bread crumbs
1 cup heavy cream, whipped
with
1 teaspoon unflavored gelatin
and
1 teaspoon rum

1. Line a loaf pan with wax paper and butter the paper, or butter the pan and dust with fine bread crumbs.

2. Beat the yolks until thick and lemon-colored, add the walnuts, salt, vanilla, and rum. Stir, fold in the egg whites, then the bread crumbs. Pour batter into the pan.

3. Bake the torte at 325° for about 50 to 60 minutes.

4. When the cake begins to cool, remove from pan and remove paper. When cold, cut into 4 layers and spread each layer with the whipped cream-gelatin-and-rum mixture.

Southern Walnut Cake

Serves 6

You may add raisins or even frost the cake, but we consider the latter gilding the lily.

¼ cup bourbon
1 teaspoon grated nutmeg
1 box yellow cake mix (9½ oz.)

1 egg
Water
1 cup chopped black walnuts

1. Soak the nutmeg in bourbon for 10 minutes.
2. Pour the cake mix into a bowl.
3. Break the egg into the spiced whiskey and add enough water to make ¾ of a cup. Pour this into the cake mix and beat well. Add the walnuts.
4. Bake in a buttered and floured loaf cake pan at 350° for about 30 minutes.

Strawberry Torte

Serves 6

2 cups hulled wild strawberries,
    lightly sugared
3 tablespoons Grand Marnier
3 egg whites
¼ teaspoon cream of tartar

1 cup sugar
1 teaspoon vanilla
½ cup black walnuts ground
    fine or chopped in blender
2 cups heavy cream

1. Combine the berries and the Grand Marnier and let stand in the refrigerator while making the meringue.
2. Beat the egg whites with cream of tartar until whites are frothy. Add sugar a tablespoon at a time, continuing to beat until the mixture will stand in stiff peaks. Add the vanilla and fold in the nut meats. Spread meringue on two buttered layer cake tins or make two rounds on a buttered cookie sheet.
3. Bake at 275° for 60 minutes. Turn off the heat. Allow meringues to cool in the oven.
4. Whip the cream and fold in the strawberries. Place one meringue round on a serving tray, spoon half the berries and cream over it; put the other round on top and finish with the rest of the strawberries and cream. Lay freshly picked strawberry leaves around the edge of the tray.

Old Fashioned Strawberry Shortcake

Serves 6 to 8

4 cups, or more, hulled wild
   strawberries, lightly sugared
2 cups flour
2 tablespoons sugar
3 teaspoons baking powder
1 teaspoon salt

⅓ cup butter or vegetable
   shortening
½ cup milk
½ cup cream
Melted butter
Soft butter

1. Let the berries stand at room temperature. In the meantime sift the flour, sugar, baking powder, and salt. Cut in the shortening. Stir in the milk and cream and mix well. Divide the dough in half.

2. Spread half the dough on a baking tin and spread with melted butter. Top with the other half.

3. Bake in a 450° oven for 12 to 15 minutes.

4. Remove cake from the oven and split it. Put the lower half on a serving platter, spread with soft butter, and spoon half the berries over it. Cover with other half and top with rest of the berries. Serve with heavy cream while biscuit is warm and crisp.

PUDDINGS, SOUFFLÉS AND CUSTARDS

Blackberry Custard Pudding

Serves 6

4 cups blackberries
1 cup butter
1½ cups sugar

1 loaf sponge cake, crumbled
6 egg yolks, well beaten
6 egg whites, beaten very stiff

1. Simmer the blackberries for a few minutes until the juice runs. Cool.

2. Cream the butter and sugar and mix in the fruit. Add the sponge cake (stale if possible) and the egg yolks. Fold in the egg whites.

3. Bake in a buttered pudding dish at 375° for 35 minutes. Serve warm with ice cream, or cold with heavy cream.

Blueberry Grunt

Serves 6

If you have never had this old-fashioned blueberry pudding you've been missing a lot!

3 cups blueberries
1 cup water
½ cup sugar
1 teaspoon lemon juice
1 cup flour

1 teaspoon baking powder
¼ teaspoon salt
2 tablespoons sugar
1 egg
½ cup milk

1. In a sauce pan, combine the water and sugar, bring to a boil, add the blueberries and lemon juice, and simmer for 3 or 4 minutes. Transfer to a shallow flame-proof serving dish.

2. Make dumpling dough as follows: Combine and sift the flour, baking powder, salt, and sugar. Beat the egg, stir in the milk, and mix into the flour. Spoon dumplings on top of hot berries.

3. Cover and let simmer for 10 minutes. Serve hot with heavy cream. A little nutmeg may be grated over the top before serving.

Strawberry Soufflé

Serves 6

1 cup wild strawberries
Sugar
3 tablespoons butter
2 tablespoons flour
½ cup cream or milk

5 eggs, separated
2 tablespoons sugar
1 tablespoon Cointreau
½ tablespoon sugar

1. Hull berries and sugar lightly.

2. Melt butter, stir in flour and cook for a minute or two. Stir in cream or milk. Cook gently until thick and hot.

3. Beat egg yolks with 2 tablespoons of sugar, then slowly add hot mixture, beating while you pour. Add berries and Cointreau.

4. Beat the egg whites until stiff, beat in ½ tablespoon sugar and fold into soufflé. Pour into a buttered soufflé dish.

5. Bake in a 350° oven for 30 minutes. Serve immediately with Strawberry Sauce (see page 243).

Blueberry Soufflé

Serves 6

2 cups blueberries
1 teaspoon lemon juice
1 cup sugar
3 tablespoons water

7 egg whites, beaten very stiff
1 tablespoon brandy
½ teaspoon grated lemon rind

1. Mash the berries or put through a blender, strain, and add the lemon juice.

2. Cook the sugar and water until it reaches 238° on your thermometer, stir in the berry juice, and let cool. Add the brandy and lemon rind to the egg whites, fold in the juice, and pour batter into a buttered soufflé dish.

3. Bake in a 400° oven for 30 minutes. Serve with Blueberry Sauce (see page 242) or Custard Sauce (see page 244).

Lemon Velvet

Serves 6

This is an unusual light dessert. The tartness of the jelly contrasts pleasantly with the custard sauce.

1 tablespoon gelatin
1 cup dandelion wine
1 cup water
3 tablespoons lemon juice
2 tablespoons grated lemon rind

7 tablespoons sugar
4 egg yolks, well beaten
Custard Sauce (see page 244) and
2 tablespoons sugar

1. Soften the gelatin in ¼ cup wine.

2. In a saucepan combine remainder of the wine, water, and lemon juice. Bring to a boil. Stir in the sugar and lemon rind. Slowly pour this over the egg yolks, mix until well blended, then place over a low fire to cook but not to boil.

3. Add the gelatin and stir until it is dissolved. Pour into a wet mold and refrigerate. Unmold.

4. Serve with a Custard Sauce, made with 2 more tablespoons of sugar than recipe calls for.

Steamed Blueberry Pudding

Serves 6

1 cup blueberries	2 tablespoons sugar
2 cups flour	¼ cup molasses
4 teaspoons baking powder	¾ cup milk
½ teaspooon salt	2 tablespoons melted butter

1. Wash and drain berries.
2. Combine the flour, baking powder, salt, and sugar. Dust a little of this over the berries and mix lightly.
3. Combine the molasses and milk, stir into the dry ingredients, and add the butter. Fold in the berries and pour the pudding into a well-greased mold.
4. Steam for 1½ hours. Serve with Orange Sauce (see page 157).

Blueberry Cottage Pudding

Serves 6

2 cups blueberries	½ cup cream
4 tablespoons butter	1½ cups flour
¾ cup sugar	2 teaspoons baking powder
1 egg	½ teaspoon salt

Topping

¾ cup sugar	3 tablespoons soft butter
1½ tablespoons flour	Cinnamon and freshly grated nutmeg

1. Wash and drain berries.
2. Cream the butter and sugar together. Beat in the egg and cream.
3. Sift the flour, baking powder, and salt, add to the first mixture, then fold in the berries. Pour the batter into a buttered pan.
4. Combine the sugar and flour, cut in the butter, add cinnamon and nutmeg to taste, and sprinkle topping on the batter.
5. Bake in a 350° oven for 20 minutes. Serve with whipped cream or Blueberry Sauce (see page 242).

Steamed Cranberry Pudding

Serves 6 to 8

This is an old New England recipe for a pudding served in restaurants and homes and enjoyed by everyone.

2½ cups cranberries
⅓ cup blanched almonds
    chopped
2 cups stale cake crumbs
½ cup sugar

2 teaspoons baking powder
½ teaspoon salt
½ cup melted butter
2 eggs, beaten with
½ cup milk

1. Wash, drain and chop the cranberries.
2. Combine the cake crumbs, sugar, baking powder, salt, melted butter, eggs, and milk. Stir in the berries and almonds.
3. Pour the mixture into a buttered and floured mold. Spread a dampened, floured cheesecloth over the pudding, then cover.
4. Steam, tightly covered, for 2 hours, keeping the water boiling. Turn pudding out on hot serving dish and serve with Hard Sauce (see page 245).

Strawberry Cobbler

Serves 6

3 cups wild strawberries
½ cup sugar
1 tablespoon cornstarch
1 cup water
Butter
1 cup flour

1 tablespoon sugar
1½ teaspoons baking powder
½ teaspoon salt
3 tablespoons butter
½ cup cream

1. Hull the berries.
2. Combine sugar, cornstarch, and water. Cook, stirring until thick and hot. Add berries.
3. Butter a baking dish, pour mixture in and dot with butter.
4. Sift together the flour, sugar, baking powder, and salt. Blend in butter. Stir in cream. (The mixture should be fairly soft.) Spoon on top of the berries.
5. Bake in a 400° oven for 25 minutes. Serve warm, with heavy cream.

Trifle

Serves 6

This is a traditional English dessert, easy to make and most delicious.

Stale cake (pound, sponge,
    butter)
Sherry
Boiled Custard (see page 244)
2 tablespoons brandy

1 teaspoon vanilla
Wild strawberry jam or
    preserve
Whipped cream

1. Place slices of cake in bottom of a serving bowl. Cover with sherry and let stand.

2. Make a boiled custard, let it cool and besides the usual teaspoon of vanilla, add 2 tablespoons of brandy.

3. Spread cake with wild strawberry jam or preserve. Pour cooled custard on top. Refrigerate until ready to serve. Standing a few hours does this dessert no harm, in fact I think it allows the flavors to blend and so improve the dish.

4. Serve topped with whipped cream flavored with a little brandy.

Plum Soufflé

Serves 6

1½ tablespoons butter
1½ tablespoons flour
1 cup cream
5 egg yolks, well beaten
½ cup sugar
Salt

2 tablespoons Cointreau
5 egg whites, beaten very stiff
Sponge Cake
½ cup wild plum jam
Powdered sugar

1. Melt the butter and stir in flour. Cook for a minute or two, add the cream, and stir until mixture thickens.

2. Combine the egg yolks, sugar, and a few grains of salt. Very slowly pour the hot mixture into the egg yolks, beating as you pour. Stir in the Cointreau. Fold in the egg whites.

3. Butter a soufflé dish and line it with sponge cake. Spread the cake with the wild plum jam. Pour batter over this and sprinkle with powdered sugar.

4. Bake in a 400° oven for 20 minutes.

FRUIT

There is no more pleasant way to end a meal than with some kind of fruit dessert; and one made with wild fruit is most prized. Wild fruit demands little else than that it be freshly picked, sweetened slightly if at all, and not chilled, lest the exquisite flavor and aroma be lost.

Here are a few simple wild fruit desserts to end a meal deliciously.

Prepared Fruit

Mulberry Dessert

Serves 4

2 cups ripe mulberries	Heavy Cream
Sugar	Sugar
Orange juice	Vanilla
2 tablespoons Cointreau	Chopped crystalized ginger

1. Sugar the mulberries to taste and allow to stand at room temperature for an hour or two.
2. Transfer to a serving dish, pour orange juice over to cover, and add Cointreau. Whip the cream, add sugar and vanilla to taste, and spoon over berries. Sprinkle with chipped crystalized ginger.

Spiced Wild Plums

Serves 6

4 cups plums	1 cup water
2 cups sugar	4 whole cloves

1. Wash and pit plums.
2. In a saucepan, combine plums, sugar, water, and cloves, bring to a boil, and simmer until they are tender. Chill.
3. Transfer to a serving bowl and sprinkle with finely chipped crystallized ginger.

Elderberry Apple Compote in Rice Ring
Serves 8

Compote

6 apples, sliced	2 cups sugar
1 quart elderberries	2 tablespoons dark rum

1. Simmer apples in water until tender, using as little water as possible. Skim out apples, add sugar, and boil for 5 minutes. Return apples to the syrup, add the elderberries, and simmer until thick, stirring occasionally, for about ½ hour. Cool.

2. Add rum. Serve in a rice ring.

Rice Ring

2 cups cooked rice	2 tablespoons cornstarch
2 cups milk	½ cup milk
¼ cup sugar	1 teaspoon vanilla
½ teaspoon salt	

1. In top of double boiler, combine rice, milk, sugar, and salt. Cook until hot. Combine cornstarch and milk, stir into rice, and cook for 15 minutes. Add vanilla and pour into an oiled ring mold. Chill. Unmold and fill with fruit.

Blackberry Mush
Serves 6

This is just as delicious when made with blueberries.

2 quarts wild blackberries	4 tablespoons cornstarch
1 cup sugar	4 tablespoons water
1½ cups cold water	

1. Wash wild blackberries or thimble berries if you think it necessary, put in a saucepan with sugar and cold water, and bring to a boil, stirring to prevent scorching. Simmer until berries are soft, from 5 to 10 minutes.

2. Combine cornstarch and water, stir into berry mixture and simmer for about 5 minutes more, or until clear.

3. Pour the mush into a serving dish and serve warm with heavy cream or Custard Sauce (see page 244).

Blueberry Mush

Follow the directions for Blackberry Mush.

Coeur à la Creme

Serves 6

This is a classic dessert, to be found in any cookbook, but is often passed over in the search for something more exotic. Let me assure you that nothing could be more delicious or more appreciated by your guests. The wild strawberries, of course, provide that unusual touch and add to its perfection.

You will need a heart-shaped basket which is available at the Bazar Français or Hammacher Schlemmer in New York, or in similar stores.

24 ounces cottage cheese	2 cups wild strawberries
1½ cups heavy cream	Sugar
Pinch of salt	

1. Line the basket with wet cheesecloth.
2. Blend the cottage cheese, cream, and a pinch of salt. Place the mixture in the basket and let drain for 12 to 15 hours.
3. Turn the cheese mold upside down on a serving dish and surround with wild strawberries, lightly sugared. Decorate with rose geranium or wild strawberry leaves.

Strawberry Pineapple Dessert

Serves 4 to 6

1 ripe pineapple	Sugar
Wild strawberries, hulled	Kirch or Cointreau to taste.

1. Cut the pineapple in half. Take out the center and dice it. Add an equal amount of strawberries, mix the two fruits, add sugar to taste, and pour in a little of either liqueur. Allow to stand in the refrigerator for a few hours.
2. When ready to serve, fill the pineapple shell with the fruit, top with scoops of pineapple ice, and decorate with fresh mint leaves.

Strawberries and Honey
Serves 4

1 quart wild strawberries   1 cup sour cream
6 ounces cream cheese   2 tablespoons Cointreau
½ cup honey

1. Using a blender or mixer, combine cheese, honey, and sour cream until perfectly smooth. Stir in the Cointreau.
2. Place strawberries in a serving dish and spoon the honey sauce over them.

Wild Plum Compote
(See page 264)
Serve with sour cream.

Strawberries Romanoff
Serves 6 to 8

This is a well-known and delicious dessert. Your guests will feel flattered—as indeed they should—if you pick wild strawberries for it.

2 cups wild strawberries   4 tablespoons powdered sugar
1 pint French vanilla ice cream   4 tablespoons Benedictine or
1 cup heavy cream   rum or kirsch

1. Hull berries and take ice cream out of refrigerator to soften.
2. Whip the cream and add sugar and liqueur.
3. Fold in ice cream, cream and berries, and serve immediately.

Wild Strawberries in Port Wine

For the best flavor these should be served at room temperature.

Wild strawberries   Port wine
Sugar

1. Wash berries if you must, hull them, and sugar lightly. Pour port wine over them.
2. Allow the berries to stand before serving.

Wild Strawberries and Cream Cheese
Serves 4

1 quart wild strawberries,   A little sugar
  hulled   Few grains salt
1 small package cream cheese
1 cup heavy cream

Combine cream, cheese, sugar, and salt, beat well and serve on wild strawberries.

FROZEN DESSERTS

Grape Sherbet
Serves 4

1 cup cream   2 tablespoons lemon juice
1 tablespoon gelatin, softened in   ¼ cup sugar
¼ cup water   Pinch of salt
1 cup grape juice

1. Heat cream in top of a double boiler, add the softened gelatin, stir, and add grape juice, lemon juice, sugar, and salt. Stir until mixture is smooth.

2. Pour into a tray and freeze.

Rose Petal Ice Cream
Serves 8

1 cup fresh, fragrant wild rose   2 egg whites, beaten stiff
  petals, chopped   1 cup heavy cream, whipped
½ cup sugar   1 teaspoon rose flavoring
½ cup water   A few drops red coloring

1. Boil sugar and water to the firm ball stage, or 242° on your candy thermometer.

2. Slowly pour the syrup over the egg whites, beating as you pour. Beat until mixture stands in soft peaks.

3. Fold in cream, rose petals, rose flavoring, and red coloring.

4. Freeze in a refrigerator tray or in your freezer.

Black Walnut Ice Cream
Serves 4
This is good topped with maple syrup.

1 cup milk

½ cup sugar

Pinch of salt

3 egg yolks, lightly beaten

1 cup heavy cream, whipped

1 tablespoon vanilla

½ cup black walnuts

1. In a saucepan combine the milk, sugar, salt, and egg yolks, stir over a low heat until the mixture comes to a boil, and remove from the stove immediately. Cool and strain.

2. Add the cream, vanilla, and walnuts. Stir. Pour into freezing trays and stir frequently during the first hour of freezing.

Frozen Strawberry Cream
Serves 6

4 egg yolks, lightly beaten

½ cup sugar

2 tablespoons flour

Salt

4 cups milk

1 tablespoon vanilla

1 quart ripe wild strawberries, hulled

Sugar to taste

1. In the top of a double boiler, combine egg yolks, sugar, flour, salt, and milk and cook over hot water until custard is thick. Cool and add vanilla.

2. Sweeten berries to taste, mash them with a fork or in a blender, combine with the cold custard, and freeze. Serve with more strawberries spooned over the top.

Wild Strawberry Ice Cream
Serves 8

2 cups wild strawberries

1/3 cup sugar

4 cups heavy cream

¾ cup sugar

Pinch of salt

1½ teaspoons vanilla

1. Crush the berries and add 1/3 cup of sugar. If they are very sweet you will need less.

2. Scald the cream and add ¾ cup sugar. Cool and add the salt and vanilla. Stir in the sweetened berries. Freeze.

Black Walnut Ice Cream Pie

Serves 6

Crumb Crust

½ cup black walnut meats   1 cup graham cracker crumbs
                                  ¼ cup soft butter

Filling

French vanilla ice cream   Wild Strawberry Sauce (see
                                  page 243)

1. Grind the nut meats very fine or chop them in the blender. Add cracker crumbs and butter, blend well, press mixture into a pie tin and bake in a 375° oven for 8 minutes. Cool the shell.
2. When ready to serve, spoon in ice cream and pour strawberry sauce over it. Decorate pie with candied borage or violet blossoms.

Crystallized Leaves and Flowers

Although there are several different ways of crystallizing leaves and flowers for use in decorating desserts, I have found the following three best. Each has its own merit. The only general rule to remember is: *don't* try to candy anything on a damp or humid day. The syrup will remain perpetually sticky.

Method I

This is the easiest of all. Whip an egg white *very* lightly, just enough so it can be picked up on a water-color brush (which you can buy at the store or borrow from your child's paint box). Brush the blossoms lightly with the egg white and sift sugar over them. Put aside to dry. I use a piece of fine wire mesh for this, but a piece of foil will do.

Pack the dry flowers in a tin box between layers of wax paper. Do not keep too long as they tend to crumble.

Method II

This produces a more durable product. At the drugstore, buy 1 ounce of powdered gum arabic and a pair of tweezers. Using the top of a double boiler, dissolve the gum arabic in ½ cup water and let it cool. Using the tweezers, carefully dip each blossom in the heavy liquid, hold it up a minute to drain, then put it on the mesh to dry. If you wish you may string the blossoms with thread and needle and hang them up. The gum arabic gives the flowers a rather leathery surface to which the syrup adheres well, and it makes the blossoms easier to handle.

Make the crystallizing syrup by boiling 1 cup of sugar with ½ cup of water and 1 tablespoon corn syrup until your candy thermometer registers 238°. Let it cool, then dip the blossoms in carefully, drain briefly and sift granulated sugar over them, covering both the top and under side.

When completely dry, pack as directed above.

Method III

This is a combination of I and II. Omit the gum arabic. Make the crystallizing syrup, cool, dip the flowers and allow to dry. Then proceed as with Method I, using the egg white and sugar.

The following candy well:

BORAGE This herb has the most entrancing star-like flowers, intense blue shaded with pink. Use the egg white-sugar method for these.

LILAC BLOSSOMS Pick the tiny stems having 3 or 4 flowerets. I use Method III for these. The white blossoms make an especially attractive decoration.

MINT LEAVES The smaller leaves are the most attractive when candied. Select perfect leaves, and add green coloring and mint flavoring to the syrup.

ROSE PETALS Select your most fragrant roses. If you are fortunate enough to have wild roses nearby, you will find that they have the most enduring fragrance of all. Add red coloring to get the desired shade of pink and as much rose flavoring as necessary.

VIOLETS You may use the wild violets, as I have done, but do not expect too much fragrance from them. I like to use them for decoration when I serve a fancy dessert, placing real leaves of whatever is available next to them. If wild violets are not easily obtainable, buy the fragrant English violets (*V. odorata*) or Parma violets from your florist. To the crystallizing syrup, add 1 tablespoon of violet flavoring and a drop of purple coloring—unless, of course, you are using white violets.

ANGELICA Everyone has bought this candied stem at Christmas time for decorating cookies. If this hardy perennial grows in your garden, you might be interested in candying it.

Cut the stem, which has ridges like celery, into 3 or 4 inch lengths. Soak overnight in brine. Drain. Put in a saucepan with 1 part vinegar to 4 parts water, to cover, and add a few drops of green coloring. Simmer until the angelica has absorbed enough green coloring, then drain it again.

Combine 1 pound of sugar and 1 cup of water, boil for 10 minutes, pour the syrup over the angelica, and let stand overnight. The following day pour the syrup off, bring to a boil, and again cover the angelica and let stand overnight. Finally simmer the stems in the syrup until tender.

They may be stored in a jar in the syrup, or drained and dried and sprinkled with granulated sugar.

LOVAGE The leaves of lovage have a rather bitter celery flavor but the root, when candied, had an interesting nutty taste. Dig the root in the fall, wash and scrape it, and slice crosswise. Simmer for 3 or 4 hours, changing the water several times. Drain and cool.

Make a crystallizing syrup of 2 cups of sugar to ½ cup of water. Add the root slices and simmer to 300°. The lovage should be clear and tender. Lay the pieces on wire mesh or tin foil to dry. You may sift granulated sugar over them while they are still moist.

SWEET FLAG One of my old cookbooks recommends preparing the root of this plant in the same way.

DESSERT SAUCES

Blueberry Sauce

1 cup water	2 cups blueberries, washed and
½ cup sugar	drained
Pinch of salt	2 tablespoons cornstarch
1 teaspoon lemon juice	4 tablespoons water

1. In a saucepan, combine the water, sugar, salt, and lemon juice. Simmer for a minute or two, add the blueberries, and continue to simmer until berries are soft.
2. Mix the cornstarch and water, and stir into the hot blueberries. Cook the sauce until thick and clear.

Brandy Pudding Sauce

2 eggs, well beaten	1 cup cream, whipped
½ cup sugar	3 tablespoons brandy
1 tablespoon butter	

1. Combine the eggs, sugar, and butter, and cook in the top of a double boiler until the sauce is thick. Cool.
2. Fold the cream into the sauce, then add the brandy. Serve with any steamed pudding, or with gingerbread or fruit cobbler. If you have made Tutti Frutti, use the liquid from that instead of the brandy.

Strawberry Sauce—I

1 cup wild strawberries, hulled   ½ tablespoon rum
Sugar

Sugar the berries lightly—sometimes they are so sweet they need practically no sugar. Add the rum. Let stand for an hour or so. Serve on ice cream or on a vanilla soufflé.

Strawberry Sauce—II

1 cup milk   ½ tablespoon flour
1 cup light cream   1 cup heavy cream, whipped
4 egg yolks, well beaten   1 cup wild strawberries
½ cup sugar   2 tablespoons strawberry syrup

1. Combine and scald the milk and light cream.
2. Combine the sugar and flour and stir into the egg yolks. Slowly pour the hot liquid into the egg-yolk mixture, stirring as you pour.
3. Cook in top of a double boiler until the sauce thickens, stirring as it cooks. Remove from the fire and allow to cool.
4. Fold in the cream, strawberries, and strawberry syrup.

Rose Petal Cream

This is an intriguing sauce to serve with fresh fruit. Try it with wild strawberries or fresh raspberries.

2 cups rose petals   A few drops rose flavoring
2 cups heavy cream   1 tablespoon Benedictine
Sugar

1. Pick the most fragrant rose petals you can find. Cut them up or run them through your blender. Pour the cream over them and let stand for an hour, no longer or they will develop a bitter flavor.
2. Strain the cream, add sugar to taste (too little being better than too much), the rose flavoring, and the Benedictine. When ready to serve, spoon mixture over the berries. Garnish with freshly picked rose leaves, washed and dried.

Custard Sauce

Cook a few rose geranium leaves in the custard to give it an interesting flavor. Remove the leaves before serving.

3 egg yolks, well beaten   Few grains salt
¼ cup sugar   2 cups milk
2 tablespoons flour   1 tablespoon vanilla

1. Combine sugar, flour, and salt, stir in egg yolks, add the milk, and cook, stirring constantly, over hot water until sauce is slightly thick. Cool.
2. Add vanilla. Serve the sauce very cold. You may add rum or any liqueur you wish, or fold in whipped cream.

Maple Sauce—I

1½ cup maple syrup   1 teaspoon grated orange rind
½ cup butter   A dash nutmeg

Combine all the ingredients and simmer for 2 or 3 minutes. Serve hot or cold on ice cream, pudding, or pancakes.

Maple Sauce—II

¼ cup maple syrup   ½ teaspoon plain gelatin
1 cup heavy cream

1. Whip the cream and mix in the gelatin. Slowly fold in the syrup.
2. Pile into a serving dish and chill.

Maple-Pineapple Sauce

1 small can (#211) crushed   ¼ teaspoon allspice
   pineapple, including juice   ¼ teaspoon freshly grated
¾ cup maple syrup   nutmeg
1 stick butter   3 tablespoons dark rum

1. Combine crushed pineapple, maple syrup, butter, allspice, and nutmeg. Simmer for 8 minutes. Add the rum.
2. Pour over vanilla ice cream.

Cold Strawberry Pudding Sauce

1 cup sugar
⅓ cup butter

2 egg whites, beaten stiff
1 cup wild strawberries

1. Cream the butter and sugar together well.
2. Fold in the egg whites, adding the strawberries last. Spoon over puddings, ice cream, or a slice of angel or sponge cake.

Grape Juice Sauce for Desserts

2 cups grape juice
⅓ cup of cream
2 tablespoons cornstarch

Few grains salt
1 tablespoon lemon juice

1. Combine the sugar, cornstarch, and salt, stir in the grape juice, and bring to a boil. Cook until sauce is thick and clear. Add lemon juice. Serve hot on fruit dumplings or steamed puddings; cold on custard, ice cream or vanilla soufflé.

Hard Sauce

Be sure to take this out of the refrigerator to soften before serving, since in spite of its name it should not be hard.

1 cup butter
1 cup confectioner's sugar

1 tablespoon rose syrup

Cream the butter until very smooth and creamy. Add the sifted sugar and continue to beat until sauce is fluffy. Add the rose syrup and mix well.

Brandy Hard Sauce

Serve this sauce at room temperature so that it melts and its flavor blends with the pudding on which it is eaten.

1 cup butter
1 cup confectioner's sugar

1 egg yolk
1 tablespoon cherry brandy

Cream the butter and gradually add the sifted sugar. Beat until sauce is light and fluffy. Beat in the egg yolk and the brandy. Serve on any hot pudding.

Wine Hard Sauce

Follow the recipe for BRANDY HARD SAUCE but omit the brandy and use blackberry wine instead. Grate nutmeg over the top before serving.

Maple Walnut Sauce

This is wonderful on ice cream or a vanilla soufflé.

1 cup maple syrup   ½ cup heavy cream
½ cup black walnut meats

1. Boil the syrup until it has reached the soft-ball stage, or 238° on your candy thermometer.
2. Beat it until it cools, then add the cream and the chopped black walnuts.

Maple-Orange Sauce

3 cups maple syrup   1 cup butter
1½ teaspoons grated orange

Combine maple syrup, orange rind, and butter. Boil for 2 or 3 minutes and serve on ice cream or waffles.

Maple Fruit Sauce

1 cup maple syrup   ½ cup mixed candied fruit

Combine and heat the syrup and fruit. Serve warm over ice cream or Meringues Glacées.

CHAPTER 12

The Sugar Maple

The early colonists learned from the Indians how to use the sap of the maple tree, and it became one of the most important means of sweetening their food. Many of us still find it a wonderful treat to gather and prepare our own maple syrup and the sweets made from it, even as our forebears did.

We tend to think of maple syrup as being the product of the sugar maple only, but I am told that the sap of the red maple, the box elder or ash-leaved maple, makes excellent syrup.

The sugar maple (*Acer saccharopharum*) and the black maple (*A. nigrum* or *A. saccharum nigrum*) produce a more generous flow of sap, so if you have these in your woods, by all means make your own syrup. Nothing you buy will ever taste as good.

You will need, first of all, to locate the correct trees. There is the story of the enthusiast who waited in vain for the sap to run, only to find he had tapped beech trees.

You need simple tapping tools: a brace and bit, a hammer, a spout for the sap to flow through, and a bucket to hang on it. Bore the hole and insert the spout, usually of metal now, though wooden spouts were originally used. The spout should be heavy enough to hold the bucket when full but not so large as to require a hole that will kill the tree or render it useless for a further flow of sap. A hole two inches deep should be enough. Those who operate a sugar bush are very careful not to injure the trees.

Your bucket may be metal or wood. There is less danger of sap fermenting in a wooden bucket, but it is difficult to keep clean, which is most important. Also, a wooden bucket must be soaked to make it tight. In a metal bucket the sap may turn sour with a sudden rise in temperature; however, there is no danger of its leaking. In either case you must keep a lid on to keep out bugs, snow, and twigs.

The sap runs best after a frosty night, and will flow for five or six weeks. Tap your trees, hang out your buckets, and put your trust in Mother Nature.

To give syrup of superior flavor, the sap should be fresh and unfermented. Once collected, boil it down to the proper concentration. Commercially, it takes 40 gallons of sap to make one gallon of syrup.

The proper concentration may be determined in several ways. You may use a hydrometer to register the density of the syrup, which should be eleven pounds to the gallon. With experience, you can tell by the color and by the way the syrup bubbles up. It used to be tested by the way it "aproned" off a wooden paddle. It can be weighed. You can also do as we do: simply boil it down until by tasting and guessing you seem to get it right. If you have a fairly large quantity of sap, you might find it fun to hunt up one of the huge old iron kettles our ancestors used and boil your syrup out of doors over a wood fire. These are still used back in the country and might be picked up at a farm auction or a country antique store.

After boiling the syrup down, strain it through cheesecloth several times and clarify by adding an egg white and one half of a cup of milk per gallon of syrup. Bring to a boil; as coagulation takes place, the milk and egg white bring any particles that escaped the cheesecloth to the surface, leaving a clear product. Skim this off and you have a clear amber syrup. Pour it into hot sterilized jars.

Opened jars should be stored in the refrigerator. If mold forms on the top, skim it off, bring syrup to a boil, and replace in a sterilized jar.

Maple Cream

This delectable spread is made by boiling the sap to 232°. I then pour it directly on my kitchen table, which is topped with a marble slab, and after it has cooled somewhat (it should actually go down to 70°) I work it with a spatula, like fondant, until it becomes thick and creamy. It is then heated in the top of a double boiler until thin enough to pour into jars.

Spread it on hot buttered scones, or use on griddlecakes instead of syrup.

Maple Sugar

To make maple sugar, boil the sap longer than when making syrup. Actually the process is similar to making fudge. The sap is boiled to 237°, then cooled to 220°. I set it in a pan of cold water to cool, beat it until it begins to thicken and grain, then pour it into molds. It must be cooked over a slow fire and watched carefully so that it does not scorch.

Soft Maple Sugar

This is made by the same process except that it is cooked to 227° and cooled to 160°. Beat it until thick and creamy and pour into glasses. It will spread like thick honey, and I don't need to tell you how it tastes on hot buttered biscuits.

To Use Maple Syrup in Place of Sugar

In substituting maple syrup for sugar in a recipe, use 1 cup syrup for ½ cup sugar and reduce the liquid used by ¼ cup.

Maple Parfait

Serves 6 to 8

1 pint heavy cream, whipped   ¾ cup shaved maple sugar
1 quart coffee ice cream

Put a scoop of ice cream into each parfait glass. Spoon the cream on top and sprinkle with maple sugar. Repeat layers until glasses are filled.

Maple Icing

This uncooked icing uses maple syrup as the liquid.

2 cups confectioners' sugar   Few grains salt
2 tablespoons soft butter   Maple syrup

Combine sugar, salt, and butter in a bowl, mix well, and add enough maple syrup to bring the icing to the proper consistency for spreading.

Maple Syrup Frosting

We like this especially on spice cake or any kind of nut cake.

1 cup maple syrup   Pinch of salt
2 egg whites   Chopped nut meats

1. Boil the syrup to the soft ball stage, or 238° on your candy thermometer.

2. Beat the egg whites stiff, then slowly pour in the syrup, continuing to beat. Add the salt. Beat until frosting is thick enough to hold its shape.

3. Spread on a cold cake and sprinkle the top with nut meats.

Maple Meringues

Makes 8 to 10 Meringues

4 egg whites   1 teaspoon vanilla
Few grains salt   1 cup black walnut meats,
1 cup maple sugar, shaved   finely ground

1. Beat the egg whites and salt until the whites are frothy, slowly add the sugar, a tablespoon at a time, continuing to beat, add the vanilla, and fold in the nut meats.

2. Cover a cookie sheet with a sheet of paper and drop the mixture on it by the spoonful.

3. Bake in a 275° oven for 50 to 60 minutes, or until the meringues are slightly brown and dry to the touch. Remove from the paper immediately. You may make Meringues Glacées by shaping into large meringues before baking, then serving them with the centers filled with ice cream and maple syrup over them.

Maple Ice Box Pudding

Serves 6

½ cup maple sugar, shaved
½ cup brown sugar
⅓ cup butter
3 egg yolks
¾ cup maple syrup
1 teaspoon vanilla
2 dozen lady fingers

1. Cream the butter with the brown and maple sugars. Beat in the egg yolks, one at a time, then slowly stir in the syrup and the vanilla.
2. Line a loaf pan with wax paper and lady fingers. Cover with the maple mixture. Then add another layer of lady fingers and more maple mixture. Repeat in layers, ending with the lady fingers.
3. Refrigerate for 24 hours. Serve with maple syrup.

Baked Peaches

Serves 8

8 ripe peaches, peeled and
   halved
8 tablespoons maple syrup
Cherry brandy
Freshly grated nutmeg

1. Arrange peaches in a baking dish, hollow side up. Put 1 spoonful of maple syrup and a little cherry brandy in each hollow.
2. Bake for 15 minutes in a 375° oven.
3. Sprinkle with nutmeg and serve.

Maple Mousse

Serves 4

1 cup maple syrup
4 egg yolks
Few grains salt
1 pint heavy cream, whipped

1. Bring the syrup to a boil.
2. Beat the egg yolks until thick and lemon colored. Add the salt, then slowly pour in the hot syrup, beating all the time. Cool.
3. Fold in the cream.
4. Spoon the mousse into a refrigerator tray and freeze.

Snow Balls with Maple Sauce

Serves 6

6 scoops vanilla ice cream   1 cup maple syrup or Maple
1 cup grated fresh coconut   Sauce

Roll balls of ice cream in the coconut to resemble snowballs.
Serve with warm maple syrup.

CHAPTER 13

Relishes, Jams, and Jellies

Wild Berries

Wild berries have a flavor the cultivated ones seem to lack. Use them freely.

While wild fruits are small and may seem at first thought to be too much trouble to harvest, their flavor is so exceptional that it is most rewarding. And there is something special about gathering them yourself, while the hot sun permeates the air with their delightful fragrance, so that you enjoy in anticipation the delicious dishes you will create when you carry them back to your kitchen.

Blackberries

Growing by the roadside or along the hedgerows we find a wild blackberry which we used to call a thimbleberry. It is long and thin, the segments smaller than those of the ordinary blackberry. It has a rich sweet flavor and can be used in many ways.

Blueberries and Huckleberries

Actually these are not the same, though they are so similar their names are used interchangeably. In some places they are called billberries and whortleberries as well. Cultivated berries appear on the market, but we prefer the wild ones. The bushes grow in damp places along the edge of open woods, or in open dry places, depending upon the variety.

There is a wild black huckleberry which does not grow here and is said to be superior in flavor. Look for it in your locality.

Cranberries

There are two varieties of cranberries: the low or marsh cranberry, the one that grows in abundance on Cape Cod and is seen in our markets, and a wild high-bush cranberry (*Viburnum trilobum*) which produces a berry good for preserves and jellies. Avoid the very similar *Viburnum opulus* which produces bitter berries.

Elderberries

The rural resident needs no introduction to elderberries. They can be made into delicious pies, jelly, jam, chutney, or wine.

Wine may be made from the flowers, which may also be added to muffins for an unusual flavor.

The unopened flowers or green fruit can be pickled, the result being something like capers.

Juniper Berries

The Juniper is a low-growing evergreen bearing pale blue berries best known as an ingredient for gin. This shrub grows wild in dry rocky places and its berries may be gathered in the fall and used immediately or dried for future use.

We like to crush 4 or 5 berries in a little soft butter. We spread this in the cavity of a wild duck or other poultry and brush the rest on the breast of the fowl.

Or put 2 berries in the bottom of the roasting pan.

If you do not have this ground juniper (*Juniperus communis*) growing near you, the dried and bottled berries can be bought at any store where dried herbs are sold.

Mulberries

We have a mulberry tree which has been denounced as a menace by friends and family. The berries ripen over a long period and the tree is filled with birds and chipmunks for what seems like most of the summer. Woe betide anyone who chooses to leave a car or to sit underneath the tree.

However, we would not part with our mulberry in spite of the strong language sometimes used in connection with it, not only because of the birds it attracts but because of its unusual fruit.

Wild Fruits

Wild Cherries

There are wild cherries in abundance in some localities. There is the black or rum cherry (*Prunus serotina*) which makes the most delectable jelly and from which the famous "cherry bounce" was made. The choke cherry (*Prunus virginiana*) and the bird cherry, also called the fire cherry or the pin cherry (*Prunus pennsylvanica*) are both good for jelly making. Mix the juice of these cherries with apple or currant juice for a delicious flavor. The sand cherry (*Prunus pumila*) contains little pectin, so must be combined with apple juice to make it jell.

Follow the general directions for jelly starting on page 265.

The ground cherry is an interesting berry which makes very good preserves. It is a round, yellow berry with a papery husk, looking like a tiny lantern. It is sometimes called the husk tomato, and in some localities is cultivated and can be found on the market.

I have a friend in whose garden it thrives, coming up each year to wander happily among the beans and tomatoes. She keeps a dish at hand for nibbling.

Wild Grapes

Grapes thrive here on the sandy bank between the beach and the house. The vines fill several roles. The roots and tangled branches create a barrier against wind and waves, preventing the erosion which could take place in stormy weather.

They provide a safe nesting site for birds. Catbirds, warblers and veeries build under their sheltering tangle and can be seen darting in and out all summer.

The fruit of the wild grape is of exceptional flavor. It makes a delicious tart jelly and can be made into wine as well.

The Hawthorn

The hawthorn is a most decorative tree, the white blossoms heralding the coming of spring and the red berries beautiful in the fall. There are hundreds of varieties of hawthorn, I am told, and we have two growing in great abundance near by: the cockspur haw, with large berries resembling small crabapples that drop from the branches while the leaves are still on the bush; and the scarlet haw, having a profusion of small red berries in clusters that remain on the branches after the leaves have fallen. These provide a gorgeous spot of color against a drab field or fence and are a beautiful sight against the snow.

Both these berries yield an interesting jelly. You will need a lot of them, since they are seedy and rather dry—but the flavor is intriguing. Let me warn you that the beautiful scarlet color disappears—your jelly will be deep gold in color. If you like, you can add red coloring matter to give it a rich red color.

Wild Plums

The Indians introduced the colonists to this delicious fruit, which they ate raw, dried, and cooked.

If you have beach plums (*Prunus maritima*) near you, you are indeed fortunate. This plum with its purplish red fruit grows low and so can withstand heavy winds. A similar plum is the sweet red wild plum (*Prunus americana*), and they both make delicious jelly, jam, preserves, and pies. They can be dried as well.

Relishes

Cranberry Sauce

4 cups cranberries   1 cup water
2 cups sugar

Boil the sugar and water together for 5 minutes, add berries and simmer until the skins pop. Cool the sauce in the pan, then transfer to a serving bowl.

Candied Cranberries

1 quart cranberries, picked over,   1½ cups sugar
    washed and drained   ¼ cup water

1. Spread the berries in a shallow baking dish, shake sugar over them, and pour in water.
2. Bake in a 350° oven for 60 minutes.
3. Cool in the syrup. The berries will be beautifully glazed and practically transparent.

Cranberry Ice

This is delicious served in the old-fashioned way with the main course of a holiday dinner.

4 cups cranberries   Juice of 2 lemons
2 cups water   Grated rind of 1 orange
2 cups sugar   2 cups cold water

1. Cook cranberries in water until skins burst. Put them through a food press or sieve, add the sugar and stir to dissolve. Add lemon juice, grated orange rind and cold water.
2. Freeze in a refrigerator tray, stirring once or twice.

Plum Chutney—I

The English, as you know, are fond of curries, and English cookbooks are full of recipes for chutneys using all sorts of fruits and vegetables as a base. Here is one for plum chutney.

2 pounds plums, pitted   2 or 3 shallots, put through
1 pound apples, cored and   garlic press
    peeled   Piece of ginger root, chopped
2 lemons   2 cups vinegar

1. In a saucepan, combine plums and apples. Grate the rind of lemons and remove the white part underneath, and slice the lemons paper thin. Add to the fruit mixture, together with the shallots, ginger root, vinegar. Bring to a boil. Simmer the chutney until it is as thick as you like it.
2. Spoon into jars. Seal and store. For a spicier chutney, see below.

Plum Chutney—II

1 pound plums, pitted
1 pound tart apples, cored
and chopped
½ pound onions, peeled and
chopped
4 cups vinegar
2 cups sugar

2 tablespoons salt
1 teaspoon cinnamon
1 teaspoon allspice
1 teaspoon cloves
1 teaspoon ginger
1 pound seedless raisins

1. Combine plums, apples, and onions.
2. Boil the vinegar, sugar, salt, cinnamon, allspice, cloves, and ginger together, add the fruit mixture and raisins, and simmer until thick, stirring to prevent sticking.
3. Spoon into hot sterilized jars and seal with paraffin.

Wild Ginger (Asarum Canadense)

The root of this interesting plant may be used fresh or dried. In making a curry, the ginger root is indispensable. It is a milder root than that which one buys in the store so it may be used more freely.

If you find a patch of heart-shaped, rather fuzzy leaves on long stems, you have probably found wild ginger. It flowers in May, but the insignificant blossom hides close to the earth and you will have to push the dead leaves aside to find it. Most books on wild flowers or edible plants will have a picture to guide you in its identification.

Ginger Apple Relish

2 pounds wild apples or wild
crab apples, peeled and
cored
Piece of wild ginger root
1 lemon, rind and juice

1 pound brown sugar
1 pinch salt
1 cup water

1. In a kettle combine apples, ginger root, lemon, sugar, and salt. Pour in water and simmer until apples are soft. You may

need to add more water as the mixture cooks, watching carefully so that apples do not scorch.

2. When the relish is as thick as you want it, spoon into hot sterilized jars and seal with paraffin.

Cranberry Relish—I

Serve with game birds.

2 cups cranberries	1 lime, seeded
1 orange	1 cup sugar

Grind the cranberries, orange and lime. Add sugar and mix well. Chill.

Cranberry Relish—II

1 pound cranberries	1 cup black walnut meats
2½ cups sugar	1 cup wild plum jam
2 tablespoons butter	Lemon juice, optional

1. Combine cranberries and sugar, put in a baking dish and cook in a 350° oven for 1 hour. Cool.

2. Melt the butter and sauté the nut meats for a few minutes.

3. Combine nuts and wild plum jam. When cold, combine with cranberries. If you want an especially tart relish, add a little lemon juice to this.

Grape Chutney

1 quart grapes, washed and drained	2 tablespoons salt
	2 cups cider vinegar
1 quart sliced apples	1 cup brown sugar
1 clove garlic, crushed	½ cup chopped blanched
1 tablespoon preserved ginger	almonds
1 tablespoon horseradish	½ cup seedless raisins

1. In a kettle, combine grapes and apples, and cook with a little water until the fruit is soft. Put through a sieve to remove seeds.

2. Cook again with other ingredients added, simmering for 1 hour, or until thick.

3. Pour into hot, sterilized jars and seal with paraffin.

Elderberry Catsup

This is a perfect accompaniment for venison or, in fact, any game.

2 quarts elderberries
Vinegar to cover
1 cup sugar
1 teaspoon cinnamon

1 tablespoon allspice
1 tablespoon cloves
¼ teaspoon cayenne pepper

1. Cook the elderberries in vinegar until the berries burst. Put through a food press or sieve, add sugar, cinnamon, allspice, cloves, and pepper. Simmer until thick.

2. Pour into sterilized jars and seal.

Elderberry Chutney

2 pounds elderberries, washed
    and drained
1 large onion, sliced
2 cups cider vinegar

1 teaspoon salt
2 teaspoons sugar
1 teaspoon ground ginger
1 pinch cayenne

1. In a kettle combine the elderberries with other ingredients and simmer until thick, stirring to prevent scorching.

2. Spoon into hot sterilized jars and seal with paraffin.

Pickles

Pickled Cherries

An interesting old recipe for pickled cherries which you might like to try.

2½ pounds cherries, stems
    removed
1 pound sugar
1 or 2 cinnamon sticks

6 or 8 cloves
2 or 3 blades of mace
Vinegar, about 2 cups

1. Place cherries in a crockery or glass container, cover with sugar and add cinnamon, cloves, and mace. Cover with vinegar. Let cherries stand, covered, at room temperature for a few days.

2. Remove the spices, place cherries in jars, and store.

Pickled Nasturtium Seeds

These little seeds are good in a martini or a salad. Use them instead of capers in a sauce to be served with lamb or fish. Pick the seeds when fully developed but before they become hard.

1 cup nasturtium seeds White wine vinegar
¼ cup salt

1. Make a brine of salt and enough water to cover the seeds. Let them soak overnight.
2. Drain and put seeds in jars. Cover with boiling vinegar and seal.

Preserves, Conserves, Dried Fruits

Marrons

These may be used in Nesselrode Sauce for ice cream.

2½ pounds prepared chestnuts 1 pound sugar
  (see pages 152-153) 3 cups water

1. Cook the chestnuts in boiling water until tender. Drain.
2. Prepare a syrup of the sugar and water, bring to a boil, and boil for 1 minute. Add the chestnuts, bring to a boil again, and bottle.
3. If you are not planning to use these fairly soon, spoon the chestnuts into hot sterilized jars, fill with the boiling syrup, and seal.

Cranberry Conserve

4 cups cranberries 2 cups black walnut meats,
1½ cups water   chopped
1 unpeeled orange, chopped 3 cups sugar
1 cup seedless raisins

1. Cook the cranberries in water until the skins burst. Add the orange, raisins, nut meats, and sugar, and simmer for 25 minutes, or until it has reached the desired thickness, stirring often.
2. Spoon into hot, sterilized jars and seal with paraffin.

Huckleberry Preserves

2 cups sugar
2 cups water
½ lemon, sliced

2 cloves
2 quarts huckleberries, washed
    and drained

1. Combine sugar, water, cloves, and lemon and boil for 5 minutes. Add the berries, bring to a boil again and boil for another 5 minutes.

2. Pour into hot, sterilized glasses and seal with paraffin.

Beach Plum Butter

4 pounds of beach plums,
    washed and pitted
Water
2 cups sugar

1 teaspoon cinnamon
1 teaspoon ground cloves
½ teaspoon allspice
1 lemon, rind and juice

1. In a kettle, crush the plums to make the juice run. As they are apt to be dry, you will need some water in which to cook them, but add as little as possible. Cook slowly until very soft, then sieve or put through the blender or a food mill.

2. Measure the pulp. Add ½ cup of sugar to each cup of pulp. Add the spices and lemon. Cook to the desired thickness, stirring often to prevent burning.

3. Pour into hot, sterilized glasses and seal with hot paraffin.

Candied Plums

1 pound sugar
½ cup water

3 pounds beach plums, cut into
    halves and pitted

1. Make a syrup of the sugar and water, add the plums a few at a time, and simmer for 15 minutes. As each batch cooks, place them on a platter and put a few more into the syrup. Continue until all are cooked.

2. Boil the syrup until very thick, pour over the plums, and put in the sun to dry.

3. When quite dry, shake sugar over them and pack in jars, with more sugar between the layers.

Dried Wild Plums

These are a great treat for nibbling, or can be used in cakes, cookies, and puddings.

Plums, washed   Boiling water

1. Cover the plums with boiling water and let stand for 20 minutes. Drain.

2. Spread the fruit on wire screening and place in the sun to dry. (It will have to be protected from insects. I use those little umbrellas of mosquito netting made to keep the flies out of the hors d'oeuvres when served out of doors.)

3. When quite dry, pack loosely in jars.

Dried Blueberries

In the old days blueberries were dried in the sun and used in muffins and cake as one would use currants.

Wild Strawberry Preserves—I

First of all, let me say that you may wash your wild strawberries if you feel you must, but they are such delicate little things that I hesitate to do anything that might take away the slightest bit of their juicy sweetness. Since they mature in the fresh air and sunshine and go right from the fields to your kitchen, I see no reason to pour water over them.

1 pound hulled wild   1 cup sugar
    strawberries

1. Using the above proportions, arrange the berries in layers with the sugar and allow to stand overnight.

2. Taking a small amount at a time, not more than 4 cupfuls, cook over a slow fire until they come to a boil, watching carefully so that they do not stick. Allow 15 minutes for cooking, then transfer to a glass bowl or crock. Repeat with another batch.

3. Let the cooked berries stand for 2 days, stirring occasionally.

4. Spoon the preserve into sterilized jelly glasses and seal with paraffin.

Wild Strawberry Preserves—II

This is the well-known "sunshine" method. It is thought to preserve the natural flavor better than any other method.

Wild strawberries, hulled   Sugar

1. Put berries in a kettle in layers with sugar, using cup for cup. Let stand for 30 minutes.
2. Place the kettle over a low fire and slowly bring to a boil. Boil for 12 minutes.
3. Spread the preserve very thin on large shallow platters, cover with glass, and place in the sun. (The glass should not touch the preserve but be just above it.) Stir the preserve once or twice a day. In 2 or 3 days the juice will have jelled.
5. Spoon into sterilized jelly glasses and seal with paraffin.

Rose Conserve

Pick roses that are full blown but not faded. Pull off the petals and place in a jar in layers, adding sugar. You can keep filling the jar as the roses bloom. Keep the jar covered.

My old cookbook does not give the amounts to use but assures the reader that it is "a very nice article to put into cakes and puddings." Try adding some orange peel and a few rosemary leaves.

Wild Plum Compote

This is delicious served with game. You may also serve it with sour cream as a dessert.

1 quart plums, pitted   Rind of ½ a lemon
½ cup light seedless raisins   Water
½ stick cinnamon   ½ cup claret
2 cloves

1. Put the plums in a saucepan and press to start the juice running. Add the raisins, cinnamon, cloves, lemon rind, and enough water to keep it from sticking. Simmer for ½ hour, stirring as necessary. Add the claret. Cool. Remove cinnamon stick and cloves.
2. Serve at once, or spoon into sterilized jars and seal with paraffin.

Strawberry Tutti-Frutti

This is an old-fashioned conserve, easy to make and delicious to eat.

2 quarts wild strawberries
2 cups sugar
1 tablespoon grated orange
    rind
Whole spices to taste—cloves,
    cinnamon, allspice

1 quart brandy
Fruits in season
Sugar

1. Start with the strawberries, sugar, orange rind, spices, and brandy. Combine in a large crock with a cover.

2. As each variety ripens, keep adding fruit and sugar in equal amounts. Cherries, hunks of fresh pineapple, peeled and sliced peaches and apricots, are all good. We find raspberries too seedy although the flavor is good. Stir often. Let stand for 2 or 3 months. Remove the spices.

3. Spoon into sterilized jars and seal. Serve over ice cream.

Jellies

General Directions for Making Jelly

Cooking: Crush the fruit and boil with as little water as possible. In the case of many wild fruits which are not juicy, quite a lot of water will be needed. However, that does not seem to affect the flavor.

Boil the fruit and water for 20 to 30 minutes, strain through a jelly bag, and measure carefully.

Add an equal amount of sugar, cup for cup, and boil for 5 minutes. Test for jelly.

Testing: This is done by pouring the liquid from the side of the spoon. If it shores off in 2 drops which come together into 1 drop, the jelly is ready to go into glasses, which should be hot and sterilized. The jelly should be skimmed first.

Another test is to use a candy thermometer. 220° is the jellying point.

Continued on next page

If your fruit does not contain enough pectin, the juice may be combined with apple juice; or liquid or granulated pectin may be added, following the directions provided by the manufacturer.

Sealing: The jelly may be vacuum sealed if you are using that kind of jar, or the glasses may be sealed with paraffin.

Melt the paraffin over hot water and pour a thin layer on the jelly. Turn each glass around, tipping slightly, so that the seal is perfect all around the edges. When the first layer of paraffin sets, pour another over it.

Cover the jelly glasses and store in a cool dark place.

Apple Jelly

Wild apples or crab apples,   Water
    cut up, stem and blossom   Sugar
    ends removed

1. Cover the apples with water and simmer until soft. Strain through a jelly bag and measure the juice.
2. To each cup of juice add ¾ cup of sugar. Boil until the liquid tests for jelly (see page 265).
3. Pour into hot jelly glasses and seal with hot paraffin.

Blueberry and Apple Jelly

2 quarts blueberries, crushed   3 cups water
½ cup water   7 cups sugar
3 pounds tart apples, cut up   1 box pectin crystals

1. Blueberries combined with apples make an interesting jelly. Make it as follows: simmer the berries with ½ cup water for 10 minutes. Place in a jelly bag, drain, and squeeze out the juice.
2. Simmer the apples with 3 cups of water for 20 minutes. Mash apples while cooking, then drain in a jelly bag and squeeze the juice out.
3. Combine and measure the juice of both fruits—it should make 7 cups. Add the pectin crystals. Bring to a rolling boil, add the sugar, and again bring to a rolling boil. Boil for 1 minute. Remove kettle from the fire and skim the jelly.
4. Pour into hot, sterilized glasses, and seal with paraffin.

Basil Jelly—I

1 cup basil leaves packed
   tightly
2 tablespoons vinegar
2 cups water

Green coloring
1½ cups sugar
½ box pectin crystals

1. Boil the basil leaves, vinegar, and water for 2 minutes. Strain out the leaves and add a few drops of green coloring.
2. Stir in the sugar and pectin and again bring the jelly to a boil. Keep at a rolling boil for 1 minute.
3. Put a basil leaf in the bottom of each hot sterilized glass and pour the hot jelly on top. Seal with paraffin.

Basil Jelly—II

Basil leaves, 3 per glass   Hot apple jelly

1. Place 2 basil leaves in the bottom of each jelly glass. Pour on the jelly and place 1 leaf on top.
2. Seal with paraffin.

Wild Crab Apple Jelly

These little apples, which actually belong to the Rose family, make a most delicious jelly and are well worth the trouble. They may be combined with any other kind of fruit.

5 pounds crab apples, cut up
10 cups water

1 box pectin crystals
4 pounds sugar

1. In a kettle, combine apples and water and simmer for 15 minutes or until apples are soft enough to mash.
2. Put them in a jelly bag. Strain, measure the juice—you should have 7 cups. If there is not enough, add a little water to the jelly bag and squeeze.
3. Return the juice to the kettle, add the pectin, stirring constantly, and cook until the juice boils. Stir in the sugar, bring to a rolling boil, and boil for 1 minute. Skim the jelly.
4. Pour into hot sterilized glasses and seal with paraffin.

Blackberry Jelly

3 quarts wild blackberries,   1 box pectin crystals
   washed   5 cups sugar

1. Put berries in a kettle and mash thoroughly so that the juice runs freely. Strain through a jelly bag and squeeze out all the juice you can. Measure it. If you do not have 3½ cups of juice, pour water through the bag and squeeze again.

2. Return the juice to the kettle, add the pectin crystals and bring to a rolling boil. Stir in the sugar and again bring to a rolling boil. Boil for 1 minute. Skim.

3. Pour into hot, sterilized glasses and seal with paraffin.

Barberry Jelly

A delicious tart jelly to serve with game.

8 cups wild barberries   6 cups water
8 tart apples   Sugar
3 oranges, juice and rind

1. Pick over and wash the barberries. Set to drain. Wash and cut up the apples, removing the stem and blossom ends. Combine in a kettle with the water and oranges.

2. Simmer until berries are very soft. Put to drain in a jelly bag.

3. Measure the juice and add ¾ cup sugar per cup of juice. Bring the juice to a boil, stir in the sugar, and cook until it tests for jelly.

4. Pour into hot sterilized glasses and seal with hot paraffin.

Cranberry-Grape Jelly

1 cup cranberry juice   1 cup wild crabapple juice
2 cups wild grape juice   2¼ cups sugar

1. For extracting the juices, see general directions (page 265).

2. In a saucepan combine the juices and boil for 5 minutes. Stir in the sugar and continue to boil until mixture jells. (See page 265 for general directions for jelly.)

3. Pour jelly into hot sterilized glasses and seal at once with paraffin.

Blackberry Wine Jelly

This is especially good with wild duck and wild rice.

7 cups sugar   2 bottles liquid pectin
1 quart blackberry wine

1. Simmer the sugar in the wine until dissolved, then bring to a full boil. Add the pectin, stirring as you pour, and again bring the liquid to a rolling boil. Boil for 1 minute.
2. Pour the jelly into hot, sterilized glasses and seal with paraffin.

Cherry Jelly

If you are fortunate enough to have a supply of black cherries or rum cherries, you can make them into a most delicious jelly.

3 pounds cherries, stems   1 box pectin crystals
  removed   4½ cups sugar
½ cup water

1. Crush the cherries, add the water and simmer for 10 minutes. Strain through a jelly bag and squeeze out the juice. Measure it —you should have 3½ cups of juice.
2. Add the pectin crystals, bring to a hard boil, and add the sugar. Again bring to a boil and boil for 1 minute. Remove the kettle from the fire and skim the jelly.
3. Pour into hot, sterilized glasses. Seal with paraffin.

Spiced Wild Crab Apple Jelly

10 cups crab apples, cut up   6 sticks cinnamon
2 cups water   36 whole cloves
2 cups cider vinegar   Sugar

1. In a kettle, combine the crab apples, water, vinegar, and the spices tied in a bag. Simmer until fruit is very soft, remove the spices, and strain through a jelly bag. Measure the juice and return to the kettle.
2. Add ¾ cup sugar per cup of juice and boil until mixture tests for jelly (see page 265). Skim.
3. Pour into hot, sterilized glasses and seal with paraffin.

Elderberry-Apple Jelly

4 cups elderberry juice   6 cups sugar
4 cups apple juice

1. Extract the juice from the elderberries and apples (see page 266, apple jelly).
2. Add the sugar and proceed according to general directions for jelly (starting on page 265).
3. Pour into hot, sterilized jelly glasses and seal with paraffin.

Elderberry Jelly

This is delicious served with biscuits for tea or with toast for breakfast. It is wonderful with game, too.

2 quarts elderberries, hulled   1 box pectin crystals
2 cups water   5 cups sugar

1. In a saucepan, simmer the elderberries and water until berries are soft. Strain through a jelly bag and measure the juice. If you do not have 3½ cups, add a little water to the bag and squeeze again to make up the difference. Return to saucepan.
2. Add pectin crystals to the juice and bring to a boil. Stir in the sugar, bring to a full rolling boil, and boil hard for 1 minute.
3. Remove from the fire, skim, and pour into hot, sterilized jelly glasses. Seal with paraffin.

Rose Hip Jelly

This is an old fashioned favorite, the recipe for which can be found in old cookbooks.

4 cups rose hips   2 pounds sugar

1. Prepare the rose hips by removing the outer covering.
2. Add just enough water to cover and bring them to a boil. Add the sugar and simmer until fruit is soft. Strain. Return to kettle.
3. Bring the juice to a boil again and test for jelly (see page 265). If not ready, boil a little longer.
4. Pour into hot, sterilized jelly glasses and seal with paraffin.

Hawthorn Jelly

Hawthorn berries   Pectin crystals
Sugar

1. In a kettle, with enough water to cover, simmer the berries until they crush easily. This will take quite some time, and they must be watched to prevent scorching. If needed, add more water as they cook.

2. Place the cooked berries in a jelly bag, drain and squeeze. If the mass seems to have cooked down until too thick and pulpy, pour a little boiling water over the jelly bag, and squeeze again. Measure the juice.

3. For each cup of juice, allow 1¼ cup of sugar and 2½ tablespoons pectin crystals.

4. Following the directions given with the pectin, mix the crystals with the juice and bring to a hard boil. Stir in the sugar, and bring to a full rolling boil, continuing for 1 minute, stirring constantly.

5. Skim the foam, pour the jelly into jelly glasses, and seal with paraffin.

Wild Plum Jelly

This is a perfect accompaniment for venison, wild duck, or in fact, any game.

5 pounds plums, washed and   1 box pectin crystals
    crushed   7½ cups sugar
1½ cups water

1. Put the plums and water in a kettle and simmer for 10 minutes, or until the juice runs freely. Drain the fruit in a jelly bag and squeeze out all the juice possible—you should have 5½ cups. If there is not enough, add water to make up this amount. Return to kettle.

2. Add the box of pectin crystals, mix well and bring to a full boil. Stir in sugar and again bring to a boil. Boil for 1 minute.

3. Remove the kettle from the fire, skim jelly if necessary, and pour into hot glasses. Seal with paraffin.

Elderberry Wine Jelly

2¼ cups elderberry wine
3 tablespoons plain gelatin
¼ cup sugar
1 lemon, juice and grated rind

1 orange, juice and grated rind
Few grains salt
¼ teaspoon coriander seeds,
    crushed
2 eggs, whites and shells

1. Soften the gelatin in ¼ cup of the wine.
2. In a saucepan, combine the rest of the wine, sugar, lemon and orange, salt, coriander seeds, egg whites, and egg shells. Simmer for 10 minutes and strain. Pour the hot wine mixture over the gelatin, and stir to dissolve.
3. Pour the jelly into a wet mold. Serve with game.

Grape Jelly with Lime or Mint

This is delicious with venison or any game.

3 cups wild grape juice
2 cups sugar

¼ cup lime juice or a bunch of
    fresh mint

1. Extract the grape juice as for jelly (see page 265).
2. Measure, combine with the sugar and lime juice or mint (which has been boiled in sugar 10 minutes and mint leaves removed) and cook until it tests for jelly (see page 265).
3. Pour into hot, sterilized glasses. Seal with paraffin.

Rose Petal Jelly

4 cups fragrant rose petals
3¼ cups boiling water
3 cups sugar

1 tablespoon lemon juice
1 box pectin crystals
1 teaspoon rose flavoring

1. Place the rose petals in a bowl and cover with the water. Let stand for 20 minutes, no longer, or they will become bitter.
2. Strain the juice into a saucepan and add the sugar and lemon juice. Bring it to a rolling boil, add the pectin and rose flavoring, and again bring to a rolling boil. Boil for 1 minute more. Skim. For a pinker jelly, add a drop or two of food coloring.
3. Pour into hot, sterilized glasses and seal with paraffin.

Wild Rose Jelly

This is a delicious, delicate jelly made from wild rose petals. If you have the patience to collect them, you will be well rewarded. You may also use garden roses for this, or use some of each, though the flavor will be a little different.

The juice of wild strawberries, used instead of the cultivated ones, is delightful in this recipe. If you like a pinker jelly, add a drop or two of food coloring.

1 quart rose petals
4 cups water
½ cup strained wild (or cultivated) strawberry juice

3½ pounds sugar
1 cup liquid pectin

1. Measure the rose petals, cover with water, bring to a boil, and boil for 15 minutes.

2. Strain through a jelly bag, add the strawberry juice, and measure the liquid. If you do not have 1 quart, add enough water to make up the difference. Return to kettle.

3. Stir in the sugar and bring to a boil. Still stirring, pour in the pectin and boil for 1 minute more.

4. Pour into jelly glasses and seal with paraffin.

Rose Geranium Jelly

Serve with chicken, pork, or turkey. This is a very delicately flavored jelly. If you like, you may tint it with food coloring used very sparingly.

Hot apple jelly

1 rose geranium leaf per glass

Place a geranium leaf in the bottom of each jelly glass. Pour in the jelly. Seal with paraffin.

Mulberry Jelly

1 quart ripe mulberries   2 cups water
1 quart unripe mulberries   Sugar

1. In a saucepan, combine the berries and water, and simmer until berries are soft. Strain through cheesecloth and measure the juice. Add an equal amount of sugar, bring to a boil, and continue boiling for 4 minutes. Test for jelly (see page 265).

2. Pour into hot, sterilized jelly glasses and seal with paraffin.

Plum Apple Jelly

Plum juice   Sugar
Wild apple or crab apple juice

1. Extract juice from fruit according to directions on page 265.

2. Use ¼ cup plum juice to ¾ cup of apple juice; use 1 cup sugar to 1 cup combined juices.

3. Follow the general directions for jelly (see pages 265-266).

Thyme Jelly

½ cup thyme leaves   Green coloring
1¼ cups water   2 cups sugar
½ lemon, sliced   ½ bottle pectin
¼ cup dandelion wine

1. Simmer the thyme, water, lemon, and wine for 10 minutes. Remove from heat and let stand for another 10 to 15 minutes. Strain. Add green coloring and pectin, bring to a hard boil, add the sugar, and boil at a rolling boil for 1 minute.

2. Pour into hot, sterilized jelly glasses and seal with paraffin.

Jams

Blackberry-Apple Jam

As some of the wild blackberries are not very juicy, a blackberry-apple jam might be a suitable product to make.

2 pounds blackberries, washed   3 pounds sugar
2 pounds tart apples, sliced
    and drained

1. Combine the blackberries and apples, place in a covered casserole, and bake in a 350° oven for 1 hour, or until fruit is soft.
2. Transfer to a saucepan, add the sugar, and boil for 20 minutes, stirring while it cooks.
3. Spoon into hot, sterilized jars and seal with paraffin.

Mulberry Jam

5 pounds mulberries   5 pounds sugar

1. Simmer berries and sugar until berries are soft and jam thick, watching carefully so that it does not stick—you may have to add a little water at the start.
2. Spoon the jam into hot, sterilized jars and seal with paraffin. You may rub the jam through a sieve while still hot. This reduces the quantity somewhat but makes it more pleasant to eat if you object to the seeds.

Wild Cherry Jam

1½ pounds cherries, pitted and   1 cup water
    chopped, about 4 cups   5 cups sugar

1. Return a few pits to fruit to add to the flavor.
2. Bring the water and sugar to a boil, continue to boil for 5 minutes, add the cherries and pits, and boil for about 1 hour or until jam is thick, skimming when necessary. (If you prefer to use pectin, follow directions on the label.) Remove the pits.
3. Pour the jam into hot, sterilized glasses and seal with paraffin.

Seedless Elderberry Jam

This jam has a delightful flavor and is perfect with game.

4 pounds elderberries   Juice of 3 lemons
4 pounds sugar   Rind of 1 lemon
Water

1. In a kettle, mash the elderberries and bring to a boil over a slow fire, adding a little water if necessary. Add 1 pound of sugar and simmer until berries are soft. Add water as needed to keep it from sticking.

2. Strain the berries to remove the seeds, add the grated rind, or zest, of 1 lemon and the juice of all; the rest of the sugar, and cook for about 30 minutes, stirring and skimming frequently. When jam has reached the desired thickness, remove from the fire.

3. Pour into hot, sterilized glasses and seal at once with paraffin.

Rose Petal Jam—I

Here is a combination of two recipes. I used one from a cookbook of my grandmother's day and one from a modern Turkish cookbook, neither of which alone suited me exactly. By using the best features of both I worked out this method of making jam.

While rose petal jam is very popular in Turkey and Syria, we seldom find it in this part of the world today. In the days when old-fashioned roses flourished in every garden and housewives used what was at hand, rose petals were used in many interesting ways.

You will find this jam delicate in flavor, tasting faintly of honey. If wild roses are used, the jam will be a pale pink. The addition of deep red roses from your garden will give it a rich red color.

2 cups rose petals   2 cups water
½ lemon, peeled   2 cups sugar

1. Wash the rose petals and drain them. Cut off the white part from the end of each petal, then cut the rest up fine with scissors. If you have a blender, run the petals through it for just a second or two and you will find them perfectly chopped.

2. Slice the lemon very thin, remove the seeds, cover with water and simmer until tender, about 4 or 5 minutes. Drain.

3. Boil the sugar and water for 10 minutes, add the lemon and rose petals, and simmer for about 30 minutes, or until syrup reaches the jelly stage, 220° on your candy thermometer.

4. Spoon the jam into hot, sterilized jelly glasses and seal with paraffin.

Rose Petal Jam—II

This recipe calls for a pound of rose petals, quite a lot to have at one time. You may need to cut it down to the amount of petals available.

1 pound rose petals, prepared   1½ cups water
   as above   3½ pounds sugar

1. Combine half of the petals and the water in a saucepan and boil for a minute or two. Strain, rubbing the petals against the side of the sieve to extract all the flavor possible.

2. Return the remaining petals to the juice, add the sugar and boil until syrup is thick.

3. Pour the jam into hot, sterilized glasses and seal with paraffin.

Chestnut Jam

This recipe comes from Algeria. You will find it unusual and delicious.

2 pounds chestnuts, shelled and   6 tablespoons orange flower
   boiled (see pages 152-153).   water (obtainable in a drug
2 pounds sugar   store)
                      ½ teaspoon vanilla

1. Chop the boiled chestnuts fairly fine and place in a saucepan.

2. Add sugar and orange flower water and cook until thick, stirring to prevent scorching. Add the vanilla.

3. Spoon into hot, sterilized jelly glasses and seal with paraffin.

Wild Plum Jam

This jam may be varied by adding orange rind and nut meats. (A quart of plums equals about 1½ pounds in weight.)

3 pounds wild plums, pitted   3 pounds sugar

1. Put the plums in a kettle with half the sugar and let stand for 24 hours.
2. Add the rest of the sugar and simmer gently until jam is thick, watching and stirring frequently so that it does not stick.
3. Spoon jam into hot, sterilized jars and seal with paraffin.

Blackberry and Beach Plum Jam

1 cup blackberries   1 cup beach plums, pitted
½ cup blackberry juice   1½ cup sugar

1. Allow enough blackberries to extract ½ cup juice (see page 265) and have 1 cup of fruit left over.
2. Simmer berries, plums, blackberry juice and sugar until the jam has reached the desired thickness.
3. Spoon into hot, sterilized jars and seal with paraffin.

Wild Strawberry Jam

Try adding a few fragrant wild rose petals to this jam.

4 cups wild strawberries,   ½ lemon, sliced paper thin
    hulled
4 cups sugar

1. Place berries in a kettle with the sugar and lemon, and simmer over low heat, stirring gently, until berries are juicy and the sugar is dissolved. Bring to a boil. Continue to boil for 8 minutes, then let stand for 1 minute and skim.
2. Pour the jam into hot, sterilized glasses and seal with paraffin.

THIS AND THAT

Canned Blueberries

This is a way of canning blueberries without sugar for pies and puddings.

Blueberries

1. Pack hot, sterilized jars with the blueberries so that they come to within ½ inch of the top of the jars. Tap and shake them down so that they are as tight as possible.

2. Put the tops on jars and process them in a hot water bath for 40 minutes. In the winter you can open a jar and make your pie, sweetening it as usual, and you will find it as delicious as the pies you made last summer from fresh berries.

Rose Honey

This is a simple way to add a delicate flavor to the ordinary honey that you find on the grocery shelf.

Honey   Petals of fragrant rose

1. Warm the honey but do not boil. Crush the rose petals and add them. Allow to stand for several days.

2. Remove rose petals and put the honey back into its jar.

Rose Petal Syrup

This is a delightful syrup that has many uses. For something different, try it in frozen desserts, cakes, and confections.

2 quarts rose petals   3¾ pounds rock candy
2½ quarts boiling water

1. Pour boiling water over rose petals and let stand for 12 hours. Strain through a jelly bag, squeezing to extract every bit of flavor.

2. Add the rock candy to the juice. (This old-fashioned sweet is still available at some confectioners.) Heat slowly until candy is dissolved. Cover the dish and allow to cool.

3. Pour syrup into bottles, cork and store in the dark.

Frozen Strawberries—I

Wild strawberries   Sugar

1. Wash strawberries in cold water if necessary, then hull them.
2. Put them in freezer cartons, adding 2 tablespoons of sugar per pint carton.
3. Place in the freezer immediately.

Frozen Strawberries—II

Allow 1 cup of syrup to 1 quart of fruit.

Wild strawberries   4 cups water
3 cups sugar

1. Prepare the wild strawberries for freezing as directed above.
2. Make a syrup using the sugar and water, cool, and chill in refrigerator.
3. Pour ¼ cup of ice-cold syrup into a pint freezer carton. Fill the carton with berries to within 1 inch of the top—you may need to add a little more syrup to cover the berries. A piece of crumpled parchment paper will keep the berries under the syrup. Put on the cover.
4. Place strawberries in the freezer immediately.

Wild Strawberry Glaze

Use this glaze on tarts or pastry of any kind. If you have any left over, it can be stored and later melted in the top of a double boiler until it is thin enough to spread.

1 cup wild strawberries,   2 apples, peeled, cored and
    hulled   cut up fine
1 cup water   Red coloring
1 cup sugar

1. In a saucepan, combine the berries, apples, water, and sugar. Cook over a low fire until the mixture jells, or until your jelly thermometer registers 220°.
2. Strain the fruit and add some red coloring if you wish.

Wild Strawberry Leather

This makes delicious nibbling and can also be melted for a glaze to use on tarts or a ham.

2 pounds strawberries, hulled   Powdered sugar
1 cup sugar

1. In a saucepan, simmer the berries and sugar over very low heat, stirring and mashing the fruit as it cooks until it is as thick as you can get it.
2. Spread on a flat dish and place in the sun to dry.
3. Sprinkle with powdered sugar, cut into squares and store it.

Strawberry Syrup

This comes from an old cookbook and is recommended for "flavoring and coloring." Try it in cakes and icings, puddings and frozen desserts.

2 quarts ripe wild strawberries   4 pounds sugar
2 quarts water   Red food coloring
1 ounce tartaric acid

1. Cover the strawberries with water, in which tartaric acid has been dissolved. Let stand overnight.
2. Strain the juice through cheesecloth and measure it. Add sugar, using cup for cup and boil for 10 minutes, skimming frequently. If you wish, add a few drops of red food coloring. Pour the juice into bottles and store.

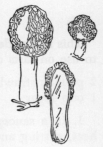

CHAPTER 14

Breads and Fritters

The use of native plants in imaginative ways goes far back in history. The Egyptians made bread from the heart of the lotus plant. The Indians ground their corn to make maize bread, then tried adding dried huckleberries and found it good. The early colonists followed their example and, using the wild ingredients growing around them, created biscuits and muffins, fritters, and tarts, all bursting with old-fashioned goodness.

Morel Tarts

8 *tarts*

If you are unable to get the morels, use any mushrooms. Serve the tarts as a luncheon dish, or as an accompaniment to the main dinner course.

Rich pastry (see page 214)
2 cups morels, sliced
2 tablespoons butter
2 tablespoons flour
1 cup light cream

Salt and freshly ground pepper
Freshly grated nutmeg
1 tablespoon sherry
Minced parsley

1. Line tart shells with the pastry and bake at 450° for 10 minutes.

2. In a skillet, sauté the mushrooms in the butter for about 5 minutes, or until tender. Remove and set them aside. Stir in the flour, cook a minute or two, then add the cream, seasonings, and sherry. When well blended, return the mushrooms to the skillet and heat thoroughly.

3. Spoon into the tart shells and sprinkle with the parsley.

Parsley Dumplings

10 to 12 dumplings

Serve these with muskrat or rabbit stew.

1 cup flour	2 teaspoons minced parsley
1 teaspoon baking powder	1 teaspoon grated onion
¼ teaspoon salt	½ cup milk

1. Sift the flour, baking powder and salt. Add the parsley and onion. Add milk and mix lightly. The dough should be soft.
2. Drop by spoonfuls into boiling salted water.
3. Boil, covered, for 15 minutes, resisting the temptation to peek under the lid.
4. Arrange dumplings around the stew in the serving dish and sprinkle more minced parsley over them.

Rose Fritters

Fresh, fragrant rose petals	½ teaspoon salt
Brandy	½ cup milk
1 egg	Powdered sugar
¾ cup flour	

1. Dip the rose petals in brandy, then in a batter made with the egg, flour, salt, and milk.
2. Fry in deep fat at 375° for one minute. Drain and dust with powdered sugar.

Plum Coffee Cake

4 cups pitted wild plums, drained	2 tablespoons melted butter
	¾ cup milk
2 cups biscuit mix	1 cup sugar
2 tablespoons sugar	½ cup melted butter
1 egg	

1. In a bowl, combine the biscuit mix, sugar, egg, butter, and milk. Beat well. Spread in a buttered 9-inch-square baking tin and arrange the plums on top. Shake the sugar over the fruit and pour the melted butter on top.
2. Bake in a 350° oven for 30 minutes.

Blueberry Fritters

12 fritters

1 cup blueberries
1 cup flour
1 teaspoon baking powder
2 tablespoons sugar

½ teaspoon salt
2 eggs, beaten with
2 teaspoons water

1. Sift together flour, baking powder, sugar, and salt. Add the eggs and water, stirring lightly into the dry ingredients. Add the blueberries. Stir gently to mix.

2. Drop by spoonfuls into fat heated to 360°, and cook until browned, or from 3 to 5 minutes. Drain on brown paper or paper towels.

3. Serve fritters piping hot with some of your home-made maple syrup.

Elderflower Fritters

Elderflowers, washed and
   drained
2 eggs, well beaten
½ cup flour
¾ teaspoon salt

¼ teaspoon freshly ground
   pepper
1 teaspoon melted butter
1 tablespoon brandy
Powdered sugar

1. Make a batter of the eggs, flour, salt, pepper, butter, and brandy. Beat well.

2. Dip flowers in the batter and fry in deep fat at 355° until crisp and brown. Drain on paper towels.

3. Sprinkle with powdered sugar and serve hot.

Beach Plum Fritters

12 fritters

12 beach plums, pitted
Brandy to cover
2 egg yolks, beaten with
1/3 cup water
1/3 cup cream

1 cup flour
¼ teaspoon salt
2 tablespoons sugar
2 egg whites, beaten stiff

1. Let the plums stand in brandy for an hour or so.

2. Combine the egg yolks, water, cream, and 1 tablespoon of the brandy. Sift together the flour, sugar, and salt. Stir the liquid in until just moistened. Fold the egg whites into the batter.

3. Drain the plums, dip each in the batter, and fry in deep fat at 370°.

4. Drain fritters on paper toweling and dust with powdered sugar.

5. Serve with plum jelly, or the brandy in which the plums were marinated.

Spinach Noodles

Serves 6

½ cup frozen chopped spinach   ½ teaspoon salt
2 eggs, beaten   Flour, about 1 cup

1. From a package of spinach, cut off enough to make about ½ cup. Allow to thaw. If too coarse, run through your blender.

2. Combine the eggs, salt, spinach, and enough flour to make a very stiff dough—this varies with the size of the eggs.

3. Roll the dough out into a very thin sheet and allow it to dry. Then roll it up and slice into thin or wide noodles, as you prefer. Lay the resulting strips on a towel to dry. Store until they are needed.

Blueberry Muffins

about 8 muffins

1 egg, lightly beaten   ½ cup sugar
½ cup milk   2 teaspoons baking powder
¼ cup melted butter   ½ teaspoon salt
1½ cups flour   1 cup blueberries

1. Combine egg, milk, and butter.

2. Sift together the flour, sugar, baking powder, and salt. Stir in the liquid until the dry ingredients are just moist. Fold in the blueberries and spoon the batter into buttered muffin tins.

3. Bake at 400° for 20 to 25 minutes.

Hush Puppies

Serves 4

The story goes that some fishermen were frying their catch over a campfire, surrounded by their hungry hounds. One of the men stirred up a cornmeal batter and fried spoonfuls of it to toss to the dogs to quiet them.

2 cups stone-ground cornmeal
1 teaspoon salt
1 tablespoon minced onion
1 egg, beaten

1½ cups water
2 tablespoons melted butter
    or bacon fat
Fat in which fish was fried

1. Mix the cornmeal, onion, and salt. Beat the egg and water, and stir into the meal. Add the butter or bacon fat.
2. Have the fat in the skillet very hot. Drop the batter in by spoonfuls. Brown on both sides.
3. Serve piping hot with panfried fish.

Blueberry Griddlecakes

Makes about 12 cakes

Try with equal parts of strained honey and your own maple syrup. Warm it for serving.

1 egg, well beaten
1½ cups buttermilk
2 tablespoons melted butter
1¼ cups flour
1 teaspoon sugar

1 teaspoon baking powder
½ teaspoon soda
½ teaspoon salt
½ cup blueberries

1. Combine the egg, buttermilk, and butter.
2. Combine flour, sugar, baking powder, soda, and salt.
3. Stir in the egg-milk mixture until well blended, then fold in the blueberries.
4. Cook these as you would any pancakes.

Cranberry Orange Coffee Cake

2 cups biscuit mix
¾ cup sugar
Grated rind 1 orange
¾ cup orange juice

1 egg, well beaten
1 cup chopped raw cranberries
Cinnamon-sugar

1. In a bowl, combine biscuit mix, sugar, orange rind, and juice. Stir in the egg and the cranberries. Pour the batter into a buttered 9-inch-square baking tin and sprinkle cinnamon-sugar over the top.

2. Bake in a 350° oven for 1 hour.

Maple Walnut Muffins

10 to 12 muffins

Biscuit mix
Milk

Maple syrup
1 cup chopped black walnut
meats

1. Use a biscuit mix, following directions for muffins with the following exception: Instead of the liquid called for, use half milk and half maple syrup, omitting the sugar. Fold in the coarsely chopped black walnuts.

2. Bake according to directions on the box.

CHAPTER 15

Beverages

The making of wine goes far back into antiquity. Wherever grapes were grown, wine was made.

Our forefathers imported wines and beer from England, but soon learned to make their own. All sorts of fruits and blossoms were used to create beverages, delightful in appearance and flavor, which were consumed freely by young and old.

Blackberry Bounce

4 quarts blackberry juice   1 quart brandy
4 pounds sugar

1. Pick enough blackberries to extract the above amount of juice (see page 265 for directions).
2. Using a preserving kettle, boil the juice and sugar for 5 minutes. Cool.
3. Add the brandy and bottle the bounce.

Blackberry Wine

10 pounds blackberries   5 pounds sugar
2½ quarts boiling water

1. Mash the berries in a crockery container, add water and allow to stand, covered, for 3 days.
2. Strain through a jelly bag and put the juice back in the crock. Add the sugar, and let the juice "work."
3. When fermentation has stopped, skim the wine, strain and bottle.

Blackberry Cordial

1 quart blackberry juice
2 cups sugar
½ stick cinnamon

1 tablespoon cloves
¼ teaspoon allspice
1 pint brandy

1. Pick enough berries to extract the above amount of juice (see page 265 for directions).
2. Measure the juice, add sugar and spices, boil for 20 minutes, strain and cool.
3. Add brandy, pour the cordial into bottles, and cork.

Cherry Bounce

2 quarts black cherries
1 pound loaf sugar
1 tablespoon whole allspice

2 inches stick cinnamon
1 tablespoon whole cloves
1 quart whiskey

1. Combine all the ingredients in a crock. Cover and allow to stand for 3 months.
2. Strain and bottle the bounce.

Clover Blossom Wine

If you have ever passed a field of clover in full blossom, you will never forget the delicious fragrance that permeates the air. It may encourage you to try this wine which I am told is exceptional.

2 quarts clover blossoms
2 quarts water
2 pounds sugar

1½ teaspoons dry yeast
1 lemon, sliced thin
1 orange, sliced thin

1. Bring the water and blossoms to a boil, continue to boil for 20 minutes. Pour mixture into a crock and allow to stand, covered, for 24 hours.
2. Strain and add the sugar, yeast, lemon, and orange. Heat to lukewarm *only*. Return to the crock, cover, and let stand for a week or so to ferment.
3. Strain the wine and bottle it.

Black Cherry Bounce

6 pounds black cherries,   1 pint brandy
    stemmed   2 cups distilled water
5 pounds sugar

1. Place the cherries, with pits left in, in a crockery container. Add the sugar and brandy, cover and let stand for 3 days, stirring frequently.

2. Cover and let stand undisturbed for 5 months.

3. Then add the distilled water, strain the bounce and bottle it.

Cherry Brandy

Black cherries   2 dozen crushed cherry pits
1 quart brandy   1½ cups sugar
1 stick cinnamon   ¾ cup water

1. Pick enough cherries to extract 1 quart of juice (see page 265 for directions).

2. Combine juice, brandy, cinnamon, and pits in a crock, and let stand for 5 days.

3. Make a syrup of the sugar and water. When cool, stir into the ingredients in the crock.

4. Strain the liquid and bottle it.

Cherry Shrub

The very word "shrub" has an old-fashioned sound that takes us back to early colonial days. Incidentally, its innocent sound is misleading.

Black cherries, stemmed   Brandy
Sugar

1. Extract the cherry juice according to directions on page 265. Measure it.

2. For each pint of juice, add ½ pound sugar and ½ pint brandy. Mix thoroughly.

3. Bottle, sealing the corks with paraffin.

Elder Flower Wine

3 pints elder flowers
3 gallons water
10 pounds sugar
2 pounds raisins

Juice of 3 oranges
Juice of 1 lemon
1 yeast cake

1. Wash and drain elder flowers and put them into crockery container.
2. Make a syrup of water and sugar, pour it hot over the elder-flowers, cover, and allow to cool.
3. Mix the orange and lemon juice with the yeast, and add to the liquid. Cover again and let stand for 10 days.
4. Strain and add the raisins. Let stand, covered, for 4 months.
5. Bottle the wine and store in a dark place for 6 months before using.

Cowslip Wine—I

This was once made in every household. It was served in the afternoon in fragile wine glasses with thin slices of seed cake.

Cowslips are more commonly known as marsh marigolds. As they do not thrive in our immediate neighborhood, we have never made this delicate wine, but it would be an interesting experiment if you have an abundance of the flowers. I give you a recipe from an old cookbook.

3 pounds sugar
4 quarts water
4 quarts marigolds

Rind and juice of 2 lemons
2 tablespoons yeast
¼ pint brandy

1. In a saucepan, combine the sugar and water, bring to a boil, then add the flowers and lemons. Pour into a crock.
2. Spread a piece of toast with the yeast and add to liquid. Cover the crock and allow to stand for 48 hours.
3. Add the brandy, cover and let stand for 8 weeks.
4. Strain and bottle the wine. It will be ready to use in another 3 or 4 weeks.

Cowslip Wine—II

1 quart cowslip flowers
1 gallon water
3 pounds sugar
1 sprig borage
1 sprig sweet briar (wild rose)

1 Seville orange, rind and
strained juice
2 lemons, rind and strained
juice
¼ ounce yeast
Brandy (optional)

1. Pick the flowers free of stalks and greens. Spread them out on trays to dry, turning frequently.

2. Boil water, sugar, borage, and sweet briar for ½ hour. Lift them out at the end of the boiling.

3. Put the orange and lemon rind into a tub, pour the boiling liquid over it and allow to cool. Stir in the dry cowslip flowers, the lemon and orange juice, and the yeast. Cover with a cloth and leave undisturbed for 2 days.

4. Turn the mixture out into a cask. Add a little brandy to taste.

5. When fermentation has ceased, bung closely and leave 3 months before bottling.

Ella's Dandelion Wine

This is a delightful wine made from the dandelion blossoms which are so prevalent that anyone can make it with little effort. The following recipe was given to me by a woman who for many years has produced the most delicate, beautiful dandelion wine. It goes down smoothly but is not as innocent as it seems.

4 quarts dandelion blossoms
4 quarts water
3 pounds sugar

3 lemons, sliced
1 yeast cake

1. Combine the blossoms and water in a crock and let stand, covered, for 9 days. Squeeze out the blossoms and strain the juice.

2. Add 3 pounds of sugar, lemons, and yeast cake. Let stand for another 9 days.

3. Strain the liquid and put it in a jug, leaving the cork out until the wine has stopped "working." Then cork up.

Dandelion Wine—II

This recipe is for a large quantity but can, of course, be adjusted to the amount of blossoms you have when you get tired picking them. For best-flavored wine, pick only the freshly opened ones. The wine improves with aging.

15 quarts dandelion blossoms   12 oranges, rind and juice
3 gallons cold water   6 lemons, rind and juice
15 pounds sugar   2½ pounds raisins
1 yeast cake

1. Simmer blossoms in water for 3 hours. Strain and return liquid to the kettle, add sugar, and again bring to a boil. Strain through cheesecloth, and when liquid has cooled to lukewarm, add the yeast. Let it stand, covered, for 3 days, skimming once a day.

2. Peel orange and lemon rind, avoiding the white part underneath. Simmer rind in a little water for ½ hour. Strain and add, together with the juice of the fruit, to the rest of the liquid. You should have 5 gallons.

3. Pour wine into a cask, add the raisins, and leave cask open for one day. Then seal tightly and let stand for 6 months before bottling.

Cherry Wine

A favorite beverage in New England in colonial days, along with cherry bounce, was this wine which also has plenty of "bounce." The recipe comes from an old cookbook.

4 pounds cherries, stemmed   1 cup sugar for each quart
1 quart boiling water   liquid

1. Crush the cherries, and put them in a jar or keg. Add the boiling water, and allow to stand for 24 hours, stirring once in a while.

2. Strain and measure liquid. Add the sugar, cover tightly, and let stand for 3 months.

3. Bottle the wine and store it.

Cherry Nectar

2 quarts black cherries   Sugar
1 quart water

   1. Boil the cherries and water for half an hour.
   2. Strain the juice through a jelly bag. Measure it.
   3. Add the sugar, cup for cup, and boil for another 10 minutes. Cool and bottle the nectar.
   4. To serve, pour over ice cream or mix with any fruit juice for a cool summer drink.

Elderberry Wine—I

7 pounds elderberries   ½ ounce ground ginger
3 gallons boiling water   6 whole cloves
To each gallon of juice add: ½ teaspoon yeast
3 pounds sugar   ½ cup brandy
1 pound raisins

   1. Stem and weigh the elderberries. Pour on boiling water and let stand for 24 hours.
   2. Mash the berries, strain through cheesecloth, measure the juice and place in a kettle. Add sugar, raisins, ground ginger, and cloves, and boil gently for 1 hour, skimming while it cooks.
   3. Cool the liquid to lukewarm, add the yeast and the brandy, pour into a wooden or crockery container, and let stand for 6 months.
   4. Strain and bottle the wine.

Elderberry Wine—II

4 pints elderberry juice   4 egg whites and egg shells
6 pints water   1 cake yeast
3 pounds sugar

   1. Pick ripe elderberries, stem, crush and strain the juice. Let stand for 24 hours to settle.
   2. Make a syrup of water and sugar, pour it hot over the elder and add the egg whites and shells. Let simmer for an hour, remove from fire.

3. When nearly cold, pour into a crockery container and add the yeast. Allow the mixture to "work," covered, for about 2 months.

4. Strain and bottle the wine. Keep it for 12 months before using.

Grape Juice

Wild grapes

Suar, ¾ cup per cup of grapes

Boiling water

1. Wash, drain and stem the grapes.

2. Have hot, sterilized quart jars ready, and in each one put 1 cup grapes and ¾ cup sugar. Pour on boiling water, to fill the jar. Put the lids on and tighten them immediately. Allow the jars to cool, then let them stand in a dark place for 2 months.

3. Strain the juice as you use it.

Strawberry Champagne Bowl

This is a beautiful and delicious thing to serve at a June wedding or any other festive occasion.

2 cups wild strawberries
1 pint champagne
Sweet woodruff, blossoms and
    leaves

1 orange, sliced thin
1 tablespoon sugar
1 quart Rhine wine
Ice

1. Pick sweet woodruff blossoms with their leaves. Put them in a punch bowl with the orange and sugar. Pour in Rhine wine and let stand for an hour or two.

2. Put a large piece of ice in the center and pour the champagne over it. Float the strawberries on top. The combination of the flavor of the strawberries and sweet woodruff, which is used to make May wine, is delightful.

Grape Wine—I

This is from an old cookbook.

Wild grapes
Cold water, 1 quart per pound
  of grapes

Sugar, 3 pounds per gallon of
  liquid
Brandy, ½ cup per gallon

1. Pick the wild grapes before they are too ripe. Stem and weigh them. To each pound of grapes add 1 quart cold water. Bruise the grapes and let stand in the water for 3 days, stirring often. Strain the grapes and measure the juice.

2. Add the sugar and pour liquid into a cask.

3. Let stand for a few days, then add the brandy.

4. After 6 months, strain and bottle. Keep for 12 months before using.

Grape Wine—II

10 pounds ripe grapes
3 quarts boiling water

5 pounds sugar

1. Stem the grapes and put them in a jar with the boiling water. When cool, squeeze "by hand," the old recipe directs. Cover the jar, and let stand for 3 days, then press out the juice.

2. Add the sugar and let stand for a week.

3. Skim and bottle the juice, corking it loosely. When it has stopped fermenting, strain the wine and bottle it.

4. Store in a cool place, laying the bottles on their sides.

Appendix

Preparation of Fish and Wild Game
AND
Useful Kitchen Aids
FOR
Fish and Game Cookery

Preparation of Fish and Game

Since the invention of the deep freeze, fish and game can be available all year round. However, whether we consume whatever is brought home from a hunting or fishing trip or freeze it to enjoy later, care in its preparation is necessary to produce a superb dish of exquisite flavor and texture.

Fish

The treatment of a fish, once you have removed the hook from its mouth, depends on your location and the distance from home. The thing to remember, under any circumstances, is that the sooner the fish is cleaned, the more delicious the flavor will be.

We fish out in the lake in front of our house, and put the fish in a net which we keep hanging over the side of the boat. This is better than a stringer which hooks the fish through the gills and sometimes kills them, or nearly so. If possible, keep them lively. When we dock our boat, we take the fish directly to the kitchen where we prepare them for cooking.

Preparation of Fish

1. Skin a bass or a carp.
2. Scale other fish—except smelt and small trout—scraping from tail to head.

3. Fillet if you wish.

4. If not, slit the belly from head to tail and carefully scoop out the entrails.

5. Wash fish thoroughly inside and out with cold water. You will find that blood clings to the backbone but can be removed by scrubbing with a small brush. I use a flat-bristle artist's brush, but a child's tooth brush is handy too.

6. Shake salt inside the cavity along the backbone.

7. Remove the head if you wish.

8. A few small gashes along the backbone will prevent the fish from curling in the skillet.

9. Refrigerate or freeze immediately.

Brook Trout

If you are fishing for brook trout in a stream, the procedure is slightly different, though the principle is the same. Clean and cool them as quickly as possible.

1. Clean the fish by slitting the belly from head to tail, then scrape out the entrails. Wash as well as you can in clear, cold water, giving special attention to the line of blood clinging to the backbone. The head is usually left on.

2. Shake salt in the cavity along the backbone.

3. Place a layer of fresh grass or willow twigs in the bottom of your creel and lay the trout on top, being careful not to crowd them. A few twigs inside the trout are a good idea, as this allows the air to circulate. Add another layer of grass and of fish.

4. Refrigerate as soon as you get home.

How to Skin a Fish

Make a cut along the dorsal fins, the lower edge of the belly, and just behind the gills, as shown in picture, top of page 299.

Holding the head of the fish with the left hand, take the upper left corner of the skin in a pair of pliers and pull it towards you.

Repeat this on the other side, then remove the head and entrails.

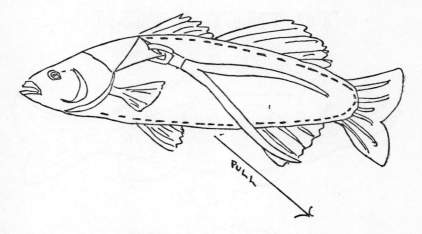

TO SKIN A FISH

How to Fillet a Fish

1. Cut through the skin from head to tail along the backbone on each side of the dorsal fin. See chart on page 300.

2. Cut a V-shaped notch behind the head, cutting to the backbone.

3. Cut through the skin just behind the gill opening. Loosen the skin and pull it towards the tail, holding the head of the fish with the left hand.

Some people do this after the fish is filleted, but we think it's easier to do it at this stage as you have more to hang on to.

4. Cut as in Step 3, but this time cut to the backbone. Turn the knife to a horizontal position and slide it along the backbone, cutting off the flesh in one slab. Turn the fish and repeat on the other side.

If you find that the fish tends to slip away from you, you can nail the head to a board. We have never found this necessary, but it might help. A workman's cotton glove on the left hand allows

TO FILET A FISH

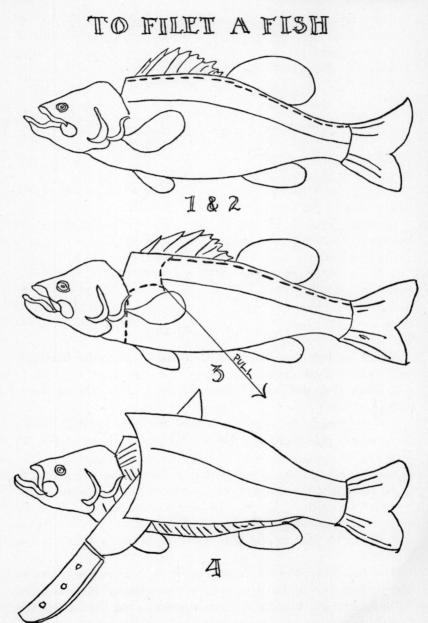

you to retain a firm grip on the fish while skinning or filleting and is a protection from the sharp gills and fins while you are working.

5. Check the fillet for any little bones that might remain in the flesh and pull them out with tweezers or a strawberry huller.

Freezing Fish

If you have more fish than you can eat or give away, you can freeze it. However, do not keep longer than 6 months in your freezer.

Small fish are frozen whole; large fish may be cut into steaks. Either may be filleted before freezing.

Large whole fish may be given an *ice glaze*. The fish should not be skinned, but otherwise prepared for cooking.

1. Place the fish, uncovered, in the freezer.

2. When frozen, dip it in as near freezing water as possible. Return to the freezer. When the fish is covered with ice, repeat the procedure, dipping and freezing, until you have built up a rather thick ice glaze. Now wrap the fish in freezer paper and return to the freezer. It will retain its moisture.

All frozen fish is better if thawed slowly before cooking. To prevent leakage while it is thawed, dip in a 10% brine solution (1 pound of salt to 4½ quarts of water) for 20 minutes. Drain, wrap, package, and freeze.

Frogs' Legs

Cut the legs from the frog, wash them, and peel the skin back—it will come off rather like a glove. Cut off the feet. Pour boiling water over the legs, drain and dry them, and they are ready to cook.

Preparation of Venison

Your enjoyment of venison, whether it be deer, reindeer, moose, elk, caribou, or antelope, depends on the care it has received in the field. Many hunters, once they have shot their deer, give little thought to its care from then on until its appearance on the table.

I believe that is the reason so many people "don't care for venison." Its gamey flavor is actually that of spoiled meat.

Quick cleaning and cooling is of the utmost importance.

First of all, lay the deer with its head downhill and cut the throat so that it will bleed thoroughly. Pumping the hind legs helps. Lay the deer flat on its back and slit the belly all the way down to within 6 inches of its tail, being careful not to cut into the intestines. Make a circular cut completely around the vent, to free it and the large intestine. Next, cut the windpipe. Then cut the diaphragm, which separates the chest from the abdominal cavity. Now grab the front legs and, giving it a jerk, roll the deer over; the insides will spill out on the ground. Cut off the heart and the liver and put aside. The liver is considered to be the choicest morsel.

Do all this quickly and thoroughly. In case of punctured organs, there will be bleeding and consequent contamination. This raises the question whether to wash the meat or not. Some hunters say that water should never be put on the meat, as it encourages the action of the bacteria promoting decay. Others wash the cavity with salt water or snow, being careful to dry it thoroughly afterward.

The carcass should be cooled quickly. If the weather prevents this, rubbing the inside with black pepper helps. It at least keeps the flies away.

Prop the carcass open with a stick so that the air will circulate. If there is a part of the meat which has been badly shot up, it should be cut away. If its condition is not too bad, you can soak it in brine overnight to remove the blood and then use it for venisonburgers.

You may skin your deer in camp or take it home for this step in its preparation. If the latter, don't make the mistake of throwing it over the front fender of your car where it will be warmed by the heat of the engine. The trunk is the best place, or, if that is not possible, the top of the car.

When you skin the deer, hang it up by the hind feet and cut the hide around the ankles. Make cuts down the inner thighs to the vent. Pull the skin down. It may be so firmly adhered that you will need to use a knife to loosen it.

If you skin the deer in the field, you can quarter it, then wrap it in cheesecloth or the tubing they use in packing houses, for easy, clean transportation. In either case, from now on it will be up to your butcher.

You will find a chart on the following page to help you identify the cuts of venison.

Hanging

This important step differs with the age and condition of the animal. Everyone agrees that, to produce the greatest eating enjoyment, the meat should be clean and fresh and preferably tender. Hanging the meat in a temperature of 35° to 40° is ideal. A week or 10 days at the most is considered right.

Preservation

The Indians and early settlers used to make "jerky"—strips of meat packed in salt for 24 hours, then smoked over a campfire. The meat was then hung out in the sun until it turned dark and dry like chips. It could be taken on a hunting trip and chewed as it was, or soaked in water and stewed. Another way often used was to pickle the meat in brine. Or if killed late in the season, the deer was hung up to freeze and the meat sawed off as needed. Fortunately we do not have to resort to these methods today.

Storing

For short-time storage in your refrigerator, cover venison loosely and use within 3 to 4 days. Organs and ground meat should be kept only 1 or 2 days.

Freezing

After your venison has hung the proper length of time, you may have it cut up, wrapped in small packages, and labeled. You may use tenderizer before freezing or sprinkle the meat with wine and herbs. It should be quick-frozen at 0° or lower, as slow freezing causes large ice crystals to form; these rupture the cells of the

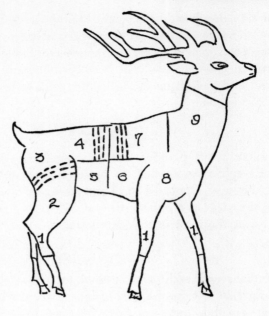

CUTS OF VENISON

1 SHANK	6 FLANK &
2 ROUND	BRISKET
3 RUMP	7 RIB
4 LOIN	8 SHOULDER
5 FLANK	9 NECK

meat and as a result vital juices are lost. We feel that the use of tenderizer before freezing also helps prevent this. The maximum storage time for frozen venison is 4 months. And remember that the venison you get out of your locker is only as good as you put in.

Cooking

This of course depends on the age of the animal and the cut of meat. Sometimes, surprisingly enough, an old buck will prove to be tender because he has not been able to exercise. Generally, though, young meat is the most tender, as you would expect.

Marinating the meat before cooking helps tenderize it. You can also pound a tough piece with a mallet to break down the fibers. The best and easiest method is to use a commercial tenderizer.

Some authorities say you should parboil venison before cooking to remove possible contamination. We feel that if it has been properly prepared, this is unnecessary.

Larding a roast is very worthwhile. Probably your butcher will do it for you, but if not, you will need a larding needle and strips of fat—salt pork is usually used but bacon will serve. Slash the roast in several places and insert the strip of fat. Tie a string around the roast over the gashes to keep them closed while cooking.

A general rule to follow in cooking: short-time cooking—10 to 15 minutes per pound—for tender cuts, and long, slow cooking for the tougher cuts. The in-between timing results in tough meat, we have found.

Thus a tender 1-inch steak should be cooked in butter in a skillet for not more than 5 minutes on each side. A 2-pound roast from the loin will take 30 minutes in a 300° oven; a rump roast of the same size will take 2 hours at the same temperature.

A cooking chart appears at top of page 306.

COOKING CHART FOR VENISON

Cut	Use for	Type of cooking
Round	Swiss steak, cubed steak, kabobs	Long slow methods Cubed steaks, brief cooking, if tenderized
Rump	Pot roast	Long, slow
Loin	Steaks, chops, cutlets	Short-time cooking
Rib	Roasts, chops	Short-time cooking
Flank	Stews and venisonburgers	Long, slow cooking
Neck	Stews	Long, slow cooking
Shoulder	Roasts	Long, slow cooking
Scraps and trimmings	Sausage	

One pound of venison with a medium amount of bone will serve 2 or 3 people. Cuts with a large amount of bone will serve 1 to 2 people per pound.

Preparation of Small Mammals

The muskrat, squirrel, opossum, and raccoon are valued as game and food in different parts of the country.

Their preparation is similar.

1. Dress immediately to prevent decay-promoting bacteria from starting to work.

2. Skin by cutting around the hind legs and down the inside of the thigh to the crotch. Loosen the skin and work towards the head. If the skin adheres firmly, as with a squirrel, a knife will be needed to loosen it. When you have reached the head, that and the feet can be cut off.

3. Cut a slit down the belly and pull out the viscera. If the intestines have been shot up, and this material has got onto the

SQUIRREL

flesh, it must be carefully cut and wiped away. Wash away any blood or hair. Look for the small yellowish fatty kernels under each front shoulder and the small of the back. If these are not removed the meat will have an unpleasant taste.

4. Cool quickly. Refrigerate as soon as possible. Any of these animals can be frozen. Tenderizer can be used before freezing or before cooking, using ½ teaspoon per pound of meat.

Small game may be eaten after 3 or 4 days.

Preparation of Wild Rabbits or Hares

The ordinary cottontail rabbit is a familiar sight in orchards and abandoned fields, or perhaps in gardens not abandoned at all.

He hides in briar patches and hedgerows. He weighs from ½ to 1 pound, while the jack rabbit can weigh as much as 20 pounds. In the northern part of the country the snowshoe rabbit is hunted.

We shoot rabbit in winter, the season being from October to March as a rule. A young rabbit, which of course is better eating, has soft ears and paws, while his claws are sharp.

It is possible to contract tularemia from a rabbit, although this is not likely. If your rabbit is lively he probably is healthy. A spotted liver in a rabbit is one symptom of the disease, and since it strikes in epidemic form, so many rabbits would be wiped out in a given area that hunters would hear of it. However, if you wish to play safe, wear gloves while cleaning it, and cook your rabbit well.

A rabbit should be dressed in the field. The simplest way to skin it is to cut the skin around the middle, being careful not to cut the flesh underneath. Take an edge on either side of the cut and push your hands apart, loosening the skin from the flesh as you go. When you get to the extremities, cut off the head and feet.

Next, cut a slit down the center of the belly and pull out the entrails.

Another way to skin a rabbit is to cut the skin around the hind legs, then inside the thigh to the crotch.

Tie the legs together, hang the rabbit up by them, and pull the skin down, working it loose as you go. Remove all shot-damaged flesh. If the animal is badly shot up, soak it in brine for 3 or 4 hours, using a tablespoon of salt to a quart of water.

As with all game, rapid cooling is important. Refrigerate as soon as the rabbit is cool.

If you use a tenderizer, pierce the flesh inside and out with a sharp fork, using ½ teaspoon of tenderizer per pound of meat.

Rabbit needs additional fat, so use salt pork or bacon in cooking. Thyme, rosemary, or marjoram blends with the flavor of rabbit to perfection.

Preparation of Game Birds

Game birds are best when cleaned immediately and eaten within 5 or 6 days.

The English, as we know, like these birds "high." One cookbook directs: ". . . they should be kept till putrefaction has commenced. Hang in feathers in a current of air and they will keep for many days." Then later on, directions are given for "removing the taint." No comment.

If you are not able to pluck your bird in the field, at least clean it if at all possible. At any rate, do not stuff it in a bag or hunting coat until it is cold.

Follow these general directions as soon as possible for all game birds:

1. Cut the throat and hang the head down to bleed.

2. Remove the feathers from the crop and tail, pulling them gently towards the tail so as not to break the skin.

3. Slit the skin over the crop and remove it.

4. Cut down to the vent and remove the entrails, separating the giblets and putting them back in the cavity or in a separate bag. Carefully cut away the oil sac at the base of the tail.

5. Stuffing the cavity with fresh cool grass helps to cool the bird and to keep some air circulating inside.

6. Refrigerate when you get them home.

If you are able to pluck the bird completely in the field, so much the better. The longer it stands, the more difficult it becomes to remove the feathers. Pull a few at a time, in the direction of the tail. If you have had a delay and the feathers have tightened, rather than break the skin in removing them, dip the bird in scalding water repeatedly until the feathers are completely soaked. (This obviously does not do for ducks, as their feathers are too well oiled.) The feathers will then come out fairly easily. Any down or pin feathers can be singed off.

Pheasant, Grouse, Partridge and Quail

Some hunters like to skin these birds, but the meat dries out in cooking as a result. If the bird is badly shot up, some of the skin will, of course, have to be removed, but keep as much intact as you can.

Woodcock

Woodcock should be plucked dry and singed. Some authorities say that this bird should never be cleaned except for the removal of the giblets. The head should be skinned and left on, the beak being used as a skewer in trussing the bird. The brains are reputed to be the most delectable part. We disregard all this and clean our woodcock but that is something for each person to decide for himself.

Ducks

In the case of ducks, pluck them dry. When you have removed all the feathers, have a kettle of boiling water ready on the stove. You will need about 2 gallons. Add ½ pound of paraffin, let it melt, and dip the duck so that it becomes coated with wax. It will take several dips to build up a sufficiently thick coat. Let the paraffin cool and harden. You may then scrape it off with a dull knife or roll it off with your fingers. The down and pin feathers will come off with it. If one or two escape, which they shouldn't, singe or pluck them.

Freezing

Game birds may be frozen like any poultry. In the case of the larger birds, cut them up and freeze in smaller packages after they have been hung the proper length of time. It is unwise to keep frozen game birds longer than 6 months, especially in the case of wild ducks, as the fat tends to become rancid and spoil the flavor.

USEFUL KITCHEN AIDS FOR FISH AND GAME PREPARATION

For Fish

Scaler
Pliers for skinning
Long oval kettle for boiling a fish whole. You may use this for
    bouillabaisse or chowder as well.
Cookie sheet or large shallow pan for baking a whole stuffed fish

For Meat

Mallet for breaking down tough fibers
Larding needle
Skewers for trussing stuffed animals
Kettle for making game stew
Roasting pan
Dutch oven

For Birds

Poultry shears
Roasting pan
Skewers for trussing stuffed birds

General

Good knives and a knife sharpener
Chopping block
Casseroles
Food mill
Blender
Cleaver
Food grinder

FROM ONE COOK TO ANOTHER

AL DENTE This is the approved method of cooking pasta. It should be cooked through, but not soft. Test by pinching a small (cool) piece between your thumb and forefinger.

APPLESAUCE Try adding freshly grated horseradish to applesauce when you serve it with pork, or grate some nutmeg over it.

ASPARAGUS Stand the bunches in water, heads up, until ready to cook. Of course, if it goes directly from garden to stove, so much the better.

BOUQUET GARNI A bunch of herbs, tied together and dropped into a dish to flavor it while it is cooking. It customarily includes parsley, a bay leaf, celery leaves, and thyme. Other herbs, such as tarragon and marjoram, may be added. Remove the herbs before you serve.

BREAD CRUMBS Use finely shredded soft bread crumbs (you can do this in a blender in a trice) in place of flour to thicken soup.

BUTTER FLAVORING Add this to baked goods and to cooking fats to improve their flavor.

CAULIFLOWER To keep the cauliflower white, add ½ cup milk to the water in which it cooks.

Take the leaves from a freshly picked cauliflower, boil them until tender, and serve with a cheese sauce.

CHEESE CAKE Try folding blueberries into it before baking.

CHOCOLATE Butter the dish before you melt the chocolate.

COOKWARE The new dishes in which you freeze, cook, and serve save time and cut down on dishwashing. When you are replacing old pots and pans, buy these new ones.

CORN   Try starting freshly picked corn-on-the-cob in cold water. Bring to a boil and boil for 5 minutes. The flavor is superlative.

CRANBERRY SHERBET   This is a quickie. Mix 1 cup cranberry sauce made of whole berries with 1 pint of soft lime sherbet. Re-freeze.

CREPES   This little French pancake has many endearing qualities for the cook who is interested in adding variety to her menus. Fill crêpes with creamed chicken or shrimp, or with slightly sugared wild strawberries. Roll up and serve warm.

CURRY POWDER   The imported curry powder has a superior flavor. Buy it when you can. It costs only a little more and is worth it.

DANDELION GREENS   Try sprinkling chopped mint leaves over them.

DILL   A liquid dill flavoring is now available. Use it in the winter, or in summer if your dill crop has failed. It has the dill-weed flavor.

EGGS   8 to 10 egg whites make 1 cup.

They whip better at room temperature, but separate more easily when cold.

When boiling eggs, pierce the ends with a needle and they will not crack.

Do not buy unrefrigerated eggs. If they have been standing on your grocer's shelf, they have been aging rapidly.

FINES HERBS   A mixture of finely chopped herbs, such as parsley, chives, tarragon, etc.

FISH   A 4-pound fish will yield about 3 pounds of fillet.

Bake fish on foil, turning the edges up to prevent the juices from dripping. If you oil the foil, the fish will be easy to remove to a platter.

Chowder may be made from frozen fillets, but the head and bones from a whole fish add an important flavor.

FLAMBÉE   Pour brandy over the food and light it. Serve when the flames have died down. This gives food so treated an indescribable flavor.

FLOWERS   Try a nasturtium leaf sandwich made with orange nut bread spread with butter.

Add nasturtium leaves to a tossed salad.

Make a marigold custard by scalding 1 cup of marigold petals in the milk. Strain and proceed as usual. Season with vanilla, nutmeg, and allspice. You will get an interesting, saffron-like flavor.

FRENCH DRESSING   Try adding a little chutney.

FRENCH TOAST   Serve with a mixture of sour cream and brown sugar.

GARLIC CROUTONS   Toast a slice of French bread, rub it with a cut garlic clove, cube it, and add to your tossed salad.

GELATIN   1 tablespoon thickens 1 pint liquid. In hot weather, reduce the liquid by 2 tablespoons for every cup called for.

To unmold: moisten the plate and the surface of the gelatin. If the mold turns out to be a little off-center, it can be slid to the proper place.

HAM BONE   Save this to make a delicious split pea soup. The stock in which you have boiled a tongue is good also.

HERB BREAD   Cut French bread lengthwise and spread generously with any herb butter—thyme, rosemary, tarragon, chives, or a blend of several. Toast in the broiler. Try sprinkling the butter with sesame seeds before toasting.

HERBS   When using fresh herbs, use three times the amount of dried ones.

HONEY   Use this on strawberries instead of sugar. Try flavoring whipped cream for desserts with honey and ground cardamom.

LEMON Lemon juice does not wilt a salad as much as vinegar does. Serve a slice of lemon with any clear soup.

MARINADE A mixture of wine or vinegar, oil, herbs, and spices, in which meat or fish is soaked. It tenderizes and flavors.

NUTMEG Grate a little nutmeg on potatoes au gratin.

OMELETS To make an omelet, have eggs at room temperature. If you must use them right out of the refrigerator, let them stand in warm water for a few minutes.

Never make an omelet out of more than 3 eggs at a time.

Water added to the eggs, rather than milk, results in a more tender, delicate omelet.

ONIONS To French fry, dip in sour cream instead of milk.

PAPRIKA This is considered by many people to be purely decorative, which is a mistake. The best paprika, which comes from Hungary, has a delicate flavor and adds to a sauce or stew. With sour cream it is almost a "must."

PARSLEY Did you ever try French-frying this for a delicious garnish?

PEACH LEAVES Drop a few into milk as you scald it for custard. They give a delicate peach flavor.

POACHING Keeping food at a simmer, not allowing it to boil. Eggs and seafood are excellent poached.

POTATOES Boiled in half milk and half water, they will mash up light and fluffy.

POTATO SOUP Make it with chicken stock and top with chopped chervil.

RADISHES Pull young, sweet radishes from your garden and serve on the cocktail tray with sweet butter to dip them in.

RICE Add 2 tablespoons of spinach puree to the rice when making a rice ring. It makes a beautiful color contrast when the ring is filled with creamed shrimp or lobster.

RIPE OLIVES Roll in bacon and broil for an appetizer.

ROLLING PIN A French rolling pin rolls out pastry quickly and efficiently.

ROUX A mixture of flour and soft butter used to thicken a sauce or gravy.

SANDWICHES To make tiny sandwiches, freeze a loaf of unsliced bread. You can then cut the slices as thin as you like.

SAUCES A first-rate sauce is more creative than a second-rate painting.
    Add a drop or two of yellow food coloring to a cream sauce for eye appeal.

SAUTÉ To sauté is to cook on top of the stove in a small amount of fat.

SEAFOOD Poach, do not boil seafood.

SMOKY SALT Added to beans, split pea soup, and gravies, gives them a lift.

SORREL The next time you cook spinach, put some sorrel in with it for an interesting flavor.

SOUFFLÉ A soufflé waits for no one. Plan to serve it immediately. A tablespoon or two of bourbon will help keep it up.

SOUR CREAM   To make sour cream out of sweet, add 2 tablespoons of lemon juice to each cup of cream.

The tang forms a pleasant contrast to fruit.

STEAK   Let a steak stand 10 minutes before carving. This will allow the juices to remain in the meat instead of running out on the platter.
Season a steak *after* broiling.

STOCK   Liquid in which meat, fowl, fish or vegetables have been cooked. Court bouillon is a specially flavored stock.

TENDERIZER   It is especially useful for game, since you are often uncertain of its tenderness.

TOMATOES   Put ripe tomatoes through your blender. Add salt and chopped sweet basil. Freeze. Serve as a first course or with the main course.

TURNOVERS   Put spoonfuls of well-seasoned creamed pheasant, duck or chicken in squares of rich pastry. Turn over, pinch the edges, and bake in a hot oven.

VANILLA   Buy the best pure vanilla extract available. Did you know that drug stores carry fine vanilla? Try it.
A vanilla bean is a good thing to have on hand. Heat a piece of it in the milk you are going to use for a custard. It may be dried and used again. Vanilla sugar is made by burying a piece of the bean in a cannister of sugar. Use this for desserts.

WHIPPED CREAM   To prevent whipped cream from separating, mix 1 teaspoon of unflavored dry gelatin into 1 pint of cream, whipped. This will give you a soft whipped cream. If you want a firmer product, use 2 teaspoons of gelatin.

ZEST   The colored part of orange or lemon rind.

Index